19 $\frac{25}{81}$

r Peter

3.6, 1982

love from

Faustus: Why, have you any pain that torture others? Mephistophilis: As great as have the human souls of men.

Urizen, *The Book of Urizen*, plate 11
Library of Congress Rosenwald Collection

Mind Forg'd Manacles

Evil in the Poetry of Blake and Shelley

MELANIE BANDY

THE UNIVERSITY OF ALABAMA PRESS
University, Alabama

Library of Congress Cataloging in Publication Data

Bandy, Melanie, 1932–
  Mind forg'd manacles.

  Bibliography: p.
  Includes index.
  1. English poetry—19th century—History and
criticism. 2. Good and evil in literature. 3. Blake,
William, 1757–1827—Religion and ethics. 4. Shelley,
Percy Bysshe, 1792–1822—Religion and ethics. I. Title.
II. Title: Evil in the poetry of Blake and Shelley.
  PR590.B26   821'.709   80–18779
  ISBN 0–8173–0046–5

Contents

Acknowledgments

For their having granted permission to quote or reprint, I am grateful to the publishers and copyright holders of the works listed here:

" 'The House of Pain': Emerson and the Tragic Sense," by Newton Arvin. Reprinted by permission from *The Hudson Review*, Vol. XII, No. 1 (Spring 1959). Copyright © by *The Hudson Review*, Inc.

On Christian Doctrine, by St. Augustine. Translated by D. W. Robertson, Jr. Copyright © 1958 by Bobbs-Merrill Co. Used by permission.

Shelley's Major Poetry: The Fabric of A Vision, by Carlos Baker. Copyright © 1948, 1974 by Princeton University Press. Reprinted by permission of Princeton University Press.

Blake: Complete Writings. Edited by Geoffrey Keynes. Copyright © Oxford University Press, 1966. By permission of Oxford University Press.

The Revolution in Physics, by Louis de Broglie. Translated by Ralph Niemeyer. Copyright © by The Noonday Press (now Farrar, Straus & Giroux, Inc.). Used by permission of Farrar, Straus & Giroux, Inc.

The Identity of Man, by Jacob Bronowski. Copyright © 1965 by Jacob Bronowski. Reprinted by permission of Doubleday & Company, Inc.

Shelley's Idols of the Cave, by Peter Butter. Copyright © 1954 by Edinburgh University Press. Used by permission.

The Labyrinth of the World, by John Amos Comenius. Translated by Matthew Spinka. Copyright © 1942 by the National Union of Czechoslovak Protestants in America. Quoted by permission.

Poor Monkey: The Child in Literature, by Peter Coveney. Published by Rockliff Publishing Corporation. Quoted by permission of the publisher. Copyright © 1957.

The Possessed, by Fyodor Dostoyevsky. Translated by Constance Garnett. Copyright © 1963 by Random House, Inc. Quoted by permission.

William Blake: His Philosophy and Symbols, by S. Foster Damon. Copyright © 1958 by Peter Smith Publisher. Used by permission.

"Burnt Norton," from *Four Quartets: Collected Poems, 1909–1935*, by T. S. Eliot. Copyright © 1936 by Harcourt, Brace and Company and by Faber & Faber, Ltd.

The Sacred Wood: Essays on Poetry and Criticism, by T. S. Eliot. Copyright © 1950 by Methuen Company, Ltd.

The Character of Physical Law, by Richard Feynman. Copyright © 1967 by Richard Feynman. Used by permission.

"Blake After Two Centuries," by Northrop Frye, *University of Toronto Quarterly* 27 (October 1957):10–21. Copyright by University of Toronto Press. Quoted by permission.

"Shelley's 'The Triumph of Life': A Critical Study," by Donald H. Reiman. Illinois Studies in Language and Literature No. 55. Copyright © 1965 by Donald C. Reiman. Used by permission.

"Introduction: Shelley's Optimism," by George M. Ridenour, in *Shelley: A Collection of Critical Essays*. Edited by George M. Ridenour. Copyright © 1965 by Prentice-Hall. Used by permission.

Coleridge on Imagination, by I. A. Richards. All rights reserved, 1950. W. W. Norton and Company, Inc., and Routledge & Kegan Paul, Ltd.

Henry Crabb Robinson on Books and Their Writers, Volume 1. Edited by Edith J. Morley. Copyright © 1938 by J. M. Dent and Sons. Used by permission.

"Shelley: Or the Poetic Value of Revolutionary Principles," *Essays in Literary Criticism*, by George Santayana. Edited by Irving Singer. Copyright © 1956 by Charles Scribner's Sons. Used by permission.

Mind and Matter, by Erwin Schrödinger. Published by Cambridge University Press. Copyright © 1959 by Cambridge University Press. Used by permission.

The Letters of Percy Bysshe Shelley. 2 volumes. Edited by Frederick L. Jones. Copyright © Oxford University Press, 1964. By permission of Oxford University Press.

The Complete Poetical Works of Percy Bysshe Shelley. Edited by Thomas Hutchinson. Copyright © Oxford University Press, 1965. By permission of Oxford University Press.

Shelley's Prose or The Trumpet of a Prophecy. Edited by David Lee Clark. Copyright © 1954 by University of New Mexico Press. Used by permission.

Shelley's Prometheus Unbound: A Critical Reading, by Earl R. Wasserman. Published by The Johns Hopkins University Press. Copyright © 1965 by The Johns Hopkins University Press.

"*Prometheus Unbound*," by Bennett Weaver. University of Michigan Publications in Language and Literature No. 27. Copyright © 1957 by University of Michigan Press. Used by permission.

The Mysticism of William Blake, by Helen C. White [1925]. New York: Russell & Russell, 1964. Used by permission.

Shelley, by Newman Ivey White. Copyright © 1960 by Alfred A. Knopf, Inc.

"Beatrice's 'Pernicious Mistake' in *The Cenci*," by Robert F. Whitman. Copyright © 1959 by *PMLA*. Used by permission.

The Apocalyptic Vision in the Poetry of Shelley, by Ross Grieg Woodman. Copyright © University of Toronto Press, 1963.

Collected Poems of W. B. Yeats. Copyright © 1933 by Macmillan Publishing Company, renewed 1961 by Bertha Georgie Yeats. Selection from "Crazy Jane Talks with the Bishop" used by permission of Macmillan Publishing Company, Bertha Georgie Yeats, Michael Yeats, and Anne Yeats.

Essays and Introductions, by W. B. Yeats. Copyright © Mrs. W. B. Yeats, 1961. Published by the Macmillan Publishing Company.

Abbreviations and Guide to Referencing System

AI	*Auguries of Innocence*
AD	*Adonais*
BA	*The Book of Ahania*
BL	*The Book of Los*
BT	*The Book of Thel*
BU	*The Book of Urizen*
CE	*The Cenci*
DC	*A Descriptive Catalogue*
E	*Europe*
EG	*The Everlasting Gospel*
EPI	*Epipsychidion*
FZ	*The Four Zoas*
GP	*The Gates of Paradise*
J	*Jerusalem*
M	*Milton*
MHH	*The Marriage of Heaven and Hell*
NR	*There Is No Natural Religion*
QM	*Queen Mab*
RI	*The Revolt of Islam*
SL	*The Song of Los*
TL	*The Triumph of Life*
VDA	*Visions of the Daughters of Albion*
VLJ	*A Vision of the Last Judgment*
WA	*The Witch of Atlas*
WW	*Ode to the West Wind*

All references to the works of Blake, without exception (including letters and annotations), are cited in the text *within parentheses* (after the first footnote reference) from *Blake: Complete Writings*, ed. Geoffrey Keynes (London: Oxford University Press, 1966). Blake's long poems, such as *Jerusalem, Milton,* and *The Four Zoas,* are cited by abbreviations followed by the appropriate plate and line numbers, e.g., J.35:46; M.25:36–37; FZ.8:3. The prose sections of *Jerusalem* and *The Marriage of Heaven and Hell,* excepting The Proverbs of Hell, do not have line numbers; therefore, page numbers follow plate number for these sections, e.g., MHH.12–13, p. 153; J.35, p. 163. Line number follows plate number for references to The Proverbs of Hell in *The Marriage of Heaven and Hell,* e.g., MHH.8:10. References to *The Gates of Paradise* are indicated by line numbers, e.g., GP.3–4, except in reference to the illustrations, where only a page number is needed, e.g., (GP, p. 301). *The Everlasting Gospel* is in sections numbered in lowercase letters *a* through *i* with line numbers; therefore, quotations are indicated by section and line number, e.g., EG.e.35. The small prose section of *The Everlasting Gospel* appearing on p. 757 of the Keynes edition is cited as EG, p. 757. *Auguries of Innocence* has only line numbers and is so cited, e.g., AI.26. Three of Blake's longer prose works—*There Is No Natural Religion, A Vision of the Last Judgment, A Descriptive Catalogue*—are referred to by abbreviations followed by the page number in the Keynes edition, e.g., NR, p. 23; VLJ, p. 63; DC, p. 125. Otherwise, Blake's prose works are cited by page number only. When the context permitted in some instances in Blake's long poems, I have supplied the name of the speaker or speakers and have deleted quotation marks and quotation marks within quotation marks.

All references to Shelley's poems, Prefaces to poems and Notes to poems (including Mary Shelley's Notes) are cited in the text within parentheses (after the first footnote reference) from *The Complete Poetical Works of Percy Bysshe Shelley,* ed. Thomas Hutchinson (London: Oxford University Press, 1965). Quotations from the prefaces and notes to poems are cited by page number only. Long poems, such as *Prometheus Unbound, The Revolt of Islam,* and *The Triumph of Life* are cited by abbreviations followed by the appropriate act, scene, line or canto, stanza, line or lines only in the case of *The Triumph of Life,* e.g.: PU.II.ii.36–37; RI.V.vii.40–42; TL.303. Brief references to *Hellas* and *Julian and Maddalo* (both titles are stated in the text) are followed by line numbers in parentheses. All references to Shelley's essays are cited in the notes from *Shelley's Prose or The Trumpet of A Prophecy,* ed. David Lee Clark (Albuquerque: University of New Mexico Press, 1954). All references to Shelley's letters are cited in the notes from *The Letters of Percy Bysshe Shelley,* ed. Frederick L. Jones, 2 vols. (Oxford: Clarendon Press, 1964).

For both Blake and Shelley, titles of short poems usually are given in the text followed by the page number in parentheses from the Keynes edition (Blake) and the Hutchinson edition (Shelley) referred to above. When the title does not appear in the text, it is listed in parentheses immediately preceding the page number, e.g.: "To Nobodaddy," p. 63. No line numbers are given for short poems.

Mind Forg'd Manacles

To my mother and to the memory of my father

Introduction

This study attempts to define and elucidate Blake's and Shelley's ideas about the origin, manifestation, and eradication of evil. William Blake, born in 1757, was thirty-five years old when Percy Bysshe Shelley was born in 1792, and he outlived his younger contemporary by five years. Shelley died in 1822 and Blake in 1827. So far as can be ascertained, they never met, corresponded, or read each other's poetry. Yet, the parallels in their thought are striking, especially their philosophical views on the nature of evil. Shelley published *Queen Mab,* his first important seminal work, in 1813. By that date, Blake had written all of his major Prophetic Books, though he did not complete *Jerusalem* until 1820. This chronology indicates the possibility of Shelley's having been influenced by Blake. Because there is no evidence of such influence, however, the comparison that I undertake in the following pages is analogical. For this reason, the parallels between the two poets seem all the more startling and suggestive. "Astonishing as many parallels are," states S. Foster Damon in noting Blake's analogical relationship to other great thinkers, "especially in the case of Shelley, they are caused by similar methods of thought under similar circumstances."[1] Shelley had his own explanation of this phenomenon:

> It may . . . well be said that Lord Byron imitates Wordsworth, or that Wordsworth imitates Lord Byron, both being great poets, and deriving from the new springs of thought and feeling, which the great events of our age have exposed to view, a similar tone of sentiment, imagery, and expression. A certain similarity all the best writers of any particular age inevitably are marked with, from the spirit of that age acting on all.[2]

Certainly, both Blake and Shelley reacted strongly to the revolutionary spirit of their time, and though at last disillusioned with the course of outer events, they kept their vision of revolutionizing man himself. In this sense, both poets attempted to write "prophetic" poetry, looking forward to an apocalyptic or utopian period in which man would discard the dusty rag-and-bone storehouse of the past and emerge in the new and glowing raiment of his true humanity.

Blake's and Shelley's ideas regarding the nature of evil remain fairly constant throughout their poetry and prose, early and late. Unless otherwise indicated, therefore, the treatment of evil within most of the following chapters is thematic, not chronological. Though Shelley's

thought has been seen as a progress from youthful Godwinian Necessi-
tarianism to mature Platonism (a growth traced by Carl Grabo in *The
Magic Plant*),[3] or to empiricism (which David Lee Clark stresses in his
edition of Shelley's prose),[4] or even to a stoicism in which Shelley no
longer struggled for a resolution of moral or metaphysical questions (so
James Rieger interprets Shelley's final poem *The Triumph of Life*),[5]
Shelley's concept of the nature of evil itself will be found to vary little
from *Queen Mab* (1813) and *The Revolt of Islam* (1818) to *Prometheus
Unbound* (1820) and *The Triumph of Life* (1822), the poem left unfinished
at the time of his death. In each of these poems (and in his essays and
letters) kings, priests, war, the desire for power, slavery, hate, deceit,
worldly ambition and gain, hypocrisy, selfishness, religion, lust, and the
vengeful Christian God are all held up to scorn. The major change from
Queen Mab and *The Revolt of Islam* to *Prometheus Unbound* and *The Triumph
of Life* lies not in Shelley's idea of what is evil, but in his greater emphasis
on what creates evil conditions in the first place—that is, on man's mind
or heart. Both *Queen Mab* and *Prometheus Unbound* look forward to the
regeneration when man will be able to replace hate and fear with love
and trust, but in Prometheus this struggle happens *within* the mind, not
in outer circumstances as in *Queen Mab,* for as soon as Prometheus casts
hate out of his heart, the outer world begins to regenerate itself according to his changed perceptions. By the time Shelley wrote *Prometheus
Unbound* he no longer saw evil as residing simply in institutions that must
be destroyed, and he tended therefore to place more and more emphasis
on imagination as the vehicle through which the outer world of nature
and man's life itself might be reformed. Such an emphasis is clearly
discernible in Shelley's last major essay, "A Defence of Poetry" (1820).
One of his earliest discursive pieces, the pamphlet "An Address to the
Irish People" (1812), calls upon men to rise and throw off the yoke of the
tyrant and, through love, to become free in their souls and bodies. And
that same call echoes and reechoes along the "stream of sound" in
Prometheus Unbound. In this poem, Shelley's stress is more on the psychological, spiritual change within Prometheus and not on a revolutionary
change in outer circumstances. But the nature of the evil remains the
same in the early pamphlet, the major poem, and the final essay. Even
when Shelley appears to discard his early belief in Necessity (stated in
Queen Mab), one can discover it in a transmuted form in both *The Revolt
of Islam* and *Prometheus Unbound*. Shelley's belief (based on feeling) in the
reformation of mankind fought a nearly losing battle with his skepticism
(based on reason) in *The Triumph of Life*. But the definition of evil has not
changed from that found in the early *Queen Mab*. The poet's attitude in
The Triumph of Life toward the possibility of eradicating evil, however, is
far more tentative than it is in *Queen Mab*.

In the same way, from the early *Songs of Innocence* (1789) and *Songs of
Experience* (1794) to the last Prophetic Book, *Jerusalem* (1804–1820),

Blake's idea of evil as a sin, error, or mistake arising from repressed energy remains constant. The heavy chain that the Earth cries out for the Bard to break in the "Introduction" to the *Songs of Experience* has been placed around her by the "selfish father" whom Blake named "Urizen" (reason) in the later Prophetic Books. The "angels" of the early *Marriage of Heaven and Hell* (1790–1793) are all Urizenic reasoners. The entire complex of ideas (jealousy, concealment, pain, repression, mystery) surrounding the character Vala of the Prophetic Books (who is analyzed in Chapter Five) can also be found in the *Songs of Experience,* especially in "My Pretty Rose Tree," "Ah, Sun-Flower," "The Lilly," "The Garden of Love," "London," "A Poison Tree" and "A Little Girl Lost." In her sexual freedom, Oothoon in *Visions of the Daughters of Albion* (1793) is like the female Emanations in *Milton* (1804–1808). The regenerated world Blake depicts at the end of *Jerusalem* is the world of the *Songs of Innocence* but deepened and intensified now through the pain and suffering of acquired "Understanding": the State of Experience. Like Shelley, Blake turned away in *The Four Zoas* (1795–1804) and *Jerusalem* from the revolutionary fervor of his early Prophecies *The French Revolution* (1791) and *America* (1793) when he realized that only a thoroughgoing psychological and spiritual change within man would yield the necessary foundation for a lasting regeneration. But the evil selfhood found in "The Pebble" of the *Songs of Experience* and any of the early Prophecies is the same one he later calls the Spectre, and again like Shelley, he stresses imaginative perception (represented by his titan Los) as a means of overcoming this Spectre. The greater emphasis on Los can be seen by comparing his smaller role in *The Four Zoas* with his broader activity in *Jerusalem*. Almost all of the first ten plates of the latter poem concern Los's efforts to subdue his reasoning Spectre and to make the Spectre work with him rather than against him.

What changes in Blake's Prophetic Books is not his definition of evil but his emphasis or perspective. In *The Book of Urizen* (1794), for example, the struggle of the Zoas (man's personified faculties) during the fall takes place between Urizen (reason) and Los (imagination). As Blake's myth developed in *The Four Zoas* (1795–1804)—a work left in manuscript—he added two other titans to his psychological representation of man: Luvah (emotion) and Tharmas (sensation). In *The Four Zoas,* Urizen and Luvah are the primary contenders. In *Jerusalem* (1804–1820) the struggle is primarily between Los and the Spectre (the most evil and restrictive form of Urizenic reasoning, in which nothing can be believed without "demonstration"). The basic outlines of the struggle, however, do not change: man is divided and must be made whole through the power of imagination.

Most of the extant letters by Blake are dated 1800 and after, when Blake was already forty-three and had completed the basic outlines of his theory of evil in *The Book of Thel* (1789), *The Marriage of Heaven and*

Hell (1790–1793), *Visions of the Daughters of Albion* (1793) and *The Book of Urizen* (1794). Thus, the letters are often useful in defining or clarifying an idea whose poetic expression Blake was then working on in *The Four Zoas* (1795–1804), *Milton* (1804–1808), and *Jerusalem* (1804–1820).

Though the concentration in this study is on Shelley's major works (*The Revolt of Islam, Prometheus Unbound, The Cenci, The Triumph of Life*), and Blake's Prophecies, I have, for the reasons listed above, used the poem, letter, annotation, essay, or other prose composition that most clearly explains the point being made. In certain instances, I have also used biographical materials, when it seemed to me that a specific idea could in this way be clarified or established more solidly, for I am attempting to deal with the concept of evil in the poets' thought as a whole. The emphasis, however, is on the major poems I have listed above.

The similarity of perception between Blake and Shelley is the subject of Chapter One, for the problem of evil—and its eradication—is very closely tied, in both poets' view, to how man sees. In his *The Mirror and the Lamp*, M. H. Abrams has pointed out the general nature of the Romantic mode of perception and how it differs from that generally accepted in all preceding centuries. The most common metaphors in use before the nineteenth century compared "the mind to a reflector of external objects." With the advent of Romanticism the mind becomes "a radiant projector which makes a contribution to the object it perceives."[6] Blake and Shelley's perception is often more radical than even this far-reaching change defined by Mr. Abrams, for both poets tend to see the object as in some sense a *creation* of the mind. In *Prometheus Unbound*, for example, when Prometheus' mind is regenerated, halcyons cease to prey upon fish and are able to feed on the formerly poisonous nightshade. Though Blake's precise idea of evil is not defined and analyzed until Chapter Two and Shelley's not until Chapter Three, this first chapter on perception is a necessary foundation for understanding all the following chapters, since those definitions themselves are firmly rooted in the poets' theories of perception.

Chapter Two delineates Blake's idea of evil under the following aspects: (1) evil as reason; (2) as negative accident; (3) as lack of action (brooding) which binds the perceiver to the past or future; (4) as indefinite (until given a form by the imagination); and (5) as a permanent state so that individuals may forever be delivered from it; for, in Blake's view, one can cast off evil only if it becomes permanently solidified. Of particular note is the discussion of the Tree of Knowledge of Good and Evil, for the separation that exists in what I refer to as the "double Tree" (in contrast to the unified Tree of Life) has far-reaching implications not only for the subject of this chapter but for the remaining ones as well. Here, as elsewhere, I use analogues freely. References

to the works of Robert Browning, Hawthorne, Emily Brontë, Wordsworth, T. S. Eliot, and Yeats are used to aid in the explanation of Blake's
notion of time. As linguists have often noted (and such is sometimes the
case with Blake and Shelley), two writers may use different words to state
the same concept. On the other hand, similar words—or even the same
words—used by two writers may express totally disparate ideas.

Chapter One deals with the affinities between Blake and Shelley's
perceptions—their views on the eradication of evil; Chapter Three turns
to an analysis of Shelley's differences from Blake on this point. Though
most of the Shelleyan evils (which I have listed above) are destroyed at
the end of *Prometheus Unbound,* mankind must still contend with fate,
time, occasion, chance, change, and death. And in Count Cenci Shelley
has created what his character Asia in *Prometheus Unbound* calls an
"immedicable" evil. Blake's Urizen, however, who is responsible in one
form or another for most of the evil and suffering in Blake's myth, is
regenerated when his "error" or "sin" of single vision (that is, the view of
reason alone) is finally brought home to him.

In Chapter Four I discuss what is perhaps the greatest, most significant, and certainly the most profound similarity between Blake and
Shelley: their idea of the evil selfhood (i.e., selfishness), its origin, and its
manifestations in the father, the priest, the king, and the orthodox
Christian God. Both poets discard the Christian God in favor of their
own concept. To Blake, God is another name for the personal Divine
Humanity (the giant Albion), while Shelley, though he infrequently uses
the term *God,* more often speaks of the impersonal Spirit of the Universe, or quite simply, Love.

In his unfallen condition, Blake's Divine Humanity, Albion, exists as
an androgynous being whose feminine portion, called Jerusalem or the
Emanation, is perfectly at one with him. Shelley's idea of the epipsyche—
the feminine half of the male psyche—is quite similar in many respects
to the Blakean Emanation. I discuss these two concepts—the Emanation
and the epipsyche—in Chapter Five. One of the greatest evils attendant
on Albion's fall from Eden is Jerusalem's separation from him—the
division of the universe from its original state of unity into a masculine
mind and a feminine nature. Essentially, this is also Shelley's view in
Prometheus Unbound. As Prometheus' epipsyche, Asia has been separated
from Prometheus because of his "fall," his curse on Jupiter. In *Prometheus Unbound* and *Jerusalem,* when the masculine-feminine components are reunited the universe also becomes whole. Cythna in *The Revolt
of Islam* and Emily in *Epipsychidion* are variations on the epipsychical
theme.

Chapter Six is very closely connected in subject matter to Chapter
Five. In this final chapter, however, I deal with Blake's and Shelley's
notions of woman and sex in a more literal, realistic sense than in the

6INTRODUCTION

preceding chapter. The poets' views on the evils of marriage and prostitution, and lust as distinguished from passion, are strikingly alike even though Shelley stresses women's equality to men and Blake tends to view the female life as a reflection of the male's. The chapter ends with an attempt to show (primarily by discussing opposing views) that Blake and Shelley's idea of the sanctity of the sexual impulse—its cosmic implications—is based on their quality of perception (previously analyzed in Chapter One). That is, "higher" and "lower" aspects of life—the spiritual and the material—may be combined through love.

Since I am cognizant of a "principle of expressive language" in a work of art (what Philip Wheelwright calls "soft focus"), I have endeavored to keep in mind that there are meanings in Blake's and Shelley's poetry that are not exact and stipulative. If strictly defined, such meanings may become more "precise" but will no longer fully represent the original ideas. Precision of this kind almost inevitably means a reduction, whereas true perception means representing the idea as fully—rather than as narrowly—as discursive language will permit. Though Wheelwright applies this principle to the language in an artistic work itself, it can profitably be applied in other ways. "There have been endless disputes about the character of Hamlet," Wheelwright states (in defining "soft focus"), "or, in semantic terms, about what the poetic and dramatic indications of Hamlet's *dramatis persona* 'really mean.' There are virtually no such disputes about Polonius. Would Shakespeare have represented Hamlet more precisely by giving as definite indications as he does of Polonius?"[7]

To be precise and exact does not necessarily imply a greater truth. In fact, modern theories even in the sciences, especially physics, point to the impossibility of such precision because the observer himself and his experiment enter into the answer to the question asked. The physical state under observation may be altered by the observation itself. Thus, Heisenberg's famous "Uncertainty Principle" states that the observer cannot know precisely at the same moment of time both the position and the speed of a particle. "Nature is a network of happenings," states Jacob Bronowski,

> that do not unroll like a red carpet into time, but are intertwined between every part of the world; and we are among those parts. In this nexus, we cannot reach certainty because it is not there to be reached; it goes with the wrong model, and the certain answers ironically are the wrong answers.[8]

Similarly, Richard Feynman, in *The Character of Physical Law*, discusses "approximate symmetries" in this way:

> You have an approximate symmetry, so you calculate a set of consequences supposing it to be perfect. When compared with experiment, it does not agree. Of course—the symmetry you are supposed to expect is approxi-

mate, so if the agreement is pretty good you say, "Nice!", while if the agreement is very poor you say "Well, this particular thing must be especially sensitive to the failure of the symmetry." Now you may laugh, but we have to make progress in that way.[9]

Mathematics itself, the most exact of the sciences, is based on unproved (and apparently unprovable) axioms, some of them contradictory. This has been demonstrated primarily by Gauss and Gödel. "It is well known that the concept of infinity leads to contradictions that have been analyzed," states Heisenberg, "but it would be practically impossible to construct the main parts of mathematics without this concept."[10]

Finally, Louis de Broglie, in *The Revolution in Physics*, stresses that the apparently clear, simple, abstract, and rigid concepts, the "idealizations" of science,

> can never be applied exactly to reality. In order to describe the complexity of reality, it may accordingly be necessary to use successively two (or several) of these idealizations for a single entity.

Thus, such concepts may be "that much less applicable to reality when they become more complete and, although we have little inclination to be paradoxical, we could hold, contrary to Descartes, that nothing is more misleading than a clear and distinct idea."[11]

The lack of "rigid concepts" does not imply a lack of meaning or lack of "truth," nor is it begging the question. It is simply a widening, a greater freedom, of perception. No one would deny that the working hypotheses of science, however tentative, make it possible to understand the world better than the perceiver could otherwise do. If light manifests itself on one occasion as a wave and on another as a particle, the scientist is not thereby prepared to deny the existence of light, but only to say that his method of perceiving it is different on the one occasion from what it is on the other.

Within the first chapter, I use a number of modern scientific concepts as suggestive analogues in my explanation of Blake's and Shelley's ideas of perception. Some of these speculations are often so startlingly close to Romantic theories of perception that they illuminate the latter in unexpected ways. It is important to realize that Blake and Shelley would find themselves in a much more congenial atmosphere in the philosophical world view that has emerged from the scientific studies of Einstein, Bohr, Heisenberg, Broglie, Schrödinger, and others than they did in their own classical, Newtonian, essentially Laplacian world view. As Robert Oppenheimer pointed out in his essay "War and the Nations" (1964):

> Those who have lived through the unravelling of the heart of the atomic paradox as it existed twenty-five or thirty years ago believe that one has come to a vision of the physical world with far more room for the human

spirit in it than could have been found in the great mechanism of
Newton.[12]

For this reason, Blake's model of the universe can perhaps be given
more attention than it otherwise would be. Even when he asserts that the
earth is flat and the sky touchable, his statements deserve notice, for they
suggest knowledge of a superior spatial dimension. If the reader quickly
"object[s] the circumnavigation" as Henry Crabb Robinson did, he
cannot hope to understand Blake's cosmology. He repeats the error of
George III, who (as reported by Gilchrist) waved off some drawings of
Blake's with an impatient and uncomprehending, "Take them away!
Take them away!"[13]

Blake and Shelley's perception—their tendency to synthesize—is
closely tied to their "abstraction," and the poetry of both poets has for
this reason been considered deficient in characterization and in a sense
of tragedy or evil. David Perkins, for example, although noting that "in a
poetry of mystical experience, [Shelley's] premises are probably unassail-
able," finds Shelley lacking in a "literary success" based on "a solid
realization of particulars, of drama, of conflict, and hence of tragedy."[14]
Similarly, Mark Schorer observes of Blake: "His concept of reordering
the personality is . . . deficient of the tragic view of evil." Thus, Blake's is
an "inadequate cosmogony."[15]

I believe this criticism must here be answered so that the reader may
approach the first chapter on perception with the understanding that
Blake and Shelley (*The Cenci* excepted) did not attempt characterization
in the usual dramatic sense. And if one approaches their poetry expecting a tragic view of evil, he will not only be disappointed but will fail to
see what it is that the poets actually are doing: they are attempting
precisely to go beyond the tragic view, to lift perception until all
divisiveness or doubleness (the basis of tragedy) is seen as illusory, until
all things (not simply the "higher" ones) are perceived *sub specie aeternitatis.* Santayana has stated the case for Shelley's perception in this way:

> If you are seriously interested only in what belongs to earth you will not be
> seriously interested in Shelley. Literature, according to Matthew Arnold,
> should be criticism of life, and Shelley did not criticise life; so that his
> poetry had no solidity. But is life, we may ask, the same thing as the
> circumstances of life on earth? Is the spirit of life, that marks and judges
> those circumstances, itself nothing? Music is surely no description of the
> circumstances of life; yet it is relevant to life unmistakably, for it stimulates
> by means of a torrent of abstract movements and images the formal and
> emotional possibilities of living which lie in the spirit.[16]

Without preconceived notions of what poetry should or should not do,
the unprejudiced reader may be able to experience this "torrent of
abstract movements and images" along what Shelley calls the "stream of

sound" in *Prometheus Unbound,* for Shelley's finest and most representative poem approximates the "absolute" condition of music as nearly as poetry (i.e., words) can.

Northrop Frye points out that one must have a taste for "this kind of metaphysical poetry," in which the usual dramatic characterization is missing:

> The heroism of Orc or the ululation of Ololon do not impress us as human realities, like Achilles or Cassandra, but as intellectual ideographs. It all depends on whether the reader has a taste for this kind of metaphysical poetry or not, on whether he is willing to read so uncompromising an address to the intellectual powers. It is not necessary to assume that qualities of poetry which are certainly not in Blake are qualities which Blake tried and failed to produce.[17]

In the same way, it can be assumed that Blake lost his early gift of lyricism and was thus forced to turn to the (as one may think) tortuous, convoluted style he employs in his Prophecies. But one need only look at the surpassingly beautiful lyric (commonly and erroneously called "Jerusalem") "And Did Those Feet in Ancient Time," which opens *Milton,* to see that Blake's lyric gift had survived intact. Other reasons must be found for his preference for the longer and more flexible line he uses in his later works; and one reason, no doubt, is its ability to render what Santayana terms "a torrent of abstract movements."[18]

This problem involving lack of characterization and a tragic view that critics have noted in Blake's and Shelley's poetry is related to the difficulty with which Shelley has been received (or not received) by the twentieth-century "New Critics." Their strictures—those of Paul Elmer More, T. S. Eliot, Mark Schorer, Cleanth Brooks, John Crowe Ransom, and others—are too well known to require documentation. For the most part, they are based on what is conceived as Shelley's "childishness" or "immaturity" and lack of paradox and irony. But, as I. A. Richards remarked,

> Our "Neo-Classic" age is repeating those feats of its predecessor which we least applaud. It is showing a fascinating versatility in travesty. And the poets of the "Romantic" period provide for it what Shakespeare, Milton and Donne were to the early eighteenth-century grammarians and emendators—effigies to be shot at because what they represent is no longer understood.[19]

Shelley's "immaturity," for example, which is no longer understood (if it ever was) actually constitutes a facet of his perception—the same or a similar facet that Jesus had in mind when he told his disciples to become as little children if they would enter the kingdom of heaven (Matthew 18:3; Mark 10:15). Ironically, the implications of this pronouncement have been most tellingly and vitally realized in Zen Buddhism,[20] but the

Romantic age of poetry in the West attempted at least something of the
child's view. Albert S. Gérard defines this element as the basic component of Romanticism:

> If one impulse can be singled out as central to the romantic inspiration, it is
> the *Sehnsucht*, the yearning toward the absolute, the aspiration to oneness
> and wholeness and organic unity, the dream of perfection. To many, both
> before and since the romantic period, this impulse has appeared juvenile.[21]

But appearance may not be reality, and the pejorative terms "immature," "childish" and "juvenile" dismiss the childlike element in Shelley's
poetry without giving any adequate explanation of it or coming to terms
with its really difficult properties. "Spiritual transformation," states
Jung, which is what the poetry of Blake and Shelley is all about,

> does not mean that one should remain a child, but that the adult should
> summon up enough honest self-criticism admixed with humility to see
> where, and in relation to what, he must behave as a child—irrationally, and
> with unreflecting receptivity.[22]

The vision of the kingdom of heaven—"regeneration" or "transformation" in the poetry of Blake and Shelley—opens only to those who
possess or can develop the child's attribute of immediate perception,
living in the moment. "Critics who dislike Shelley . . . are often hostile to
youth (they say 'adolescence'), and rationalize their difficulty with the
poet by calling him immature," writes George M. Ridenour.

> But what we call maturity often seems to be made up of equal parts of
> cowardice and exhaustion. We finally give up our own insistence that the
> world be a human world and then make fun of the people who are still
> working at it. We tell them they are immature.[23]

Blake and Shelley's childlike perception based on energy and immediacy
is discussed in Chapter One.

Each new age (and that of the Romantics was no different), in its
tendency to dismiss the standards of the previous era, reminds one of
the March Hare, the Dormouse, and the Mad Hatter's tea party.
Though the table is a large one, the three are all crowded together at one
corner of it. " 'No room! No room!' they cried out when they saw Alice
coming." And the only possible answer belongs to Alice: "There's *plenty*
of room!"—for the "abstraction" of Blake and Shelley as well as for
tragedy and the paradox and irony that have become, by and large, the
touchstones of the twentieth-century critics' judgment. Because we shall
probably never understand things in a final way, the critics of the
twenty-first century will no doubt repudiate these criteria. For "truth" or
"worth" cannot be defined so rigorously in art (they have not been so far
even in the sciences) that old critical icons shall remain standing. Only a

Brave New World could give us such uniformity, together with the destruction of art itself. The study of elementary particles has opened up a more vibrant and stranger world than we formerly knew, consisting primarily of opposites, time reversals, paradoxes, and contradictions. For the most part, the scientist of our time does not resist these antitheses but accounts for them through the enlargement of his first basic principles, theories, and assumptions. The wise literary critic, I believe, can do no less than follow this example and accept both the wave and the particle as they manifest themselves in the force field of literature. More importantly, the critic has to try, at least, to turn in the direction of the light that creates these "opposites," despite the fact that we see through a glass, darkly.

The Romantic spirit, which can never be a pejorative term to those who fully understand its implications, is revealed essentially in this endeavor. It is an attempt to discover the hidden unity within and among all phenomena. It reveals connections and shows the part in relation to the whole. "Stop this day and night with me and you shall possess the origin of all poems," in the words of Whitman, is the invitation of those who expound and experience these connections. If one can combine sensation, thought, feeling, and imagination in this creative act, his consciousness expands into freedom.

Chapter One

The Narrow Chinks of the Cavern

If the doors of perception were cleansed every thing would appear
to man as it is, infinite.

For man has closed himself up, till he sees all things thro' narrow
chinks of his cavern.

(The Marriage of Heaven and Hell)

Blake's and Shelley's theories about the nature of evil and its eradication
depend on and are determined by their ideas of perception. It is
important, therefore, to establish the basic properties of that perception.
The nature of Blake's vision and, in part, Shelley's vision, as well, may be
explained (and often has been) by their reactions to the eighteenth-century Lockian-Newtonian universe, to which both were heir. But over and
above "reaction" stand poetic minds keenly poised to receive and interpret the slight, subtle intimations that come from what Gogol termed
"man's inner world, full of sounds and holy secrets." It is noteworthy
that Blake told Crabb Robinson that all persons partake of this visionary
capacity but lose it for lack of cultivation.[1]

The view that imaginative vision can overcome what man believes to
be the ingrained evils of the world is largely unqualified in the work of
Blake. The reader is always struck by the coherence and unity of his
apocalyptic vision, both in his prose and verse and in casual statements
made to his friends throughout the course of his entire life. On his death
bed, he sang hymns to the glorious vision of regeneration—to that other
world that was not merely a "vegetable glass"—that was opening out
before him,[2] as it opened out to St. John the Divine on the isle of Patmos.
Shelley, on the other hand, found such a total inclusiveness difficult to
attain, and his work contains passages of uncertainty and even despair
amid his firmer statements of belief.

In many of their major poems, the poets set forth a quality and kind of
vision they believed could regenerate the universe and destroy its
seemingly ineradicable and inevitable evils. They believed that the
perceiver is not simply a passive recording instrument but to a large
extent creates, through the quality of his perception, the nature of the
outer world. He projects preexisting schemata onto the things he per-

ceives around him and by and large sees things as he *expects* to see them. The twentieth-century psychologist terms these schemata "mental sets." In *Art and Illusion,* a study of perception in relation to painting, Ernst Gombrich analyzes an experiment dealing with such mental sets. If the results of this experiment (devised by Adelbert Ames) are applied to Blake's and Shelley's perceptions, it becomes apparent that their mental sets contain schemata and projections of a highly imaginative character that go well beyond the ordinary person's perceptive abilities. In the poets' views, however, any person may develop such abilities by studying art. As a matter of fact, Blake and Shelley attempt to raise the reader's perception through their art so that evil can be overcome. Although Gombrich does not consider perception in its relation to evil, the ideas derived from his discussion of the Ames experiment can be applied to understanding the role of perception in Blake's and Shelley's poetry.

The experiment Gombrich discusses involves three peepholes through which a person looks with one eye at each of three objects (one within each peephole) displayed in the distance. Each time, the person sees a "tubular chair." But if he goes round and looks at these objects from another angle, he sees that only one of them is actually a chair. The object on the right

> is really a distorted, skewy object which only assumes the appearance of a chair from the one angle at which we first looked at it; the middle one presents an even greater surprise: it is not even one coherent object but a variety of wires extended in front of a backdrop on which is painted what we took to be the seat of a chair.

Even undeceived, however, if the person looks again through the peepholes he still sees three chairs because the mind imposes the "known" upon the "unknown": the perceiver cannot imagine (or see) the other, strange shapes with which he is unfamiliar even after he has seen them. Gombrich explains the implications of the experiment in this manner:

> It is important to be quite clear at this point wherein the illusion consists. It consists, I believe, in the conviction that there is only one way of interpreting the visual pattern in front of us. We are blind to the other possible configurations because we literally "cannot imagine" these un-likely objects. They have no name and no habitation in the universe of our experience. Of chairs we know, of the crisscross tangle we do not. Perhaps a man from Mars whose furniture was of that unlikely kind would react differently. To him the chair would always present the illusion that he had the familiar crisscross in front of his eye.
>   One of the facts that Ames [the experimenter] and his associates want to drive home with these demonstrations is, as they put it, that "perceptions are not disclosures." What we can see through the peephole does not directly and immediately reveal to us "what is there"; in fact, we cannot

possibly tell "what is there"; we can only guess, and our guess will be influenced by our expectations. Since we know chairs but have no experience of those crisscross tangles which also "look like" chairs from one point, we cannot imagine, or see, the chair as a crisscross tangle but will always select from the various possible forms the one we know.

The example illustrates the inherent ambiguity of all images and also reminds us of the reasons why we are so rarely aware of them. Ambiguity . . . can never be seen as such. We notice it only by learning to switch from one reading to another and by realizing that both interpretations fit the image equally well.[3]

First, Gombrich states that the major inference drawn from the experiment is that the viewer tends to believe in only *one* way of interpreting the visual pattern in front of him because he *cannot imagine* the other objects. However, a viewer such as a Blake or a Shelley, whose mental set is based upon a wider category of expectation than the ordinary person's, does not have to impose the known upon the unknown. Because he *can* imagine other visual patterns "unlikely shapes," he might be able to see the crisscross tangle. In other words, he might be able to see what is really there even through the peephole, without the necessity of going round and looking from another angle. Such a perceiver is not limited to one way of seeing. His imaginative fluidity permits him to see, in many cases, something other than the expected or the familiar and to see what is really there under two or more aspects at once. The object might "really" be a chair and imaginatively a crisscross tangle or vice versa. Seeing only "one way" is reminiscent of the frog's limited vision, whose eyes are set to receive a specific kind of stimuli, such as the movements of small crawling bugs. Because of this "set" for movement, the frog starves when provided only with dead (and hence motionless) but quite edible flies.[4] On the other hand, Blake can see a tree filled with angels or the sun as a company of the heavenly host or a thistle as an old man because his mental set possesses a wider category of projection than does the ordinary person's. The esemplastic imaginative faculty does not only *modify* perception, as Coleridge states; in Blake and Shelley's view, it also *transforms* what is perceived, often radically. As a matter of fact, such a transformation takes place within the Ancient Mariner: outer objects previously seen as evil and ugly are subsequently seen as good and beautiful. The objects themselves have not changed; the way he perceives the objects has changed. Richard Haven has stated with great clarity the meaning of this transfiguration, a meaning that also holds true for Blake and Shelley's perception:

> The world of time and space is the world of ordinary consciousness, at least for modern Western man. It is our way of locating things and selves in relation to each other, and it underlies our definition of those things and

selves. The Mariner does not go from this place to that place, from this time to that time. What changes is not his location but his relation to the world around him, the structure, so to speak, of his experience. The watersnakes whose beauty he blesses are the same creatures whose loathsomeness repelled him. The world of lovely lights and sweet sounds is the same "place" as that in which his anguished soul was an alien. The consciousness that shrank in upon itself in an agony of isolation is the same as that which opens in a gush of love. The realist looks to experience, but in experience, the Mariner discovers, there is another dimension than time and space, a dimension in which the boundaries between subject and object, between *I* and *it* are not fixed but fluid.[5]

This same "fluid" ability accounts for the typically Shelleyan universe in *Prometheus Unbound*. In this universe all inanimate things are passionately alive, intensely human; and while some are more comfortable in viewing such perception under the form of metaphor, Gombrich also points out: "to our emotion, a window can be an eye and a jug can have a mouth; it is reason which insists on the difference between the narrower class of the real and the wider class of the metaphorical, the barrier between image and reality."[6]

Secondly, Gombrich states that Ames and his associates wished to stress that "perceptions are not disclosures"; that is, what the viewer sees does not necessarily reveal "what is there." The implications of this finding have been clearly summed up by the mathematician Jacob Bronowski:

> In the physical and in the logical worlds, what we have seen happen is the breakdown of the plain model of a world outside ourselves where we simply look on and observe. It has turned out that you can approximate to physics when you make this separation, but there comes a point when the approximation breaks down. When that point was reached in astronomy, Einstein's laws took the place of Newton's. For Relativity derives essentially from the philosophic analysis which insists that there is not a fact and an observer, but a joining of the two in an observation.[7]

Thus, the most recent frontier that has opened in perception cannot be bounded by concepts such as the "real" world of "objects" versus the world of imaginative forms, for there will be a constant interaction of the two, "outer" flowing to "inner" (an arbitrary, if useful, distinction), and "inner" continually transmuting, magnifying or otherwise transforming the "outer." "Admittedly our sense perceptions constitute our sole knowledge about things," the physicist Erwin Schrödinger writes:

> This objective world remains a hypothesis, however natural. If we do adopt it, is it not by far the most natural thing to ascribe to that external world, and not to ourselves, all the characteristics that our sense perceptions find in it.[8]

This "subject" and "object" problem is much the same as the problem of "matter" and "energy" used to be in the realm of physics. The twentieth-century scientist has got round this problem by falling back on the vision of the observer: the world of solid objects is an illusion created by our perception. The receiving apparatus, the brain, imposes preexisting schemata. Objects, however, are "really" made up of centers of energy in constant motion that we "know" but cannot see. Material particles cease to be material in the splitting of the atom, and while the scientist can count them, he does not know what they are. In this connection, Bronowski points up the inherent limitations of what Blake terms the Newtonian or "single vision" view of the universe by drawing attention to the discrepancies between the description of the world given by "an axiomatic system" and that world itself, which contains places where "there will be holes which cannot be filled in by deduction, and at other points two opposite deductions may turn up."[9]

Thirdly, Gombrich points out that the Ames experiment illustrates the inherent ambiguity of all images and that the viewer learns to be aware of such ambiguity *not in itself* but by switching from one interpretation to another and seeing that both fit the image equally well. Perhaps the most famous of these ambiguous images, reproduced in many basic psychology texts, is that of the picture of two persons in black silhouette facing each other on opposite sides of the frame. The silhouettes also form a white vase in the center of the picture. As one looks, one can, with practice, switch quickly back and forth between these two interpretations of the image. One does not, however, see both of them simultaneously. Similarly, in physics, light manifests itself as a wave or as a particle, depending on the nature of the experiment, i.e., on how the experimenter chooses to look at it. Both models are considered equally valid; each "fits the image." Blake, however, apparently possessed the ability to see this ambiguity in itself, to hold two contraries within his mind at once. The essential quality of Shelley's perception, on the other hand, lies in its quickness; as Harold Bloom has said, "the sight or sound too keen for more than a flash of apprehension is the staple of his imagination."[10] And the reader needs a similar acuteness if he is to recognize that sight or sound in its true meaning. Once the reader realizes this, he will not be content with a small amount of effort on his part, but will see, as Northrop Frye says in relation to Blake, that such a poet "demands an energy of response."[11] Only with such responses can one see through "inherent ambiguity" into the essential oneness on which it is grounded.

In their poetry, both Blake and Shelley make their readers aware of an imaginative perception that somehow transforms what it appears to receive from the so-called outer world. "All things exist as they are perceived—at least in relation to the percipient," Shelley states in "A Defence of Poetry."[12] Similarly, Blake speaks for the imaginative transformation of the universe as first perceived by the physical eye, the "single vision" which sees outer objects only. This eye is to be looked through, not with. "Experiments have acquainted us with a paradoxical fact," states Vitus B. Dröscher. "Man can see 'correctly' only because of his imagination. The human eye, optically speaking, is a piece of bad workmanship."[13] What appears as truth to its partial view may be untrue to a full imaginative vision. Thus, while other men may see the sun as "a round disk of fire somewhat like a Guinea," Blake, perceiving with the inner eye of the imagination, sees it as "an Innumerable company of the Heavenly host, crying 'Holy, Holy, Holy is the Lord God Almighty.' "[14] In like manner, Blake reduces the vast interstellar distances considered by astronomy to manageable human dimensions:

> Being irritated by the exclusively scientific talk at a friend's house, which talk had turned on the vastness of space, he cried out, "It is false. I walked the other evening to the end of the earth, and touched the sky with my finger."[15]

Blake could do this because "What is Above is Within" (J.71:6). These seemingly terrible reaches of space—silent distances that so terrified Pascal—as seen by single vision, shrink "the organs / Of life till they become Finite & itself seems Infinite" (M.10:6–7). The imaginative faculty of the poet, however, in transforming his vision, leads to a heightened awareness of the infinite within himself. Northrop Frye has stressed the intensity of consciousness necessary for such an insight:

> By vision [Blake] meant the view of the world, not as it might be, still less as it ordinarily appears, but as it really is when it is seen by human consciousness at its greatest height and intensity. It is the artist's business to attain this heightened or transfigured view of things, and show us what kind of world is actually in front of us, with all its glowing splendours and horrifying evils. It is only the direct, metaphorical, and mythical percep- tions, which work without compromise with unimaginative notions of reality, that can clearly render the forms of such a world.[16]

Blake sees all things as existing within the Divine Humanity, the titan of his work whom he calls "Albion." The outer world of nature—such as the round disk of fire that the sun appears to be—is perceived as being "outer" only since Albion's fall from his previous condition of unity in Eternity:

> For all are Men in Eternity, Rivers, Mountains, Cities, Villages,
> All are Human, & when you enter into their Bosoms you walk
> In Heavens & Earths, as in your own Bosom you bear your Heaven
> And Earth & all you behold; tho' it appears Without, it is Within,
> In your Imagination, of which this World of Mortality is but a
> Shadow. (J.71:15–19)

Peter Fisher points out that " 'nature' to the Druid and the Deist was the basic reality containing a scale of being including man, but to Blake, 'nature' was the lowest degree in a scale of visionary perception which man himself included."[17] The fundamental difference must be borne in mind in order to understand Blake's theory of perception. In a similar vein, Milton O. Percival remarks that nature, to Blake, "is the outward image of man in a state of absence from God."[18]

The outer world, thus, is a projection from within man; it appears to be separate from the perceiver but is in reality a thoroughly human world that can be transformed at any time through apocalyptic vision. Ross Greig Woodman has noted this projection in Shelley's idea of the imagination: "the objects with which man lives are not the existential objects of the external world, but the projected forms of his own psyche. The imagination recreates the universe into a human form."[19] *Prometheus Unbound* contains such an animated, human universe. Energetic and passionate, all its parts yearn toward one another to be joined through love, and such a renovation comes about only because Prometheus has achieved sight: he has perceived truth and therefore it prevails. "[Error] is Burnt up the Moment Men cease to behold it," states Blake (VLJ, p. 617), and this burning up of error can clearly be seen in *Prometheus Unbound*. For example, Ocean reveals to Apollo what will happen within his realm because of the dethronement of the evil Jupiter. This regeneration comes about through Prometheus' changed vision:

> Henceforth the fields of heaven-reflecting sea
> Which are my realm, will heave, unstained with blood,
> Beneath the uplifting winds, like plains of corn
> Swayed by the summer air; my streams will flow
> Round many-peopled continents, and round
> Fortunate isles; and from their glassy thrones
> Blue Proteus and his humid nymphs shall mark
> The shadow of fair ships, as mortals see
> The floating bark of the light-laden moon
> With that white star, its sightless pilot's crest,
> Borne down the rapid sunset's ebbing sea;
> Tracking their path no more by blood and groans,
> And desolation, and the mingled voice
> Of slavery and command; but by the light
> Of wave-reflected flowers, and floating odours,
> And music soft, and mild, free, gentle voices,
> And sweetest music, such as spirits love.[20]

Similarly, the moon and the earth join in a contrapuntal song in celebration of unified sight through love, much like the singing sun that Blake sees.

The major foundation of Blake's theory of perception lies in the fourfold aspect of vision. In this fourfold aspect, man's complete powers of perception—imagination, emotion, reason, and sensation—act in unison. Man's vision must be raised to the fourfold level if he is to transform his universe.

Blake defines the four ways of seeing in a letter to his friend Thomas Butts dated November 22, 1802. In this letter, he poetically divides perception into its outer (lower) and inward (higher) aspects and into four gradations, indicating that his vision is always at least twofold, containing both the outward sight (the object as usually seen) and inward vision (the imaginative meaning of the object in human terms). Thus, when a "frowning Thistle" appears in his path, he sees it as "an old Man grey" who cautions him against turning back to his real poetic work for fear of "Poverty, Envy, old age" and death. (Blake was at this time living at Felpham under the oppressive patronage of William Hayley.) Similarly, he sees his titan Los appear in the form of the sun, and Blake laments that he is no longer under the warmth and light of the sun of Imagination (fourfold vision) represented by Los (pp. 816–818). Nevertheless, he still sees with at least twofold vision. Single vision—a view Blake says he never descends to—is the very lowest form of sight, essentially a perception in which one is actually asleep or blind; he sees mechanically without that energy necessary to transform the object into a living thing, as Blake does when he sees the sun or a thistle. It is the blindness that Voltaire and Rousseau experience when they throw the sands of mockery against the wind. Blake associates Voltaire and Rousseau with "natural religion," i.e., Deism, which denies the visionary capacity of the seer (such as St. John the Divine's, or Isaiah's or Ezekiel's) and discounts his revelations:

Mock on, Mock on Voltaire, Rousseau:
Mock on, Mock on: 'tis all in vain!
You throw the sand against the wind,
And the wind blows it back again. (p. 418)

Threefold vision combines the outward and inward aspect of twofold vision and adds an emotional or loving component. If the perceiver can see the twofold aspect of an object with emotion or love, he can burst through the seeming barrier of subject-object into the highest plane of imaginative vision.

The highest vision (which combines the other three: the object itself; the object in a human aspect; the object perceived emotionally) is fourfold (imaginative) because in it all the powers of man (whom Blake calls "Albion") are blended and in harmony. Blake terms these powers

"Zoas": Urthona-Los (imagination, intuition, poetic genius); Luvah (love, passion, feeling, heart); Urizen (mind, reason); and Tharmas (sensation, body). Single vision, on the other hand, exists when the cold faculty of reason dominates over the others, a condition that Blake terms "Newton's sleep" because he associates this view with Newton's rigid and mechanical universe of law (p. 818). Although in Blake's myth all the Zoas strive for domination over Albion after his fall from Eternity, Urizen is largely responsible for the initial catastrophe because he is the first to separate himself from Eternity and the other Zoas, to battle for dominion, to seek solids without fluctuation, to divide, measure and weigh, to impose rule and law, to look into the future and attempt to control it. Thus, single vision is always the inflexible view of the reason that sees the sun as a round disk of fire somewhat like a guinea.

Single vision versus fourfold vision may be more concretely illustrated by noting Henry Crabb Robinson's response to Blake's contention that the earth was flat. Crabb Robinson, a barrister, spent much of his spare time traveling about London playing whist and collecting the sayings of the great literary men (Wordsworth, Coleridge, Lamb, for example) to whom he was introduced. He met Blake in 1825, two years before the poet's death. When he and Blake showed up at the same dinner party, it was a real occasion for Crabb Robinson's diary because he thought Blake mad, although he admired his artistic ability. When Blake asserted that the earth was flat, therefore, Crabb Robinson "objected the circumnavigation," but at that moment they were called to dinner and Blake's reply was lost.[21] What Blake probably meant is that he saw the earth as an "infinite plane" (M.15:32); or as G. R. S. Mead explains:

> Three-dimensional space is for normal sight bounded by surfaces; those who have inner vision ("four-dimensional" sight) say that the contents of an object—e.g., a watch—appear, in some incomprehensible way, spread out before them as on a surface.[22]

Blake refers to the "flat Earth" in *Milton,* and states that the view of the world "As of a Globe rolling thro' Voidness . . . is a delusion of Ulro" (M.29:16)—that is, a delusion created by Albion's fall into the natural world where he retains only five of his previously infinite senses. The astronomer William Bonner, in *The Mystery of the Expanding Universe,* observes that "a four-dimensional structure is the *ultimate reality,* but our *mode of perception* makes us split it into three spatial dimensions and one of time."[23] The analogy with Blake's four Zoas is by no means exact (and it is not meant to be), but the astronomer's idea of "ultimate reality" having a fourfold structure that is somehow *split* by our mode of perception is surprisingly close to Blake's idea of an original fourfold vision that Albion loses in his fall. Perhaps those who can combine the three spatial dimensions and the one of time in their usual way of seeing the world around them are able to see subject and object, the past and the future, from a unified instead of a split perspective. If one could travel at the speed of light, for example (or perceive imaginatively at that speed—to "burst," in Shelley's term), time would no longer remain what it is for us on the comparatively slow-moving earth. "A light ray, i.e., a wave carrying a photon," explains the scientist Charles Noël Martin,

> which has exactly the same speed as light, is completely severed from time (according to our standards). While it leaves a star, one aeon away from us, to be observed on earth one billion years later, the photon itself "experiences" its own departure and arrival as simultaneous events.[24]

In Blake's view, the fall has produced the inversion, restriction, and shrinking of man's formerly infinite, fourfold perceptive powers. Out of his infinite senses he could expand or contract at will, man in his fall from Eternity retains only five. In *The Four Zoas* Blake indicates how such an inversion came to pass.

As previously stated, the Zoas are the four powers—reason, imagination, emotion, and sensation—of Albion (Man). In their original state in Eternity these powers operate in concert. Within the circle of being, Albion, Tharmas (sensation) is in the West, Luvah (emotion) in the East, Urizen (reason) in the South, and Urthona (imagination)—called Los after the fall—in the North. Though Urthona's place is in the North, Blake considers it the Nadir, the deepest point of the cosmos, the basis or foundation of the cosmic man, Albion, in imagination. Urizen's position in the South is the highest point, the Zenith, the head of Albion. Luvah's position is in the East, the Center (the heart), and Tharmas' is in the West, Circumference (body or sensation). These seem to be their eternal positions (J.12:54–58). However, as S. Foster Damon interprets the fall of the Zoas, Urizen *rises* into the Zenith, usurping Urthona's place, and Urthona *sinks* to the Nadir. In the regeneration, Urthona assumes his rightful place in the North and Urizen returns to the South.[25] Milton O. Percival, on the other hand, sees the Zenith, Urizen's realm, as *originally* the highest point. When Urizen falls, he sinks *below* the North so that the poles become inverted.[26] In any case, whether Urizen rises or sinks, an inversion of right and left has taken place in his usurpation of Urthona's realm. The original instigators of the fall are Urizen and Luvah.

Both Urizen and Luvah function as the ambitious Satans of Blake's myth. Actuated by "foul ambition" (FZ.4:141–142), Urizen, wishing to usurp Urthona's position in the North, gives his own "horses of Light into the hands of Luvah" (FZ.4:113): "deep in the North I place my lot," he says to Luvah, "Thou in the South" (FZ.1:491–492). Though Luvah at first declines Urizen's offer (FZ.1:504–513), Urizen "with darkness overspreading all the armies, / Sent round his heralds secretly commanding to depart / Into the north" (FZ.1:535–537). Urizen seems willing to give up his steeds of light at this point, but later he accuses Luvah of stealing "the wine of the Almighty" (apparently symbolizing the desire for domination)—a wine Luvah gave to Urizen in exchange for the latter's steeds. Urizen, in his own words, drunk on the "immortal draught," fell from his "throne sublime" (FZ.5:237). Luvah, after Urizen was intoxicated, then "*siez'd* the Horses of Light" (FZ.1.264, italics mine), instead of simply accepting them from Urizen. In any case, whether the horses were a gift on Urizen's part or whether Luvah stole them as Urizen asserts, the horses themselves realize they are in the wrong position: "How rag'd the golden horses of Urizen, bound to the chariot of Love" (FZ.7b.201). In other words, regardless of how the two Zoas see their falls, reason (South) attempts to take the place of the imagination (North), and love or emotion (East) attempts to take the place of reason (South).

This contention and displacement within Albion—the Microcosm and the Macrocosm—bring about his fall from Eternity. With his Zoas in upside-down positions, Albion's vision also becomes distorted: metaphysically and psychologically he stands on his head so that right and left become inverted.[27] Blake states that "the Modern Church [i.e., Urizenic religion] Crucifies Christ with the Head Downwards" (VLJ, p. 615); that is, it has inverted the true right and left and placed the Divine Vision Jesus in the position that fallen man assumes in his birth. A Gnostic text, *The Martyrdom of Peter,* in which Peter himself speaks, throws much light on Blake's conception:

> "Fitly wert Thou alone stretched on the cross with head on high, O Lord, who hast redeemed all of the world from sin. I have desired to imitate Thee in Thy passion too; yet would I not take on myself to be hanged upright. For we, pure men and sinners, are born from Adam, but Thou art God of God, Light of true Light, before all aeons and after them; thought worthy to become for men Man without stain of man, Thou hast stood forth man's glorious Saviour. Thou ever upright, ever-raised on high eternally above! We, men according to the flesh, are sons of the first man (Adam), who sunk his being in the earth, whose fall in human generation is shown forth. For we are brought to birth in such a way, that we do seem to be poured into earth, so that *the right is left, the left doth right become*; in that our state is changed in those who are the authors of this life. *For this world down below doth think the right what is the left.*"[28]

Albion's failure in perception and the revolt among his Zoas come about because he refuses to behold the divine vision of unity. Because of this, Urizen can ultimately achieve dominance within him.

In *The Four Zoas,* Los states that "Refusing to behold the Divine Image which all behold / And live thereby, [Albion] is sunk down into a deadly sleep" (FZ.1.290–291). Essentially, Albion has turned "his Eyes outward to Self, losing the Divine Vision" (FZ.2:2). Similarly, in *Jerusalem,* Los sees that "Albion had turn'd his back against the Divine Vision" (J.39:14), the first movement of his fall into the natural world of the five senses. When Albion loses the Divine Vision, the principle of unity is broken and the universe he contained within himself flees away from him (J.70:32), often taking on the form of that mighty polypus that Blake describes in *Milton* (34:24–31) and *Jerusalem* (15:4–5; 49:24–25). The serpent form that nature thus takes is associated with the suffering and constriction that prevail in the fallen world. Man loses the sense that all things are a part of his own nature and proceeds to restrict, solidify, or destroy them. When this Urizenic view holds sway, he becomes guilty of

> clouding with a cloud,
> And building arches high, & cities, turrets & towers & domes
> Whose smoke destroy'd the pleasant gardens, & whose running kennels
> Chok'd the bright rivers. (FZ.9:166–169)

Only at the apocalypse does man, who "looks out in tree & herb & fish & bird & beast" collect "the scatter'd portions of his immortal body" (FZ.8:561–562). Until that time, however, he continues to rend and wrench his universe into the various perverted forms it wears, not realizing that he is rending his own body. This is why both Blake and Shelley stress raising the perception through art. Shelley, for example, asserts that when the outer world assumes dominance over the inner one in this manner, the only answer is to activate the poetic faculty (whom Blake calls "Los") that lies dormant within us:

> The cultivation of poetry is never more to be desired than at periods when, from an excess of the selfish and calculating principle, the accumulation of the materials of external life exceed the quantity of the power of assimilating them to the internal laws of human nature.[29]

This "accumulation of the materials of external life," brought about by restricted vision, creates a suffering world in the highest degree. And not the least of the sufferers in that world is man himself, for the pain he inflicts ultimately recoils upon him, so closely are all things interrelated:

> Each outcry of the hunted Hare
> A fibre from the Brain does tear. (AI.13–14)

In the fallen world, love (as a form of energy) is especially restricted, as Blake indicates in *The Marriage of Heaven and Hell.* Thus, the Zoa who represents Love—Luvah—is bound down and tortured by the Sons of Albion on a "Stone of Trial." In torturing Luvah, however, the Sons of

Albion discover, like Prometheus in his hate for Jupiter, that they are
also torturing themselves:

> they rejoice over Luvah in mockery & bitter scorn.
> Sudden they become like what they behold, in howlings & deadly
>   pain:
> Spasms smite their features, sinews & limbs: pale they look on
>   one another;
> They turn, contorted: their iron necks bend unwilling towards
> Luvah: their lips tremble: their muscular fibres are cramp'd
>   & smitten:
> They become like what they behold! (J.65:74–79)

Similarly, one of the most terrifying aspects of the fall is that Los must
bind Urizen after the latter separates himself from Eternity. Blake sees
the fall not only in terms of Urizen's displacement of Urthona and
Albion's loss of the Divine Vision: Urizen is also guilty of separating
himself, closing himself off, from Eternity. After he performs this
action, Los must bind him with the five senses (symbolic of man's
"natural" or "unspiritual" condition) in order to keep him from falling
into the Void of Non-Entity (Blake's name for total annihilation).
Though this action is necessary, in performing it Los "became what he
beheld"—that is, he becomes bound and restricted (FZ.4:203), though
the imagination always has means, such as artistic endeavor, of overcoming restriction. As Los becomes what he beholds, so too does Prometheus
see himself in his torturing Furies, who are the outward embodiment of
his inward hate: "Whilst I behold such execrable shapes / Methinks I
grow like what I contemplate" (PU.I.449–450). Thus, neither Blake nor
Shelley sees the universe with a vision that divides subject and object, the
outer world from the mind which projects it: whatever is projected
returns to the beholder and he becomes like it. In Shelley's view, for
example, no one is less free than the tyrant, who in enslaving others also
becomes a slave: "for none of Woman born, / Can choose but drain the
bitter dregs of woe, / Which ever from the oppressed to the oppressors
flow" (RI.VIII.xv.3332–3333). This statement from *The Revolt of Islam* is
made by Cythna to the mariners who rescue her after her escape from
the sea-cave where she has been confined by the tyrant; and she
indicates—as in Luvah's Stone of Trial—that man builds or projects out
of his own mind the altar on which he himself is bound and sacrificed:

> Man seeks for gold in mines, that he may weave
> A lasting chain for his own slavery;—
> In fear and restless care that he may live
>   He toils for others, who must ever be
>   The joyless thralls of like captivity;
> He murders, for his chiefs delight in ruin;
>   He builds the altar, that its idol's fee

May be his very blood; he is pursuing—
O, blind and willing wretch!—his own obscure undoing. (RI.VIII.xiv)

Of course, in man's fallen state, a perception capable of overcoming this blindness is extremely difficult to develop, and only the most titanic Losian labors in art suffice to turn ordinary single sight into imaginative vision. For much of the outer creation reflects the fallen nature of man, especially his unbelief in the divine vision he has lost:

The Bat that flits at close of Eve
Has left the Brain that won't Believe.
The Owl that calls upon the Night
Speaks the Unbeliever's fright. (AI.25–28)

Once fourfold vision is achieved, however,

                                  the scaly newt creeps
From the stone, & the armed fly springs from the rocky crevice,
The spider, The bat burst from the harden'd slime, crying
To one another: "What are we, & whence is our joy & delight?" (FZ.9:606–609)

Both Blake and Shelley maintain the view that a world not trans- formed through imaginative vision is inevitably a world of suffering.[30] In *Prometheus Unbound,* for example, the universe falls into such a condition because Prometheus gives in to his hate for Jupiter—a drastic failure of vision—and Prometheus lies stretched out on his painful rock in the Indian Caucasus much as Albion does on his oozy rock in the natural world amid the Sea of Time and Space. In both instances, we see clearly the condition of the universe before the fire of regeneration cleanses it. Albion lies

Upon the Oozy rock inwrapped with the weeds of death.
His eyes sink hollow in his head, his flesh cover'd with slime
And shrunk up to the bones; alas, that Man should come to this!
His strong bones beat with snows & hid within the caves of night,
Marrowless, bloodless, falling into dust, driven by the winds.
O how the horrors of Eternal Death take hold on Man!
His faint groans shake the caves & issue thro' the desolate rocks,
And the strong Eagle, now with numming cold blighted of feathers,
Once like the pride of the sun, now flagging on cold night,
Hovers with blasted wings aloft, watching with Eager Eye
Till Man shall leave a corruptible body. (FZ.8:514–524)

Prometheus experiences a similar state, and cries out in his initial address to Jupiter:

The crawling glaciers pierce me with the spears
Of their moon-freezing crystals, the bright chains

> Eat with their burning cold into my bones.
> Heaven's winged hound, polluting from thy lips
> His beak in poison not his own, tears up
> My heart; and shapeless sights come wandering by,
> The ghastly people of the realm of dream,
> Mocking me: and the Earthquake-fiends are charged
> To wrench the rivets from my quivering wounds
> When the rocks split and close again behind:
> While from their loud aybsses howling throng
> The genii of the storm, urging the rage
> Of whirlwind, and afflict me with keen hail. (PU.I.31–43)

In this striking similarity, it is apparent that Shelley's titan as well as Blake's has experienced a failure of vision, a failure overcome in both cases through a loving perception that blesses all creation.

Before such a change, however, most things remain, in their condition of suffering, inimical or silent. All fluid movement has been lost.[31] The voices from the Mountains, Springs, Air, and Whirlwinds that reveal to Prometheus the effects of his curse speak of being "stained with bitter blood," of "many a rending groan," of the descent of darkness, and finally of being forced into a hellish silence:

> for dreams of ruin
> To frozen caves our flight pursuing
> Made us keep silence—thus—and thus—
> Though silence is as hell to us. (PU.I.79;85;103–106)

When the oppressive tyrant Urizen (the single view of the reason) who is largely responsible for most of the "rending groans" in Blake's myth, explores his dens in the Sixth Night of *The Four Zoas,* the living creatures of the fallen world—in this case a scorpion and a lion—will not speak to him and indeed attack him instead:

> Oft would he stand & question a fierce scorpion glowing with gold;
> In vain; the terror heard not. Then a lion he would sieze
> By the fierce mane, staying his howling course; in vain the voice
> Of Urizen, in vain the Eloquent tongue. A Rock, A Cloud, a
>   Mountain,
> Were now not Vocal as in Climes of happy Eternity
> Where the lamb replies to the infant voice, & the lion to the man
>   of years
> Giving them sweet instructions; where the Cloud, the River & the
>   Field
> Talk with the husbandman & shepherd. But these attack'd him sore,
> Siezing upon his feet, & rending the sinews, that in Caves
> He hid to recure his obstructed powers with rest & oblivion. (FZ.6:131–140)

In a universe not reformed through vision, all things exist in separation. Urizen speaks, but his voice is only "inarticulate thunder" (FZ.6:124) to his creatures; for the voice and the word are divided. The voice speaks, but the word is not uttered.[32] In the transformed universe, however (that of the visionary), the lion easily understands the word and guards the lovely Lyca in Blake's "The Little Girl Lost" and "The Little Girl Found" (pp. 112–115); or he watches over the sheepfold in "Night" (pp. 118–119).

This transformed universe is heralded by song and sound, music and the dance; joy and movement break through the constriction, silence, and suffering. The Chorus of Hours in Act Four of *Prometheus Unbound* before Prometheus' regeneration

> were hounds
> Which chased the day like a bleeding deer,
> And it limped and stumbled with many wounds
> Through the nightly dells of the desert year.

After Prometheus' release, the Hours no longer stumble or limp but dance in harmony:

> But now, oh weave the mystic measure
> Of music, and dance, and shapes of light,
> Let the Hours, and the spirits of might and pleasure,
> Like the clouds and sunbeams, unite. (PU.IV.73–79)

Similarly, when Ione questions "What is that awful sound?" Panthea replies:

> 'Tis the deep music of the rolling world
> Kindling within the strings of the waved air
> Aeolian modulations. (PU.IV.185–188)

In his discussion of *Prometheus Unbound,* Bennett Weaver has subsumed its entire structure under "song." Speaking of the plays of Seneca, Jonson, and Racine, he states:

> There is a structure of crystal and of frost, there is a structure of water and wind. The one is static; the other is fluid. The one is fixed; the other is moving. The structure of *Prometheus Unbound* is one that moves, and moves away from circumstance toward song.[33]

In the following observation from his Notes to *Hellas* (1822), Shelley recognizes the difficulty of setting forth his vision of joyful renewal: "Prophecies of wars, and rumours of wars, etc., may safely be made by poet or prophet in any age, but to anticipate however darkly a period of regeneration and happiness is a more hazardous exercise of the faculty which bards possess or feign" (p. 479). In this "hazardous exercise" he chose song or sound as the most effective means of raising his readers' perception—if it could be raised—into a higher awareness. This effort can certainly be experienced in the lyrics of the Fourth Act of *Prometheus Unbound*. Glenn O'Malley has demonstrated the synesthetic design of the poem that he calls the "stream-of-sound," using Shelley's own term. The Fourth Act is "a cosmic vision in which Shelley floats a series of intricate apparitions on an uninterrupted stream-of-sound." The "stream" comprises the earth's atmosphere: spray, vapors, the ocean, clouds, dew, rain, streams, electrical phenomena, and represents physical life; the "sound" comprises all song and harmony and represents love.[34] In this blend, the entire universe moves and sings, and the physical or "lower" world becomes one with the spiritual "higher" one: the barrier between inner and outer, subject and object, no longer exists.

In Blake and Shelley's perception, true permanence resides in all fluid forms: a song that dies away on the wind, a flowing stream, or a cloud that constantly changes shape. "I change, but I cannot die" says Shelley's Cloud (p. 602, 1.76). Keats, feeling that he would be unremembered, desired to have the following epitaph: "Here lieth one whose name was writ on water." But the permanent songs of the Piper in the "Introduction" to the *Songs of Innocence* are written on water, lightly and delicately, not in a heavy book which the child (who speaks to the Piper out of a cloud) must struggle to lift. The Fairy who dictates *Europe* to Blake "bribes" the Poet into feeding him on love thoughts by offering to write a book on leaves of flowers (E.III.14–15). In Blake's final illustration to the Book of Job, Job and his family have discarded their heavy books and sitting position in favor of light musical instruments. They are all now standing up in poses of extraordinary buoyancy.

One must possess an unusual capacity of vision to "see" such a transformation. "I see Every thing I paint in This World," Blake wrote to The Rev. Dr. Trusler,

> but Every body does not see alike. To the Eyes of a Miser a Guinea is more beautiful than the Sun, & a bag worn with the use of Money has more beautiful proportions than a Vine filled with Grapes. The tree which moves some to tears of joy is in the Eyes of others only a Green thing that stands in the way.

He adds: "As a man is, So he Sees" (p. 793). In this connection, Peter F. Fisher states, "man's possibilities lie in developing his powers of perception and not in identifying himself with what he has already observed. If he allows himself to think that his particular degree of perception is unalterable, so it becomes."[35] Such unalterability is the state of solidification that Urizen creates wherever he goes (until the apocalypse), and it is symbolized throughout Blake's myth by the Druid stone of human sacrifice set up by Urizen and his priests and kept supplied by Rahab (mystery religion) and Tirzah (restrictive moral law)—a stone that makes those who behold it equally rigid and inflexible. It is a way of perceiving in which object and subject become totally unrelated; Urizen raises his "world of solid obstruction" (BU.4:23). The hope of release lies in the Losian poet, who realizes, in the words of Nicholas Berdyaev, that "truth does not face a ready-made reality outside itself, it is the creative transforming of reality." He adds: "Truth means change, it is the transfiguration of given reality."[36] Although he is more skeptical than Blake regarding the possibility of this transfiguration,[37] Shelley nevertheless indicates that what he terms his "early materialism" (i.e., ideas based on those of Locke, Hume, Hartley, and Holbach) ultimately failed to satisfy him; and he states in his "Essay on Life":

> whatever may be [man's] true and final destination, there is a spirit within him at enmity with nothingness and dissolution. This is the character of all life and being. Each is at once the centre and the circumference, the point to which all things are referred, and the line in which all things are contained.[38]

Thus, despite his doubts, one position that Shelley often takes, as in *Prometheus Unbound,* is that the mind possesses the ability to transform creation. Such a position is affirmed, for example, in *Julian and Maddalo.* Shelley (as Julian) attempts to reveal this power to Byron (as Maddalo):

> We might be otherwise—we might be all
> We dream of happy, high, majestical.
> Where is the love, beauty, and truth we seek
> But in our mind? and if we were not weak
> Should we be less in deed than in desire? (172–176)

Similarly, Blake contends that "Mental Things are alone Real; what is call'd Corporeal, Nobody Knows of its Dwelling Place: it is in Fallacy, & its Existence an Imposture. Where is the Existence Out of Mind or Thought? Where is it but in the Mind of a Fool?" (VLJ, p. 617).[39]

Even before the apocalypse that comes at the end of Blake's myth, one may learn to see in a way that lifts the barriers from the doors of perception. Man, although fallen, still retains within himself the necessary energy to overcome the dead weight of Ulro if he will but use it instead of listening to the Urizenic voice of caution and restriction. While wreaking great havoc, the violent forms in the nature he sees around him nevertheless point to an eternal aspect of himself that his reason can suppress only intermittently and ineffectually: "The roaring of lions, the howling of wolves, the raging of the stormy sea, and the destructive sword, are portions of eternity, too great for the eye of man" (MHH.8:7). Therefore, "the wrath of the lion is the wisdom of God"

(MHH.8:4). It is wisdom because wrath may break up Urizen's solids
when other methods have failed. The appearance of wrath indicates that
energy is not totally suppressed, that a revolution is possible.

One may also achieve sight through the energy expended in artistic
creation. Los—the titan in Blake's myth who represents imagination—in
building his city of art, Golgonooza, pours his energy into his art and
achieves a vision through which the apparently solid, finite, and restricted world becomes fluid, infinite, and expansive. Similarly, the
energy in Shelley's burning fountain in *Adonais* (1821) pours down on
the Poet's frail bark below and splits open the skies to reveal the eternal
One. In the poetry of both poets, the reader often experiences a
characteristic "bursting" movement, an informing, centrifugal breath
that succeeds in breaking up usual and ordinary modes of perception.[40]
This bursting (a term Shelley himself uses) movement can be felt
especially in Stanza XLIII of *Adonais,* as the one Spirit's plastic stress

> Sweeps through the dull dense world, compelling there,
> All new successions to the forms they wear;
> Torturing th' unwilling dross that checks its flight
> To its own likeness, as each mass may bear;
> And bursting in its beauty and its might
> From trees and beasts and men into the Heaven's light. (AD.XLIII.381–387)

Blake also sets the universe into energetic motion, revealing a place
where all is breathing, living and divine. The Fairy in *Europe* tells the
Poet: "I'll sing to you to this soft lute, and shew you all alive / The world,
where every particle of dust breathes forth its joy" (E.III.17–18). Similarly, the Fairy in *Queen Mab* reveals to Ianthe that the world around her
is alive down to its smallest particle:

> I tell thee that those viewless beings,
> Whose mansion is the smallest particle
> Of the impassive atmosphere,
> Think, feel and live like man. (QM.II.231–234)

This aspect of Shelley's imagination is more noticeable, perhaps, in this
early work, but it was a faculty he never entirely lost, as a reading of
Prometheus Unbound will reveal. Carl Grabo has remarked:

> the animated universe of his subsequent and greater verse displays the
> same imaginative faculty which endows even inanimate things with a
> peculiar and characteristic life. In Shelley existed, along with his critical
> intellect, a primitive power of animating the common phenomena of
> earth, a power kin to that of the myth-makers in the dawn of the human
> imagination.[41]

This same power can also be seen in the poetry of Blake, and especially in the Lilly, the Cloud, the Worm and the Clod of Clay in *The Book of Thel,* who disclose to the maiden who fears to enter into vegetated existence that "our steeds drink of the golden springs / Where Luvah doth renew his horses" (BT.3:7–8)—that is, even the so-called lowest forms of existence or being take part in the universal love by which all things are related. "If a thing loves," Blake states, "it is infinite" (p. 91).

Blake places emphasis on energy because it raises the level of perception so that the inflexibility of the reason is broken through. In this attempt "Rintrah roars & shakes his fires in the burden'd air" at the beginning of *The Marriage of Heaven and Hell* (2:1). "The tygers of wrath are wiser than the horses of instruction" (MHH.9:5) because the tigers are engaged in the destruction of single vision while the horses are perpetuating it through Urizen's solidified laws and customs. Such solidification appears especially in the Gradgrindian education of the child which obliterates the imagination. Blake was grateful that he escaped the horses of instruction: "Thank God, I never was sent to school / To be Flog'd into following the Style of a Fool" (p. 550). The Urizenic school, like standing water, is poisonous (MHH.9–6). Only the swift intensity of the imagination can keep perception (and its objects) free and flowing. Blake replies to Lavater's aphorism "He submits to be seen through a microscope, who suffers himself to be caught in a fit of passion" with "& such a one I dare love" (p. 85), for this at the least is an impulse towards breaking up the restrictions of reason so that a higher insight may be achieved. For in Blake's Eden, among the Eternals, wrath gives place to love and there is continual forgiveness and mutual sacrifice.

Thus, the highest state of Eden or imaginative insight—the Losian view of the universe—is achieved by an understanding based on energy. It cannot be achieved by "holiness," that is, by moral codes that set standards of behavior. "Men are admitted into Heaven," states Blake, "not because they have curbed & govern'd their Passions or have No Passions, but because they have Cultivated their Understandings" (VLJ, p. 615). Similarly, he told the uncomprehending Crabb Robinson that "there is suffering in heaven, for where there is the capacity of enjoyment there is the capacity of pain."[42] Urizen, throughout Blake's Prophetic Books, attempts to curb and suppress the passions in favor of a rigid moral code based on the idea of "good"—an abstraction that tends to harden into a law that is applied everywhere and on all occasions with equal rigor: "One law for the lion and ox is oppression" (MHH.22–24, p. 158).

José Ortega y Gasset, in his essay "The Sportive Origin of the State," affirms a Blakean view of energy when he states, "all utilitarian actions aiming at adaption, all mere reactions to pressing needs, must be considered as secondary vital functions, while the first and original activity of life is always spontaneous, effusive, overflowing, a liberal expansion of pre-existing energies." This "liberal expansion of pre-existing energies" could stand as a definition of Blake's fourfold vision, which flows from the perceiver himself to transform the world out of its present state and into its imaginative form. In the same essay, Ortega points out an instructive example of liberality:

> A billiard ball colliding with another imparts to it an impulse in principle equal to its own; cause and effect are equal. But when the spur's point ever so lightly touches its flank, the thoroughbred breaks into a gallop, generously out of proportion to the impulse of the spur.[43]

The billiard ball world is Urizen's world, whose children

>   wept, & built
> Tombs in the desolate places,
> And form'd laws of prudence, and call'd them
> The eternal laws of God. (BU.28:4–7)

Superfluity, abundance, quickness, intensity, an overflowing quality, on the contrary, are characteristic of the Losian world of the poet; for, as Northrop Frye has indicated regarding Blake's dislike of the "Military" classical virtues and his preference for Hebrew prophecy in their stead: "dignity and prudence" are not "essentially imaginative" qualities.[44] In his laws of prudence Urizen includes "stern demands of Right & Duty instead of Liberty" (FZ.1:37). The wheel of his religion (Urizen represents the orthodox Christian God created by reason as well as reason itself) moves "From west to east, against the current of / Creation"—for the reason creates all restrictive religious codes—and man is "shrunk up / Into a little root a fathom long" (J.77:4–5; 10–11). The idea of duty, as in Blake's first two or three illustrations to the Book of Job, is particularly pernicious because it is necessarily a restriction placed upon the free-flowing nature of love. In Blake's view, Job's error consists in his self-righteousness (like that of the angels in *The Marriage of Heaven and Hell*), an error finally purged by his great sufferings. Shelley expresses a similar idea about duty, for duty is based on the containment of energy—a kind of slavery to the lowest common denominator in human relationships that both poets attempt to combat. To Shelley, one of the worst conditions of slavery and superstition that can obtain within the human spirit is to refrain from harming another because of duty or from fear of punishment. There is no worth in such a coercive virtue. Rather, one who is "the willing author of extensive benefit" requires no other reason than "the happiness of mankind" in performing any act.[45]

In Blake's view, man cannot expect to see truly and to overcome evil and suffering until he understands how to right himself out of the inverted position assumed in his fall. Blake's poetry is in large part an attempt to reveal how this may be accomplished. "The Nature of my Work is Visionary or Imaginative; it is an Endeavour to Restore what the Ancients call'd the Golden Age," he states (p. 605).

In *The Marriage of Heaven and Hell* Blake attempts to set man's vision to rights by inverting the invertors: the angels are the actual devils; the so-called devils represent the true good. The powerfully imaginative, nonreasonable, paradoxical thrust needed to break out of habitual patterns of thought and perception is indicated primarily in *The Marriage* by the prophets Isaiah and Ezekiel. The Old Testament prophets dine with Blake—"A Memorable Fancy"—and answer his questions about the nature of their perceptions. Isaiah states that he did not see God "in a finite organical perception" but that his "senses discover'd the infinite in every thing." Ezekiel then confirms the idea that the infinite may be discovered in *every thing* without exception by answering Blake's question: "Why he eat dung, & lay so long on his right & left side?" Ezekiel replies: "the desire of raising other men into a perception of the infinite" (MHH.12–13, pp. 153–154). Thus, the so-called "lower" aspects of life are seen as lower only because of faulty vision; in reality, they are inextricably tied to the "higher" or spiritual aspects. True vision implies "marrying" them so that soul and body, for example, become one. Blake states that his method of raising perception will be to melt *apparent* surfaces away in order to reveal reality:

> But first the notion that man has a body distinct from his soul is to be expunged; this I shall do by printing in the infernal method, by corrosives, which in Hell are salutary and medicinal, melting apparent surfaces away, and displaying the infinite which was hid.
>
> If the doors of perception were cleansed every thing would appear to man as it is, infinite.
>
> For man has closed himself up, till he sees all things thro' narrow chinks of his cavern. (MHH.14, p. 154)

As Asloob Ansari has pointed out, in the fall "the upward and the downward, whose identity is insisted on so repeatedly by all mystical doctrines, now stand unrelated."[46] These appear in one form as Heaven and Hell, and Blake's "marriage" is an attempt to display "the infinite which was hid" precisely in the "hellish" or "devilish" downward sphere. Glenn O'Malley, in his study *Shelley and Synesthesia*, concludes that Shelley's "elaboration of synesthetic themes in his most intensely philosophical contexts points up sharply a concern, not to escape the 'material' and the sensuous, but to test and demonstrate how one order of experience can relate to other and supposedly higher ones."[47] In *Adonais*, for example, the "upward" "one Spirit" sweeps down to impress itself on all earthly forms. These forms—trees, beasts and men—thus become like the one Spirit who then "bursts" or rises from them back into the light of heaven: a continuous interaction of the two "separate" spheres, the spiritual and the material (AD.XLIII.381–387). To Joseph Barrell, "this aspect"—the relation of the upward to the downward—"is indeed no other than the peculiar Romantic desire to link the transcendental with the earthly."[48] Most of the proverbs in *The Marriage of Heaven and Hell* serve just such a function:

> The pride of the peacock is the glory of God.
> The lust of the goat is the bounty of God.
> The wrath of the lion is the wisdom of God.
> The nakedness of woman is the work of God. (MHH.8:2–5)

The swiftness and power of the imagination are closely connected with this lower or "evil" region of wrath or "hell." Energy, in all its forms, springs up from it. Blake walks among the fires of this realm "delighted with the enjoyments of Genius, which to Angels [the self-righteous—those who attempt to suppress their energies] look like torment and insanity" (MHH.6–7, p. 150). At the end of *The Marriage*, however, one angel is converted by a devil: the angel embraces a flame of fire and, being consumed, rises as Elijah. In becoming a devil—making contact with energy (fire)—the angel also becomes a prophet, poet or visionary, for without this "lower" faculty one cannot see truly.

The descent that Asia makes to the realm of Demogorgon in *Prometheus Unbound* is essentially a descent to discover what C. M. Bowra terms the "spiritual energy" at the "centre of being."[49] As Northrop Frye notes, in *Prometheus Unbound* "the beneficial comes mainly from below":[50]

> To the deep, to the deep,
>   Down, down!
> Through the shade of sleep,
> Through the cloudy strife
> Of Death and of Life;
> Through the veil and the bar
> Of things which seem and are
> Even to the steps of the remotest throne,
>   Down, down! (PU.II.iii.54–61)

If this volcanic depth can be tapped, the remote sky-god created by reason (or thought without affection), who is Jupiter in *Prometheus Unbound* and Urizen in Blake's Prophetic Books, can be overcome and there can be a rejoining of "down" and "up."

In Blake's myth, Urthona represents this power of "spiritual energy." As a smith, he works at his fiery forge deep within Albion's being, and Blake refers to him throughout the Prophecies as "dark Urthona."[51] To see properly, Albion must reactivate Urthona, much as Asia must rouse Demogorgon in *Prometheus Unbound*. In *The Four Zoas*, Urthona's hammer beats on his anvils incessantly within the depths of Albion's being in his attempt to give error a definite form so that it can be cast out, in his efforts to rouse Albion from his stupor on the oozy rock of the world of Generation (the "caverned" world the viewer sees before the imagination—fourfold vision—transforms it). At the regeneration, all the nations of the earth are ground in Urthona's mills and are thus purified, and he himself sounds his hammer "In the deep caves beneath; his limbs renew'd, his Lions roar / Around the Furnaces & in Evening sport upon the plains" (FZ.9:840–842). However, Urthona does not appear in the fallen world as himself, but only in his "vehicular" form, Los—that is, poetry, painting and prophecy (more generally, art), which represent the influx of the imagination into the fallen world and give it whatever fluidity and beauty it possesses: Spirit (Urthona) manifests itself in Art (Los). In the apocalypse, Urthona-Los wins the struggle brought on by the fall not by destroying Urizen but by convincing him to give up his stranglehold on futurity and to live in the eternal present. For Urizen attempts not only to *see* into the future but to *control* it as well, whereas true perception finds the infinite in the present, fleeting moment; in a space—opening into Eternity—less than a globule of man's blood; in a time less than a pulsation of the artery, in which all the poet's work is done (M.28:62–63; 29:1–3; 21–22), or in the smallest object, such as a grain of sand (AI.1). The fleeting moment that appears so impermanent (like flowing water or the changing shapes of clouds) is actually the only permanence:

> He who binds to himself a joy
> Does the winged life destroy;
> But he who kisses the joy as it flies
> Lives in eternity's sun rise. (p. 179)

Los wields Urthona's hammer when he builds Golgonooza, a spiritually unified city of art and regeneration similar to the New Jerusalem in the Book of Revelation.

Blake reveals his titan Urizen constantly in the process of solidifying the "upward" into a law of "holiness" so that the vision of unity among opposites is lost, as well as the totally unpredictable and quick quality of imaginative sight. If one reads with attention, he can see that Dostoevski's portrait of the "prophet" Semyon Yakovlevich in *The Possessed* tells a great deal about Blake's Ezekiel and the function of the prophet in general. Semyon loves tea, and

> As a rule, he did not take tea alone, but poured out some for his visitors, but by no means for all, usually pointing himself to those he wished to honour. And his choice always surprised people by its unexpectedness. Passing by the wealthy and the high-placed, he sometimes pitched upon a peasant or some decrepit old woman. Another time he would pass over the beggars to honour some fat wealthy merchant. Tea was served differently, too, to different people, sugar was put into some of the glasses and handed separately with others, while some got it without any sugar at all.

Similarly, he has one visitor beaten with a broom, gives a gold coin to a rich merchant, and shouts an obscenity at one of the ladies in the group.[52] Semyon, like Blake's Los or the devils in *The Marriage of Heaven and Hell,* possesses no moral precepts by which he passes judgment either on the high or the low: he is indifferent to these divisions and instead acts immediately according to how he feels at the moment. In his presence, one might suddenly *see* that the divisions the world makes between rich and poor are not real ones but more or less on the same level as having tea with or without sugar. In other words, such actions, by their unpredictable nature and failure in conformity to conventional notions of value, tend to break down (or up) the usual and ordinary mode of perceiving that Blake terms "single vision." These actions are often powerful enough to melt apparent surfaces away and to reveal that even dung must be seen under the aspect of the infinite. To Urizen and his priests, however, some things are "holy" while others are not.

A refusal to separate things into moral categories is no doubt what Blake meant by his cryptic statement to Crabb Robinson, "what are called the vices in the natural world are the highest sublimities in the spiritual world."[53] To some extent, of course, Blake may have enjoyed having a bit of fun with his literal friend, but if he here meant the joining of what is considered "low" with what is considered "high" his statement is certainly consistent with his poetry. M. Esther Harding, in speaking of *Pilgrim's Progress,* makes a very close analogy to Blake's idea of the "marriage" of heaven and hell and throws a good deal of light on his statement to Crabb Robinson:

> Thus, in this Celestial City, the opposites are united, the marriage of the Bride and Bridegroom takes place eternally. Christ and his Church, the Godhead and the Manhood become one, and incidentally the joys denied on earth are enjoyed in their eternal form in heaven; surely a hint that those things which are most desired on earth, often in such a debased form that they become the greatest hindrance on the path, are to be found in heaven in a new form so that they can be enjoyed.[54]

The Kabbalah expresses the same thought in its well-known formula, "That which is below is like that which is above."[55] A. E. Waite in his commentary rephrases this same thought in relation to evil: "For the Spirit of Evil imitates the Spirit of Good, and that which it occasions below in malice the spirit of good fulfills in holiness above."[56] A similar assertion is made by Jacob Boehme, whom Blake referred to as a "divinely inspired man."[57] In Boehme's "light world" or God's kingdom, the "dark world" is hidden as a mystery. It is the opposite pole of the light world and contains the power, force, fire and energy—like Blake's hell in *The Marriage of Heaven and Hell*. Again, as in the Kabbalah, the terms Boehme uses differ from Blake's but the idea remains the same: "That which in the dark world is a pang, is in the light world a pleasing delight; and what in the dark is a stinging and enmity is in the light an uplifting joy."[58]

As one can see by these four analogues, Blake's statement to Crabb Robinson about the vices of the natural world being the highest sublimities in the spiritual world, as well as Ezekiel's eating of dung to raise men's perception into the infinite, is not "Romantic perversity," or "Romantic agony" in Mario Praz' term. This "satanic" (or Byronic) element does not exist in Blake's poetry.[59] He does not agonize over his feelings of guilt or hint darkly at unnameable crimes. His hell is one in which he delights in the fire of genius. All the so-called "lower" or material aspects of life are seen in relationship to the "higher" or spiritual aspects: the "marriage" of heaven and hell. This lower realm of "hell" that Urizen attempts to suppress in his fallen position of dominance contains the energy, as fire, needed for a true perception. Los's creative forge also contains this fire, and he labors incessantly throughout the Prophetic Books to reveal the divine reality concealed in all things. If such an unveiling does not take place, Albion continues to be suppressed under the inversion of Urizen's usurpation and single vision.

It is primarily the quality of the child's vision that can restore the universe to its original state of unity and joy, a quality compounded of exuberance, love, enthusiasm, energy, intuition, and immediacy. Essentially, this is another definition of Blake's fourfold vision. Though Shelley does not employ that term, he stresses this same childlike view as being necessary to achieve true spiritual sight.

Rationality, for the most part, has always been considered by Western civilization as the supreme faculty of man to which the others should be subordinate. Blake sees the child before it is taught that rationality should be superior as very closely connected in its vision to the "hellish" realm of libidinous energy which the adult attempts to suppress. Thus, Blake's view of the child's innocent vision is not sentimental or "Victorian." As Peter Coveney has indicated in his study of the concept of the child in nineteenth-century English literature:

The Romantic image of the child started with Blake's free acceptance of its innocent sexuality. It is ironic that a literary image initiated in this way should have become one of the most powerful obstacles to the acceptance of the sexual character of the child a century later [i.e., with the Victorians].[60]

To Blake, in the crushing of all forms of energy, man reveals his fallen nature and his single vision. The fire in Blake's hell appears in an artistic as well as a sexual expression. (The sexual aspect of energy is more fully discussed in Chapter Five.) Blake walks among the fires, delighted with the enjoyment of genius, and brings back many Proverbs of Hell to show that the quickness and fullness of being possessed by the child are to be preferred over the prudence that confines one to the "object" world of single vision. The child, in his daring energy, arrives on the scene open and responsive to the immediate and emotional content of an object. In his willing acceptance and response to what he sees, the child indicates his ready and generous presence in a way that reveals its "prophetic" quality of true sight:

Little Lamb,
Here I am. (p. 123)

So Abraham's "Here I am" indicates his willingness to be the means of transmitting God's word to his people.

By and large, the child has not yet come under the dead weight of custom, the Urizenic tendency towards solidification, and thus he is capable of Losian insight. Blake states that "Knowledge is not by deduction, but Immediate by Perception or Sense at once" (p. 774), and because the child has developed little if any deductive power, nothing intervenes between him and the object he looks at, so that "at once" becomes highly significant. The child can see "at once" because he sees with feeling. In a lecture on Wordsworth, H. W. Garrod pointed out that "the path from sense to imagination does not pass through the intellect. It passes through the affections."[61] If the path passes to intellect, immediate knowledge is blocked, for the deductive process must be accomplished step by step.

In his annotations to Swedenborg's *Divine Love and Divine Wisdom,* Blake clearly points out the function of the affections:

Think of a white cloud as being holy, you cannot love it; but think of a holy man within the cloud, love springs up in your thoughts, for to think of holiness distinct from man is impossible to the affections. Thought alone can make monsters, but the affections cannot. (p. 90)

The affections do not block the imagination; on the contrary, they permit it to expand and envelop the object, to make it human, to make it knowable. It might be said that Blake loves the sun in just such a manner for it to appear to him as a company of the heavenly host. In *The Burning Fountain* Philip Wheelwright asserts that such emotion is also a vital necessity for the reader, if he is to obtain the insight that a poem offers:

> My thesis is that truly expressive symbolism—in a poem, for example— means, refers, awakens insight, *in and through*, the emotions it engenders, and that so far as the emotion is not aroused the full insight is correspond- ingly not awakened.[62]

If spontaneity, immediacy, affection are not there as a thing is seen, if a delay takes place in understanding, the reason has an opportunity to interpose and cut off the sight in its imaginative totality, leaving only, as in Blake's example of a tree, a green thing that stands in the way. The child, however, has not yet learned to put up any very intensive barriers between inner and outer, higher and lower, good and evil, subject and object. "The world is given to me only once, not one existing and one perceived," states Professor Schrödinger. "Subject and object are only one. The barrier between them cannot be said to have broken down as a result of recent experience in the physical sciences, for this barrier does not exist."[63] Because Blake does not set up such a barrier, the tree can appear to him as it is to the inward eye; in other words, it too is part of the Divine Humanity, part of Albion's scattered body. The trouble with Urizen throughout the Prophetic Books is that he looks to the future, in Dr. Johnson's words, to supply the deficiencies of the present, "in spaces remote / Seeking the Eternal which is always present to the wise; / Seeking for pleasure which unsought falls round the infant's path" (FZ.9:170–172). But if one perceives the outer world with Newtonian single vision, he sets up a universe that Northrop Frye describes as follows:

> The world outside us, or physical nature, is a blind and mechanical order, hence if we merely accept its conditions we find ourselves setting up blind and mechanistic patterns of behaviour. The world outside is also a fiercely competitive world, and living under its conditions involves us in unending war and misery. Blake's lyrics contrast the vision of experience, the stupefied adult view that the evils of nature are built into human life and cannot be changed, with the vision of innocence in the child, who assumes that the world is a pleasant place made for his benefit. The adult tends to think of the child's vision as ignorant and undeveloped, but actually it is a clearer and more civilized vision than his own.[64]

Blake indicates his acceptance of the child's clear vision in replying to Dr. Trusler's statement that he needed "somebody to elucidate" his ideas:

> I am happy to find a Great Majority of Fellow Mortals who can Elucidate My Visions, & Particularly they have been Elucidated by Children, who

have taken a greater delight in contemplating my Pictures than I even hoped. Neither Youth nor Childhood is Folly or Incapacity. Some Children are Fools & so are some Old Men. But There is a vast Majority on the side of Imagination or Spiritual Sensation. (p. 794)

In *Prometheus Unbound,* the great change that takes place within the universe after Prometheus' regeneration is partly delineated in terms of the childlike joy and exuberance of the Spirit of the Earth, not unlike that of the children in the *Songs of Innocence.* We learn from Panthea that this Spirit loved Asia as a mother, "and with her / It made its childish confidence, and told her / All it had known or seen, for it saw much, / Yet idly reasoned what it saw" (PU.III.iv.19–22). As spring arrives, as love pours into the formerly constricted world, as Aeolian music sounds from the mountains, the Spirit of the Earth runs like a child to Asia and tells her how its world has changed since the regeneration of Prometheus:

> and when the dawn
> Came, wouldst thou think that toads, and snakes, and efts,
> Could e'er be beautiful? yet so they were,
> And that with little change of shape or hue:
> All things had put their evil nature off:
> I cannot tell my joy, when o'er a lake
> Upon a drooping bough with nightshade twined,
> I saw two azure halcyons clinging downward
> And thinning one bright bunch of amber berries,
> With quick long beaks, and in the deep there lay
> Those lovely forms imaged as in a sky;
> So, with my thoughts full of these happy changes,
> We meet again, the happiest change of all. (PU.III.iv.73–85)

When energy is not expressed with this childlike openness, however, it turns inward to become the source of outer devastation. In speaking of this inner childlike world of desire that we suppress, Northrop Frye states that it is not quite so securely bound as we would like to believe:

> Every so often it breaks loose and projects itself on society in the form of war. It seems odd that we should keep plunging with great relief into moral holidays of aggression in which robbery and murder become virtues instead of crimes.[65]

In Blake's "A Poison Tree" the speaker's wrath ends when he expresses his anger to his friend, but grows when he conceals the same feeling from an enemy. Thus turned inward, the energy is perverted into "soft deceitful wiles" by which the foe is destroyed. Similarly, libidinous (specifically sexual) energy not accepted and expressed with its true innocence can become the source of destructiveness and death. In *Jerusalem,* for example, the warriors cry out in despair that they are "drunk with unsatiated love," that they "must rush again to War, for the

Virgin has frown'd & refus'd" (J.68:62–63. The warriors are under the power of the chaste Tirzah (restrictive moral law) who passes her knife of flint "over the howling Victim" (J.67:24–25) on the altar where this energy is circumscribed. In order to avoid such terrible expressions of suppressed energy, the adult must learn to see with the open vision of the child.

The child possesses the ability to see in its first intuitional, unified stage. In the regeneration that takes place in *The Four Zoas*, for example, Tharmas and his feminine consort Enion—who represent the physical, outer aspect of the world (and the body of man)—become little children in the "Gardens of Vala" (FZ.9:510–511), the pastoral setting of the renovated world. This signifies that the first Edenic state of man and his vision are in the process of restoration. Once that restoration is complete, "Tharmas brought his flocks upon the hills, & in the Vales / Around the Eternal Man's [i.e., Albion's] bright tent, the little Children play / Among the wooly flocks" (FZ.9:838–840).

This early quality of perception found in the child is thus not based on a knowledge acquired through study. When the disciples asked Jesus, "Who is the greatest in the kingdom of heaven?" he placed a child in their midst (Matthew 18:1–3) and said, "Whosoever shall not receive the kingdom of God as a little child, he shall not enter therein" (Mark 10:15). Blake turns this statement into direct metaphor. "That is heaven," he said, pointing to a group of children at play.[66] To Blake, the whole idea of Christianity lies under the heading "Forgiveness of Sins" rather than under that of morality or moral precept (p. 774) acquired through study, and only a childlike consciousness and awareness are fluid enough to create the conditions under which such forgiveness can take place. Commenting on Berkeley's *Siris*, Blake states:

> Jesus supposes every Thing to be Evident to the Child & to the Poor & Unlearned. Such is the Gospel. The whole Bible is fill'd with Imagination & Visions from End to End & not with Moral Virtues; that is the business of Plato & the Greeks & all Warriors. The Moral Virtues are continual Accusers of Sin & promote Eternal Wars & Dominency over others. (p. 774)

Such moral virtue (instead of vision) is exemplified to perfection in Blake's illustrations to the Book of Job. In the beginning of the series, Job and his family sit and read heavy Urizenic books while light musical instruments hang unused on the tree behind them. Job gives charity, not out of the spontaneous flow of loving feeling, but as a duty. After his great sufferings and new insight, however, Job stands before the altar in the position of the crucifixion (a position Blake always uses throughout the Prophecies as a symbol of the giving up of selfishness). And in the final illustration, the entire family stands to play the formerly unused instruments: we are in the joyful, sounding world of the child.[67]

Blake depicts the imaginative and immediate quality of the child's vision in his engravings of 1793: *For Children: The Gates of Paradise*. (When he wrote additional legends for the series, *circa* 1818, he called the same engravings *For the Sexes: The Gates of Paradise*.) The eleventh illustration depicts an "Aged Ignorance"—a blind old Urizenic man—clipping the wings of a child who is greeting or reaching out for the Losian sun of the imagination. The legend underneath reads: "Perceptive Organs closed, their Objects close" (p. 767). In no other illustration, perhaps, has the artist so vitally stated the symbolic connection between the child's quality of vision and true perception and between the viewer and the object he perceives. If the viewer's "perceptive organ," the eye, is imaginatively closed, the object itself will appear closed: that is, the object will appear as object only as it does to single vision. In this view, the sun always appears as a round disk of fire and never as a company of the heavenly host. If the viewer has achieved fourfold vision, however, the object is not seen as "closed" but as a living organism that within itself opens out into the infinite: "How do you know but ev'ry Bird that cuts the airy way," a "mighty Devil" writes in *The Marriage of Heaven and Hell*, "Is an immense world of delight, clos'd by your senses five?" (MHH.6–7, p. 150).

Shelley's twelve-year-old Cythna in *The Revolt of Islam* combines the immediate perception of the child and a knowledge not gained through study. Like Blake, Shelley believes the development of such a vision would aid the perceiver to burst out of the world of closed objects into a world—literally the same world but differently perceived—where all forms are remade by the imagination. Cythna possesses this "new lore" of imaginative understanding:

> New lore was this—old age, with its gray hair,
>   And wrinkled legends of unworthy things,
> And icy sneers, is nought: it cannot dare
>   To burst the chains which life forever flings
>   On the entangled soul's aspiring wings. (RI.II.xxxiii.955–959)

Cythna's child (who is born after the tyrant confines Cythna in a cave by the sea) also possesses this "new lore" of immediate vision, symbolized primarily by the light of the sun, stars, or moon filtering down into the cave. Cythna tells Laon about the birth of her child and its growth:

> I watched the dawn of her first smiles, and soon
>   When zenith-stars were trembling on the wave,
> Or when the beams of the invisible moon,
>   Or sun, from many a prism within the cave
>   Their gem-born shadows to the water gave,
> Her looks would hunt them, and with outspread hand,
>   From the swift lights which might that fountain pave,
> She would mark one, and laugh, when that command
> Slighting, it lingered there, and could not understand. (RI.VII.xx)

In addition to playing with the light, the child teaches Cythna to play with the "golden shells" within the cave, which are similar to the "mystic shell" in *Prometheus Unbound* that holds the "lulled music" of regeneration to be poured down upon the world by the Spirit of the Hour. Cythna says:

> and on a day
> When I was happiest in that strange retreat,
> With heaps of golden shells we two did play,—
> Both infants, weaving wings for time's perpetual way. (RI.VII.xxi.3015–3018)

At the end of the poem, after Cythna and Laon's death by fire, this child whom she had thought lost to her, now a "winged shape," glides toward Laon and Cythna in a boat of "hollow pearl, / Almost translucent with the light divine / Of her within" (RI.XII.xxi.4630–4632). Here, the light and the shell—the playthings of the child in the cave—are combined in a most ingenious and typically Shelleyan manner. The three embark in the boat, and after three days and nights arrive at the Temple of the Spirit.

Thus, in Shelley's poetry as in Blake's, the child's way of perceiving functions as a guide out of limited awareness into the expansiveness of true spiritual understanding. This childlike quality of perception could burst open the cavern of single vision and reveal the world and its objects, man and nature, as infinite, harmonious, articulate, and loving.

Chapter Two

The Sleep of Ulro

But many doubted & despair'd & imputed Sin & Righteousness
To Individuals & not to States, and these Slept in Ulro.
(J.25:15–16)

If reduced to the use of one word in defining Blake's idea of evil, one would be forced to choose the word *reason*. In his distrust of reason, Blake reveals himself as more of a "Romantic" than Wordsworth, Coleridge, or Byron, all of whom retain much of the preceding century's rationalism in their thought. Only the Shelley of *Prometheus Unbound*, perhaps, can match Blake in that soaring imaginative flight which leaves concepts far behind. Indeed, Blake and Shelley finally give up "reasonable" narrative itself as tending to restrict this flight. Compare, for example, *The Four Zoas* with *Jerusalem* and *The Revolt of Islam* with *Prometheus Unbound*. However, the idea of reason as a force creating separation and rigidity (as in Urizen) is peculiar to most of the Romantics (both in England and on the Continent) and to their quality of vision.

For Coleridge, for example, the imagination (comparable to Blake's Los) is the "esemplastic" power that reconciles opposite or discordant qualities, while the products of the mere reflective faculty (Blake's Urizen) partake of death.[1] This condition of separation and death Blake terms "Ulro," a condition of sleep and error on the very edge of Non-Entity. Similarly, Shelley contends that poetry, as a function of the imagination, "subdues to union, under its light yoke, all irreconcilable things." Like Coleridge and Blake, he places the imagination in the highest place as "the principle of synthesis." In "A Defence of Poetry," he defines reason as "the enumeration of quantities already known," whereas "imagination is the perception of the value of those quantities, both separately and as a whole. Reason respects the differences, and imagination the similitudes of things."[2]

E. D. Hirsch, in an analogical study of Wordsworth and Schelling, finds that the poet and the philosopher are essentially in agreement regarding reason:

> Artificiality is a name for productions of the meddling intellect, of thought in isolation from the whole. When Wordsworth speaks opprobriously of custom, he means artificial or arbitrary custom. He means convention which has become a law unto itself like the isolated intellect which produced it.

Indeed, "the root of all evil is consciousness operating in separation, consciousness denying its connections." Hirsch points out that both Schelling and Wordsworth lost this earlier view as they grew older. He partly accounts for this loss by noting their reactions to the deaths of persons close to them.[3] Seemingly, their vision could not sustain the shock of evil when it was personally brought home to them.

Both Shelley and Blake, in contrast, maintained their early enthusiasm for the imagination and its possibilities, although Shelley, to be sure, did not live to feel the hardening of that poetic artery of which Blake speaks; and one cannot make out an absolute, conclusive case regarding a change of mind on the basis of the fragment *The Triumph of Life*, the poem he was working on at the time of his death. It is beyond dispute, however, that the elderly Blake was quite as intense in his claims for the imagination and in his denigration of reason as the young Blake had been. One need only look at his Job illustrations or glance at a few of the pages of *Jerusalem* to be convinced. A brief biographical reference can make this point quite clear. On learning of the death of the sculptor Flaxman, a friend of Blake's, Crabb Robinson called on the poet,

> desirous to see how, with his peculiar feelings and opinions, he would receive the intelligence. It was much as I expected. He had himself been very ill during the summer, and his first observation was with a smile: "I thought I should have gone first." He then said: "I cannot consider death as anything but a removing from one room to another."[4]

Blake was at this time (1825) sixty-eight years old; he died two years later. Blake and Shelley in maintaining their Romantic idealism have become representative of what a life lived according to the dictates of the imagination might be like.

Another major Romantic—Keats—goes even further in the denial of reason as the final arbiter of truth when he states, "axioms in philosophy are not axioms until they are proved upon our pulses."[5] The pulse is part of the divine energy (discussed in chapter one) that Blake and Shelley believe so necessary to true perception, and it is on the pulse that one understands love and forgiveness—the two cornerstones of both poets' thought. The pulse is the flash of understanding Blake speaks of when he states that knowledge is not by deduction but immediate by sense or perception at once, the pulsation of the artery. The interchangeability of "sense" and "perception" indicates that Blake, like the Romantic poets who came after him (especially Keats), had moved very far away from the Lockian view of the senses. In Locke's system, as Basil Willey points out, "the mind, though *passive* in perception, becomes active in all the subsequent processes of reflection, which include compounding, comparing, and abstracting *from the ideas that sensation has impressed on it.*"[6] To the Romantic, however, the mind contributes actively and at first to the perceived object; and, in Coleridge's words, "sensation itself is but vision nascent."[7] Hence, Keats can "prove" an axiom imaginatively upon the pulse.

Blake was even more insistent than the poets who succeeded him in the belief that "reason is the only evil."[8] In commenting on Bacon's essay *Of Truth,* Blake once again asserts that true vision is not the result of elaborate and intricate thought processes. "Self-Evident Truth is one Thing and Truth the result of Reasoning is another Thing. Rational Truth is not the truth of Christ, but of Pilate. It is the Tree of the Knowledge of Good and Evil" (p. 397). Eating of this Tree makes the viewer, like Urizen, "Self-clos'd, all repelling," a "soul-shudd'ring vacuum" a "self-contemplating shadow" (BU.3:3–5;21). The separation of the two contraries Good and Evil (which the Tree symbolizes) leads in the hands of Urizen to the solidification and abstraction of "good" into a rigid law of "holiness" (self-righteousness) that has no relationship to its opposite "evil" (energy). This is why Blake attempts to "marry" Heaven (Good) and Hell (Evil).

The separation that exists in the Tree of Knowledge of Good and Evil is fostered by all systems of education. Thus, as we have seen, Blake places much emphasis on the very young child's vision before he has attended school. One should read and study, as Blake did when he attended drawing school (and, indeed, as he did throughout his life), in freedom, not "under a cruel eye outworn," as the school boy does in Blake's poem by that title (p. 124). As T. S. Eliot has pointed out, there are two kinds of education:

> It is important that the artist should be highly educated in his own art; but his education is one that is hindered rather than helped by the ordinary processes of society which constitute education for the ordinary man. For these processes consist largely in the acquisition of impersonal ideas which obscure what we really are and feel, what we really want, and what really excites our interest. It is of course not the actual information acquired, but the conformity which the accumulation of knowledge is apt to impose, that is harmful.[9]

In Blake's view, the child should not be forced to acquire such impersonal ideas or indeed to attend school at all. " 'There is no use in education,' " he remarked to Crabb Robinson.

> "I hold it wrong—it is the great sin—it is eating of the tree of good and evil. That was the fault of Plato: he knew nothing but of the virtues and vices and Good and Evil. There is nothing in all that. Everything is good in God's eyes."

Though Blake continued by stating that he was no judge of absolute evil, Crabb Robinson asserts that on many occasions "he spoke as if he denied altogether the existence of evil and as if we had nothing to do with right and wrong, it being sufficient to consider all things as alike the work of God."[10] But this is precisely what Urizen's "brethren and sons" in the fallen world do not do. Instead, they devise schools and form instruments in their attempt to measure what can be known only through the imagination—or more correctly by the imagination and reason (and sensation and emotion) acting in concert. Urizen commands "all the work with care & power & severity" (FZ.2:127–134). This work, however, in the most literal sense belongs to Satan because it perpetuates the divisiveness created by the fall and symbolized by the Tree of Knowledge of Good and Evil.

In his engraving *The Laocoön* (circa 1820), Blake asserts that acceptance of this Tree leads away from the path of art into power, empire, money, "Demonstration," and Natural Religion or Deism: "Good and Evil are Riches and Poverty, a Tree of Misery, propagating Generation and Death." Quite explicitly, he maintains that "Money . . . is The Great Satan or Reason, the Root of Good & Evil in the Accusation of Sin" (p. 776). The religion of Jesus has nothing to do with this separation, for "Christianity is Art & not money" and "Art is the Tree of Life" (p. 777).

Blake is here speaking on a different level from the usual Christian interpretation of the love of money as the root of all evil. He states regarding his painting *A Vision of the Last Judgment:*

> Some people & not a few Artists have asserted that the Painter of this Picture would not have done so well if he had been properly Encourag'd. Let those who think so, reflect on the State of Nations under Poverty & their incapability of Art; tho' Art is Above Either, the Argument is better for Affluence than Poverty; & tho he would not have been a greater Artist, yet he would have produc'd Greater works of Art in proportion to his means. (VLJ, p. 612)

The artist is not concerned with riches and poverty in themselves or with the power that the former confers, but only with having the money he needs in order to produce his works—and Blake had little enough. Only someone who has never experienced the despair of not being able to procure the best materials will speak lightly of poverty. For the most part, as Blake saw, the materials of the world are not used to further art—and hence true religion—but go into "Caesar's Laurel Crown" (AI.98). For, as he points out, "there will always be as many Hypocrites born as Honest Men, & they will always have superior Power in Mortal things" (VLJ, p. 616). Riches should serve art and life, rather than death and empire: "When Gold & Gems adorn the Plow / To Peaceful Arts shall Envy Bow" (AI.101–102). The plow is a creative instrument in Blake's myth, preparing the way for the seed of the apocalypse, part of that "simple workmanship" the fallen world contemns in favor of its involved Satanic wheels (FZ.7b:175–186). In the apocalypse, riches express man's inner, spiritual splendor. The "Words of the Mutual Covenant Divine" appear "On Chariots of gold & jewels," and the formerly evil serpent becomes "clothed in gems & rich array" (J.98:41–42; 44).

Acceptance of Urizen's separation between Good and Evil leads to questions of morality, of goodness and badness, but these are "secondary considerations, & belong to Philosophy & not to Poetry, to Exception & not to Rule, to Accident and not to Substance; the Ancients call'd it eating of the tree of good & evil" (p. 778).[11] In fact, the last Judgment begins

> when all those are Cast away who trouble Religion with Questions concerning Good & Evil or Eating of the Tree of those Knowledges or Reasonings which hinder the Vision of God, turning all into a Consuming Fire. When Imagination, Art & Science & all intellectual Gifts, all the Gifts of the Holy Ghost, are look'd upon as of no use & only Contention remains to Man, then the Last Judgment begins. (VLJ, p. 604)[12]

This Tree is destroyed in the apocalypse (J.98:47). Thus, one can see why Blake insisted on wisdom rather than on goodness or "holiness" (J.91:55–58). The latter hinders the vision of God because it makes for separation, whereas wisdom or understanding creates unity and wholeness. "The Fool shall not enter into Heaven let him be ever so Holy" (VLJ, p. 615). For this reason, Los refuses to "Reason & compare: my business is to Create" (J.10:21).

The Sons of Albion in the fallen world, following Urizen's example, are also guilty of separating good and evil:

> And this is the manner of the Sons of Albion in their strength:
> They take the Two Contraries which are call'd Qualities, with which
> Every Substance is clothed: they name them Good & Evil;
> From them they make an Abstract, which is a Negation
> Not only of the Substance from which it is derived,
> A murderer of its own Body, but also a murderer
> Of every Divine Member: it is the Reasoning Power,
> An Abstract objecting power that Negatives every thing.
> This is the Spectre of Man, the Holy Reasoning Power,
> And in its Holiness is closed the Abomination of Desolation. (J.10:7–16)

The abstract, reasoning power (Urizen) is thus responsible for tearing apart the contraries or qualities that exist in harmony in Eternity. And this "Spectre of Man" is perhaps the best definition of Blakean—and to some extent Romantic—evil.

Urizen in *The Four Zoas* is responsible for Albion's inverted vision because he usurps Urthona's rightful place in the North. But he also originates evil from another perspective (*The Book of Urizen*) by separating himself from the other Eternals. He rises in Eternity (or falls out of it) as a "shadow" who is "unknown, abstracted, / Brooding, secret"—four of the most evil qualities in Blake's thought (BU.3:1;6–7). Urizen divides and measures space (BU.3:8–9); his Satanic, rolling wheels "sound in his clouds"; and his hills are covered with hail, ice and snow (BU.3:30–33), in contrast to the fiery sun and forges of the imaginative Los. "I have sought for a joy without pain," Urizen states as his quest, "For a solid without fluctuation" (BU.4:10–11).

Urizen, in his attempt to keep things down to their very lowest denominator, in his fear of desire, closely resembles the First Spirit in Shelley's "The Two Spirits: An Allegory."[13] The First Spirit—certainly a spirit of negation—cautions the Second Spirit about the "Shadow" (the same term Blake applies to Urizen) which "tracks thy flight of fire." The First Spirit warns the Second of night, hail, lightning, rain, and hurricane if it should persist in its imaginative flights, for this journey is always fearful to one of single vision, who fears that he will lose all he has gained (which he clutches desperately and possessively to his breast) and obtain nothing in return. But the Second Spirit, like Los, perseveres in its aspirations through the power of love:

> The deathless stars are bright above;
>   If I would cross the shade of night,
> Within my heart is the lamp of love,
>   And that is day! (p. 615)

The Second Spirit does not place its trust in the outer "Guinea sun" of single vision, which is subject to the vicissitudes of nature and to ultimate dissolution. Instead, it creates its own day by carrying its inner light deep within: its "lamp of love" is very much like Los's "globe of fire" (J.31–3).

By the role that Urizen plays in Blake's myth, the reader can readily see that Urizen's attempt to restrict and solidify is misguided. Without contraries, Blake states, there is no progression (MHH.3, p.149). Contraries must be "married," not separated as Urizen believes. One of the "Auguries of Innocence" (which reveal how man may be restored to Eternity) points out rather explicitly that joy and pain, like other contraries, ought not to be separated if man wishes to live fully, intensely and rightly:

> Man was made for joy and woe;
> And when this we rightly know
> Thro' the world we safely go.
> Joy and Woe are woven fine,
> A Clothing for the Soul divine;
> Under every grief & pine
> Runs a joy with silken twine. (AI.56–62)

When Urizen unravels this double twine—especially the twine of good and evil—it requires all the poet's Losian imagination to recombine them. Hence, as Blake's Ezekiel reveals when he eats dung, what is considered evil or "lower" must be reunited with its contrary, just as Urizen himself must finally become one again with Urthona-Los. Basically, therefore, a separation created by reason acting in isolation causes the appearance of evil in the universe. Urizen not only initially separates himself from the other Eternals, but constantly strives to turn the contrary "good" into a solid without fluctuation. In the Mystery religion that he institutes[14] such rigidity prevents the continual forgiveness of sins that to Blake totally sums up Christianity. The living flowers of the garden of love harden into tombstones and the hard pebble replaces the loving, pliable clod of clay.

It is always important to keep in mind, however, that reason becomes evil only in separation from man's other faculties and that Urizen is not destroyed in Blake's myth, for all contraries are equally true. In this connection, Peter Fisher has pointed out the importance of accepting paradox as a tool in understanding Blake:

> The moral judgment abhors a paradox, but it is only in paradox that the recurrent nature of life and its unique identity can both be understood. To fall short of this paradox is to become committed to the half-truths of formal logic and dogmatic theology where, to get a final answer, it is necessary to eliminate the contrary aspect of every problem.[15]

Similarly, Philip Wheelwright contends that "it is possible that overprecision distracts a seeker from apprehending the object or situation in its full nature."[16] The eye has a blind spot directly in the center, and if one believes, with Emerson, that natural facts are symbols of spiritual ones, he may prefer the quick, perhaps oblique glance of the imagination to the direct stare of formal logic. In Blake's words, "every Natural Effect has a Spiritual Cause, and Not / A Natural; for a Natural Cause only seems" (M.26:44–45). When the Rev. Dr. Trusler wrote to Blake that he needed "somebody to Elucidate" his ideas, Blake replied:[17]

> But you ought to know that What is Grand is necessarily obscure to Weak men. That which can be made Explicit to the Idiot is not worth my care. The wisest of the Ancients consider'd what is not too Explicit as the fittest for Instruction, because it rouzes the faculties to act. (p. 793)

Thus, at the Apocalypse, Urizen as a contrary is regenerated as a radiant youth from the suffering old man Blake depicts him to be up until that time, and he again takes the reins of his horses of light and his chariot of fire, for the true function of reason is to illuminate, not to restrict. Moreover, sin, error, mistake—what Blake admits as evil—are all easily forgiven (J.20:23–24). When Urizen says simply, "I have Erred" (FZ.9:225), the universe begins to dynamically regenerate itself. It is not sin, error or mistake that is displeasing to God, as the orthodox have thought, but "Unbelief & Eating of the Tree of Knowledge of Good and Evil" (VLJ, p. 615). Blake reserves his strongest condemnation for unbelief in the Divine Humanity, the world of imagination which is preeminently the child's world:

He who mocks the Infant's Faith
Shall be mock'd in Age & Death.
He who shall teach the Child to Doubt
The rotting Grave shall ne'er get out. (AI.85–88)

Also, Blake's attitude toward his artistic creation of Urizen is worth noting, in view of Urizen's evil role in the myth. Almost the last of Blake's artistic efforts on his death bed (he also drew his wife) was to color a relief etching of Urizen (the frontpiece to *Europe* known as "The Ancient of Days"). According to Gilchrist, this work was a "singular favorite" of Blake's and he labored long and patiently over the final coloring, exulting when he at last achieved the results he desired.[18] The reader should bear in mind, when he sees the suffering Urizen of the Prophecies, Blake's loving relationship to his "Prince of Light," for Blake never intends to leave the impression that one can get along well and be whole without reason. Reason in Eternity and reason in the fallen world, however, are not the same. In the former, it illuminates; in the latter, it restricts.

Blake tends to identify evil with reason as it acts in separation from the other faculties in order to bind and restrict. This evil (a sin, error, or mistake) does not exist in Albion's original eternal state, but arises because the reasoning power separates the contraries "Good" and "Evil," symbolized by the Tree of Knowledge of Good and Evil. This separation causes a fall within Albion that brings about the appearance of the natural world, the "Vegetable Glass" (VLJ, p. 605) or "shadow" of Eternity (M.29:22). Evil is thus a "negative accident" belonging not to Eternity but to this natural world. This negative sin, error, or mistake can be overcome by forgiveness, suffering, and art.

Blake maintains that "everything is atheism that assumes the reality of the natural and unspiritual world."[19] Evil makes its appearance in the natural world because all things are divided; they are not perceived under their eternal aspect; Albion does not see that rivers and mountains are his own body. "Error is Created," Blake affirms. "Truth is Eternal. Error, or Creation, will be Burned up, & then, & not till Then, Truth or Eternity will appear. It is Burnt up the Moment Men cease to behold it" (VLJ, p. 617). Eternity exists "Independent of Creation which was an act of Mercy" (VLJ, p. 614). Man would fall even further, into Non-Entity, but the creation of the natural world stops him at the level of his five senses. Los, who is "Lord of the Furnaces" (J.8:26) in his attempt to solidify and cast out error, tries to convince his sons that Satan is only an appearance:

> Will you suffer this Satan, this Body of Doubt that Seems but Is Not,
> To Occupy the very threshold of Eternal Life? if Bacon, Newton,
>   Locke
> Deny a Conscience in Man & the Communion of Saints & Angels,
> Contemning the Divine Vision & Fruition, Worshiping the Deus
> Of the Heathen, The God of This World, & the Goddess Nature,
> Mystery, Babylon the Great, The Druid Dragon & hidden Harlot,
> Is it not the Signal of the Morning which was told us in the
>   Beginning? (J.93:20–26)

When evil becomes contained and formed into Bacon, Newton, and Locke, the Mystery religion of Urizen, and the Druid Dragon, then it can no longer obstruct the threshold to Eternity, for it can then be understood (by those who have developed fourfold vision) as "seeming" rather than as reality.

In a passage similar to the above, spoken by the Eternals, Blake indicates, however, that negative evil becomes reality to those who accept it as such, for there is nothing else but mind—spiritual body or form. Moreover, through this acceptance, the negation then assumes a power over them and their vision. In its limited and suffering aspects, the fallen world everywhere reveals the dire results of this assumption:

> Then those in Great Eternity who contemplate on Death
> Said thus: "What seems to Be, Is, To those to whom
> It seems to Be, & is productive of the most dreadful
> Consequences to those to whom it seems to Be, even of
> Torments, Despair, Eternal Death; but the Divine Mercy
> Steps beyond and Redeems Man in the Body of Jesus." (J.36:50–55)

This is not to imply that sin, error, mistake and their consequent pain cannot come into being in Eternity (for it is certainly from Eternity that Urizen emerges); and, as Blake told Crabb Robinson, "There is suffering in heaven, for where there is the capacity of enjoyment, there is the capacity of pain."[20] Urizen's separation, however, is a more drastic one than those that usually occur. The Sons of Eden may fall into error, but they have much assistance in overcoming it and the forgiveness of their Brothers—for there is continual forgiveness of sin in Eternity, as well as mutual sacrifice (a mental, not a physical, act). Also, they may seek restful repose with their Emanations in Beulah, the feminine world that surrounds Eden (M.30:13–14). In *Jerusalem,* for example, the immortal Bard of Oxford (S. Foster Damon believes he may be Shelley),[21] brings "leaves of the Tree of Life" to the fallen Albion and attempts to revive him by suggesting that he repose in Beulah:

Thou art in Error, Albion, the Land of Ulro.
One Error not remov'd will destroy a human Soul.
Repose in Beulah's night till the Error is remov'd.
Reason not on both sides. (J.46:10–13)

Albion, in reasoning on both sides, exemplifies the error that exists in the Tree of Knowledge of Good and Evil.

Mary Shelley, in her note to *Prometheus Unbound*, speaks for both Shelley and Blake when she states: "The prominent feature of Shelley's theory of the destiny of the human species was that evil is not inherent in the system of creation, but an accident that might be expelled" (p. 271). Similarly, Shelley affirms in the Preface to *The Revolt of Islam* that the poem illustrates "the transient nature of ignorance and error, and the eternity of genius and virtue" (p. 32). Although the resurgence of evil is still a possibility at the end of *Prometheus Unbound*, Prometheus has succeeded through love, forgiveness and union with Asia in renovating the universe. Similarly, the idea of evil as accident is contained in one of Blake's strongest objections to Lavater's *Aphorisms on Man* (a work he generally approved). Lavater, he states, "makes every thing originate in its accident; he makes the vicious propensity not only a leading feature of the man, but the stamina on which all his virtues grow. But as I understand Vice it is a Negative" (p. 88). Again, in speaking to Crabb Robinson about "absolute evil" Blake pleads ignorance; and the most he would concede is "that there is error, mistake, etc., and if these be evil then there is evil, but these are only negations."[22] This close parallel in Blake's and Shelley's thought—that evil is negative or accidental—is based on the similar nature of their perception: they believe that evil might be expelled because they see it as being *within* the mind of man himself and therefore within his ability to cast out.

Blake distinguishes between "negations" and "contraries" (J.17:33–37).[23] The former can be destroyed, the latter cannot. If the two contraries Good and Evil are not separated (as they are in the fallen world in the Tree of Knowledge of Good and Evil) they function in harmony; for Evil as a contrary (not as error or sin) is the energy that makes the Good movable. To separate these contraries constitutes a negative "error" or "mistake" that can be destroyed in the Void of Non-Entity. Urizen makes this mistake when he separates himself from Eternity and attempts to restrict each contrary (joy-pain, solidity-fluidity) until it has no contact with its opposite. Although Urizen's error can be destroyed, he himself cannot, for he is the contrary of Urthona-Los and a necessary part of the whole.

Before he finally realizes or understands his error (and this understanding is the foundation of true perception), however, Urizen is reduced to a "dragon of the Deeps" (FZ.9:138) with a "scaly form" (FZ.9:162), for he tends to fall into more and more evil forms as his

error of separation progresses and solidifies. Albion himself, roused by
Los from his Ulro sleep on the oozy rock of Generation, threatens to cast
Urizen "out into the indefinite / Where nothing lives, there to wander; &
if thou returnst weary, / Weeping at the threshold of Existence, I will
steel my heart / Against thee to Eternity, & never recieve thee more"
(FZ.9:146–149). Before such power, and because he was "anxious . . . /
To reassume the human" form (FZ.9:162–163), Urizen gives in. As he
speaks the words of his repentance, "he shook his aged mantles off / Into
the fires" and "rose into the heavens in naked majesty, / In radiant
Youth" (FZ.9:190–193).

Thus, even Blake's greatest evil-doer—the aged, manacled, cold and
brooding Urizen—becomes regenerated, for Blake contends, in Los's
words, that "things are so constructed / And built by the Divine hand
that the sinner shall always escape" (J.31:30–31). Vengeance for sin or
mistake, rather than forgiveness, is the religion of Satan, the selfhood, a
religion that blazes forth from the "serpent altars" of the fallen world
(built by the Sons of Albion) where love (Luvah) is continually sacrificed.[24] Los, however, understands that love and forgiveness are the true
ways back to Eternity:

> If I should dare to lay my finger on a grain of sand
> In way of vengeance, I punish the already punish'd. O whom
> Should I pity if I pity not the sinner who is gone astray?
> O Albion, if thou takest vengeance, if thou revengest thy wrongs,
> Thou art for ever lost! What can I do to hinder the Sons
> Of Albion from taking vengeance? or how shall I them perswade? (J.31:33–38)

Herein, propounded by the imagination, lies one of the secrets of
overcoming evil; and both Blake and Shelley, with certain lapses—as in
Shelley's poem to the magistrate who deprived him of his children by his
first wife Harriet (pp. 542–544) and in some of Blake's notebook
epigrams meant only for his own eyes (pp. 538–559)—attempted to live
without hatred. One of the most concise expressions of this attempt
(which Lamb admired) is found in Shelley's brief "Lines to a Critic." In
this poem, he indicates that he accepted Blake's distinction between the
sinner and his state—the only path to forgiveness:

> I
> Honey from silkworms who can gather,
>   Or silk from the yellow bee?
> The grass may grow in winter weather
>   As soon as hate in me.
> II
> Hate men who cant, and men who pray,
>   And men who rail like thee;
> An equal passion to repay
>   They are not coy like me.

III

Or seek some slave of power and gold
   To be thy dear heart's mate;
Thy love will move that bigot cold
   Sooner than me, thy hate.

IV

A passion like the one I prove
   Cannot divided be;
I hate thy want of truth and love—
   How should I then hate thee? (p. 550)

In *The Revolt of Islam*, Laon makes the mistake of killing some of his enemies. Having suffered intensely for that act and having been taught in the ways of love by the old hermit who rescued him from his place of torment, Laon returns to the city to rejoin his small band of patriots. When this group is attacked by the tyrant's men, Laon rushes between them to prevent violence and a spear transfixes his arm. He then addresses both sides:

Oh wherefore should ill ever flow from ill,
   And pain still keener pain for ever breed?
We all are brethren—even the slaves who kill
   For hire, are men; and to avenge misdeed
   On the misdoer, doth but Misery feed
With her own broken heart! O Earth, O Heaven!
   And thou, dread Nature, which to every deed
   And all that lives or is, to be hath given,
Even as to thee have these done ill, and are forgiven! (RI.V.xi)

Like Laon, Urizen gains an insight into his error through his suffering, since the more he imposes his moral rules of conduct, the more bound and restricted he himself becomes. In this way, Urizen illustrates quite precisely what Blake means by the term *understanding*. In an almost illegible annotation to Swedenborg's *Divine Love,* Blake appears to be saying that there is no "good will" existing in man, that will takes the form of persecution and selfishness (as it does in Shelley's Cenci) and is therefore evil. God, he states, is not will but understanding, which may flow into the will and reform it. "Understanding or Thought is not natural to Man," he asserts; "it is acquir'd by means of Suffering & Distress, i.e. Experience. Will, Desire, Love, Pain, Envy, & all other affections are Natural, but Understanding is Acquired" (p. 89). In the light of this statement, it is apparent that the state of Experience is to be passed through into this understanding. If one remains in the state of Experience, he becomes increasingly restricted to its one-sided, single vision and to more and more of its pain, its hard pebblelike quality. Shelley's Prometheus, for example, has endured the pain of a very similar state for three thousand years, until he finally acquires understanding by means of suffering and distress: "misery" states Prometheus, "made me wise./ The curse / Once breathed on thee [Jupiter] I would recall" (PU.I.58–59). Like Los, Prometheus has come to understand that hatred and vengeance cannot be the true way but only that of love and forgiveness, and these may be acquired by suffering. Throughout the Prophetic Books, Los continues to perform his creative labors, "tho' in terrible pains" (J.62:42).

However, although Blake indicates that suffering may be a way to understanding, it is not an end in itself, and the artist performs more in spite of than because of it. Blake's attitude here is very similar to the apparent contradiction I have noted in his statements about riches and poverty; or in his contention that creation, the "vegetable glass," the caverned world of the five senses, is error, while at the same time he celebrates that same creation and the human body as the "chief inlet of Soul in this age," (MHH.4, p. 149), and affirms that every particle of dust, the clod of clay and the worm, are one with the Divine Vision. These "opposites" or aspects of the "contraries" are resolved through the power of the Imagination. Similarly, he makes the assumption of the child's innocence, while he also maintains that "Man is born a Spectre" (J.52, p. 682). The child's innocence is not moral goodness, however; he simply understands more than the adult, at least until the adult has suffered through the separative state of Experience into an even higher state of understanding than his original innocence. Although there was plenty of art flourishing in London, "yet no one brings work to me," Blake wrote to William Hayley (October 7, 1803). While attempting to be "content that it shall be so as long as God pleases" (p. 829), Blake cries out,

> some say that Happiness is not Good for Mortals, & they ought to be answer'd that Sorrow is not fit for Immortals & is utterly useless to any one; a blight never does good to a Tree, & if a blight kill not a Tree but it still bear fruit, let none say that the fruit was in consequence of the blight. (p. 830)

In the state of Generation (the world seen with the five senses) one simply makes do with what is given him, suffering or Experience, and tries to turn it to the account of Eternity: "Eternity is in love with the productions of time" (MHH.7:10). And, as Blake said in the same letter to Hayley: "Yet I laugh & sing, for if on Earth neglected I am in heaven a Prince among Princes." This statement indicates more clearly than any other, perhaps, Blake's attitude toward the suffering one must endure in the fallen world: only Art could raise his existence to the level of laughter or song. Like his titan Los, he "kept the Divine Vision in time of trouble" (J.30:15). In this way, he understood how to make both contraries work for rather than against him: "Joys impregnate. Sorrows bring forth" (MHH.8:9). Art exists precisely for this function: to raise the level of perception until the error of separation can be overcome. Through Los, who howls in pain before his fiery, creative forges, Albion learns to recombine his scattered body.

In the effort to overcome separativeness, to subdue Urizen, Blake does not invoke the Greek Muses, the daughters of memory who represent the binding down of man to the natural or unspiritual world— that is, to separation—but calls upon Jesus himself, the Poetic Genius or Human Imagination:

> Trembling I sit day and night, my friends are astonish'd at me,
> Yet they forgive my wanderings. I rest not from my great task!
> To open the Eternal Worlds, to open the immortal Eyes
> Of man inwards into the Worlds of Thought, into Eternity
> Ever expanding in the Bosom of God, the Human Imagination.
> O Saviour pour upon me thy Spirit of meekness & love! (J.5:16–21)

Similarly, Shelley asserts that poetry "creates anew the universe."[25] By such recreation, both Shelley and Blake attempt, in Coleridge's words, to bring "the whole soul of man into activity," to create "a tone and spirit of unity, that blends and (as it were) *fuses* each [faculty of the soul] into each by that synthetic and magical power, to which I would exclusively appropriate the name of Imagination."[26] Without such a fusion of his faculties (Blake personifies these as the Zoas), Albion remains in his uninspired or fallen condition on his cold, hard, wet rock amid the Sea of Time and Space. To Blake, this is man's natural (not Eternal) state. In the fallen world, Albion reaches the "Limit of Contraction"—Adam, the physical body, and the "limit of Opacity"—Satan, as low as error, sin or mistake can fall (FZ.4:271–273).

In this fallen, opaque world—until it is illumined by the imagination— evil takes on magnified proportions because of Albion's propensity to brood over his mistakes; instead, Albion should take some quick, definite action such as artistic creation. Brooding is closely connected with Blake's notion of the collapse of past and future time into the present. If one can be released from living in the past *or* future, he becomes free to live in the present moment, i.e., in Eternity.

In the tendency to brood, Albion has been well taught by Urizen, who broods in secret after his separation from the other Eternals (BU.3:7;25). When the chained Orc (revolutionary energy) causes the universe to pulsate, Urizen sits by him "fix'd in envy" and "brooding & cover'd with snow" (FZ.7a:28). He wears a "brooded smile" when he asks Los to submit to him as the ruler of the universe (FZ.1:321–322). Similarly, Albion sits after his fall "Brooding on evil" (J.42:2). The evil Hand of Blake's Prophecies—a type of the reasoning faculty—possesses

Three awful & terrible Heads,
Three Brains, in contradictory council brooding incessantly,
Neither daring to put in act its councils, fearing each-other,
Therefore rejecting Ideas as nothing & holding all Wisdom
To consist in the agreements & disagreements of Ideas,
Plotting to devour Albion's Body of Humanity & Love. (J.70:4–9)

Brooding places one in opposition to himself until he is incapable of effective action: "Expect poison from the standing water" (MHH.9:6).

"In the beginning," says Faust in one memorable statement of a Romantic credo, "was the Deed." And to Blake, salvation comes with action, movement, swiftness, intensity, energy—all opposites of restriction or solidification and all characteristic of Los's activities. The accidental evil (error, mistake) that comes into existence in the fallen world Blake defines as

omission of act in self & the hindering of act in another; This is Vice, but all Act is Virtue. To hinder another is not an act; it is the contrary; it is a restraint on action both in ourselves & in the person hinder'd, for he who hinders another omits his own duty at the same time. Murder is Hindering Another. Theft is Hindering Another. (p. 88)

As Northrop Frye points out, "in most orthodox theories of conduct, the evil side of man's nature is associated not with passivity but with 'passion,' " [27] as in most stories of the Double.[28] By giving the world the "Bible of Hell," Blake presents the contraries in a new way, thus raising one's perception out of the fallen world of Generation. This effort to build Jerusalem in England is probably the reason why the Prophetic Books very nearly burst their containing form and why so many feel uneasy in reading them. As T. S. Eliot says in *Burnt Norton*, "Words strain, / Crack and sometimes break, under the burden."

Evil as a contrary (not as error or mistake) "is the active springing from Energy" (MHH.3, p.149). In the separation that occurs in the Tree of Knowledge of Good and Evil, this energy becomes something to be suppressed instead of expressed, with disastrous results for man and his world. When one understands that Blake is speaking of evil as a contrary, his statement that "Active evil is better than passive good" (p. 77) becomes clear. Orc, for example, the son of Los, functions as an active evil of this kind in the Prophecies, for energy breaks out in the holocaust of revolution if it is suppressed too long, just as it erupts into war or other cruelties of human sacrifice. One form of the bound act appears in the "secret shadows" of the youth's or maiden's chamber in *Visions of the Daughters of Albion*; and Oothoon, who suffers under Urizen's rigid and selfish code of morality, asks of him:

Are not these the places of religion, the rewards of continence,
The self enjoyings of self denial? Why doest thou seek religion?

Is it because acts are not lovely that thou seekest solitude
Where the horrible darkness is impressed with reflections of
    desire? (VDA.7:8–11)

Urizen's priestly, Druidic religion is based on the circumscribing of this
energy, else it could not exist at all. To him and his priests "acts are not
lovely." Rahab (Urizen's mystery religion) and Tirzah (restrictive moral
law) bind the howling victims down as they do Luvah on the Stone of
Trial and pass their knives of flint over them, sadistically pitying and
enjoying their cries of pain. In this, Rahab and Tirzah are very much like
the Furies who torment Prometheus: they live and only can live from the
agony of their victim (PU.I.465–473).

In Albion's fall, all act becomes a crime, and he attempts to stem the
tide of flowing energy—which he sees as sin—by condensing the hills
and valleys into "solid rocks, stedfast, / A foundation and certainty and
demonstrative truth" (J.28:10–11). In Northrop Frye's words regarding
Thomas Paine's distrust of imagination, Albion has come to believe "that
the deader a thing is the more trustworthy it is; that a rock is a solid
reality and that the vital spirit of a living man is a rarefied and diapha-
nous ghost."[29] Only the active Los can control the Reasoning Spectre of
demonstration to the extent that he keeps before Albion's eyes the lost
vision of Eden, for the "outward Creation"—that is, the natural or
unspiritual world where Abstract Philosophy holds sway—"is hindrance
& not Action" (VLJ, p. 617). Creation is a type of error, mistake or
hindrance of action (Blake defines evil in each of these ways) and will
finally be consumed at the Last Judgment. But Blake does not accept
"act" as deed only. He objects, for example, to Francis Bacon's statement
that good thoughts "are little better than good dreams, except they be
put in act" by replying: "Thought is Act. Christ's Acts were Nothing to
Caesar's if this is not so" (p. 400). Thought is act because "Mental Things
are alone Real" (VLJ, p. 617).

Lack of action—that is, brooding—creates the condition under which
Abstraction or Negations can come into existence. Rahab, who in one
sense represents the memory of sin or mistake, sits hidden within the
Hand who has three heads, "Brooding Abstract Philosophy to destroy
Imagination, the Divine- / Humanity" (J.70:19–20). This "Abstract Philosophy" is the same as that created by Albion's sons when they separate
the two contraries Good and Evil and create from them an "abstract" or
"negation." Their thought becomes taken up with "agreements and
disagreements," the characteristic concerns of the separative faculty,
reason. "All Quarrels arise from Reasoning," Los asserts (J.64:20). The
Zoa Tharmas complains to his consort Enion after Albion's fall:

Why wilt thou Examine every little fibre of my soul,
Spreading them out before the sun like stalks of flax to dry?

The infant joy is beautiful, but its anatomy
Horrible, Ghast & Deadly; nought shalt thou find in it
But Death, Despair & Everlasting brooding Melancholy. (FZ.1.47–51)

If one broodingly examines the fibres of the soul with single vision in search of sin, he remains "abstracted" and divided: "Serpent Reasonings us entice / Of Good and Evil, Virtue and Vice" (GP.5–6). In *Jerusalem*, Albion sees this philosophy of the abstract descend upon his own head after he has taught it to his sons; for the son, learning from the father, turns the same hatred back to him: "O my Children, / I have educated you in the crucifying cruelties of Demonstration / Till you have assum'd the Providence of God & slain your Father" (J.24:54–56). Similarly, in *The Book of Ahania*, Urizen's son Fuzon cries out:

"Shall we worship this Demon of smoke,"
Said Fuzon, "this abstract non-entity,
This cloudy God seated on waters.
Now seen, now obscur'd, King of sorrow?" (BA.2:10–13)

In this case, however, the father, Urizen, successfully crushes his son's revolt (BA.3:39–44) and crucifies him on his Tree of Mystery, as he later does Los's son Orc (FZ.7a:162–165). Plate 8 of Blake's illustrations *For Children: The Gates of Paradise* (1793) depicts an aged Urizenic figure who sits on a thronelike structure (in another sense he is the orthodox Christian God) with a sword in one hand. He leans his forehead in sorrow upon his other hand while his son aims a spear at his heart. The legend reads: "My Son! My Son!" (p. 209; p. 766). Many years later (about 1818), when Blake wrote additional legends for the same illustrations (which he called *For the Sexes: The Gates of Paradise*), he expanded the same legend to read as follows:

In vain-glory hatcht & nurst,
By double Spectres Self Accurst,
My Son! my Son! thou treatest me
But as I have instructed thee. (GP.27–30)

Thus, education partakes of the Spectre in that it is always concerned with the doubleness of the Tree of Knowledge of Good and Evil. The abstract or negation into which these qualities, Good and Evil, harden as a result of such education is then turned back upon the instigator, and the cycle perpetuates itself generation after generation.[30]

Such division keeps one involved in what Blake terms the "Ratio"—comparing one thing to another and thus turning them into abstractions. In this way, one repeats the same round over again without seeing the truth. "It is a dangerous illusion," states F. R. Leavis in commenting on Blake, that we can attain to the real by an abstracting process, or that perception is a matter of passive exposure to an objective world of which science gives a true report. The eye is part of the brain, and the brain is a representative of the living whole, an agent of the psyche: perception is creative.[31]

For this reason, Los says his business is to create, not to compare.

The "infant joy" that exists before examination—the child's fourfold vision—can restore wholeness, for the child has not yet been taught Demonstration or Abstract Philosophy; he does not examine but perceives, and he lives in the eternal moment, the pulsation of the artery, considering neither remembrance nor futurity. Blake used these two terms interchangeably, since to go either backward or forward constitutes the same movement of error. One must live in the Now, which is all that ever exists. This interchangeability of terms (indicating more clearly than anything else Blake's attitude toward the opposites engendered by eating of the Tree of Knowledge of Good and Evil), can be seen unequivocally in his deletions of "remembrance" and the additions of "futurity" in those lines from *The Four Zoas* in which Urizen is finally regenerated:

> Then Go, O dark [remembrance *del.*] futurity! I will cast thee forth
> from these
> Heavens of my brain, nor will I look upon [remembrance *del.*] futurity
> more.
> I cast [remembrance *del.*] futurity away, & turn my back upon that
> void.
> Which I have made; for lo! [Remembrance *del.*] futurity is in this
> moment. (FZ.9:180–183)

Both the past and the future are contained in the present moment, as Eternity itself is, and one cannot for that reason bind it in any way; he can only recognize it and let it go:

> He who binds to himself a joy
> Does the winged life destroy:
> But he who kisses the joy as it flies
> Lives in eternity's sun rise. (p.179)

Edward J. Rose, writing on *Jerusalem*, maintains that Blake's most complex poem is "based upon a one-to-infinity relationship" rather than a one-to-one relationship; and thus becomes "a system of linked analogies ending in a final identity, the metaphorical present."[32] This "metaphorical present" is Blake's Eternity.

The collapse of the past and the future into an Eternal Now (or the failure to do so) has been expressed often in the century and a half since Blake's death by English and American authors who share Blake's vision of other dimensions that we can see now only through a glass, darkly.

Porphyria's lover in Browning's poem, for example, attempts to trap and hold the joyous moment Blake speaks of; but like Hawthorne's Aylmer in *The Birthmark*, who "failed to look beyond the shadowy scope of time, and, living once for all in eternity, to find the perfect future in the present,"[33] he obtains nothing but a dead body, the type of "perfection" that constitutes the world of Ulro. In *Wuthering Heights,* Heathcliff dies at the window that symbolizes the conjunction of past and future, of time and eternity, of the world we usually see and that other world which obscurely rises before our consciousness through the influence of art. Matthew in Wordsworth's "The Two April Mornings" feels pain because his grief for his dead daughter has passed. But the more subtle aspect of the poem lies in his reaction to the living girl whom he sees on the first April morning. She is a "pure delight" because he does not wish to bind her to him, something that restricts us not only to time but to its griefs as well. T. S. Eliot in *Burnt Norton* not only collapses the future and past into the present—

> Time past and time future
> What might have been and what has been
> Point to one end, which is always present

—but also seems to feel that such a vision is the only way to redeem time in time, to overcome evil. As we rise to the height of this vision "above the moving tree"—the cyclic pattern or dance of the universe—to "the still point," we accept the opposites, the garlic and the sapphires; and though we still hear below us the boarhound and the boar, they are nevertheless through our clarified perception "reconciled among the stars."[34] Those who remain bound to single sight are incapable of this vision. And, unfortunately, as Yeats affirms in a lyrical passage from "William Blake and His Illustrations to *The Divine Comedy*," the world is almost always "incapable":

> the truth Blake preached and sang and painted is the root of the cultivated life, of the fragile perfect blossom of the world born in ages of leisure and peace, and never yet to last more than a little season; the life those Phaeacians, who told Odysseus that they had set their hearts in nothing but in "the dance and changes of raiment, and love and sleep," lived before Poseidon heaped a mountain above them; the lives of all who, having eaten of the Tree of Life, love, more than did the barbarous ages when none had time to live "the minute particulars of life," the little fragments of space and time, which are wholly flooded by beautiful emotion because they are so little they are hardly of time and space at all.[35]

These little fragments of space and time cannot be discerned through the "Reasoning Power" (J.10:13). Those who use only this limited vision, like the Sons of Urizen, "In ignorance . . . view a small portion & think that All, / And call it Demonstration" (J.65:27–28). Hazard Adams, in his *Blake and Yeats: The Contrary Vision*, points out that Crabb Robinson and Robert Southey did not respond with enthusiasm to Blake's *Jerusalem* because they demanded "a standard floor plan."[36] They could not place England in Jerusalem; eternity could not intersect time.

By the wise, the eternal moment may be found within each day; and, if found, it raises all the other moments to Eternity:

> There is a Moment in each Day that Satan cannot find,
> Nor can his Watch Fiends find it; but the Industrious find
> This Moment & it multiply, & when it once is found
> It renovates every Moment of the Day if rightly placed. (M.35:42–45)

If one can do this, he releases himself from brooding on evil and becomes free. One dies to his past experiences immediately. This requires great energy and attention on the adult's part (the child can accomplish the feat more easily), but it is the only way the mind can be renewed (like the child's) and the only way one finds it possible to love. For if one attempts to love while clinging to the memory of his former experiences (his own sins or those of others), he will fail. Blake advises, therefore, "Drive your cart and your plow over the bones of the dead" (MHH.7:2). One can work (the plow signifies artistic creation) only by forgetting the past and living in the moment of time that Blake calls the pulsation of the artery. There is no method in this, only perception. That is why he discarded the Greek Muses (the Daughters of Memory) and substituted his own Daughters of Beulah (Inspiration) in their stead. Similarly, Shelley's Cythna in *The Revolt of Islam* counsels the mariners to forget past sins and so become truly free, for the past (as in Blake's Proverb) belongs to death:

> Reproach not thine own soul, but know thyself,
> Nor hate another's crime, nor loathe thine own.
> It is the dark idolatry of self,
> Which, when our thoughts and actions once are gone,
> Demands that man should weep, and bleed, and groan;
> O vacant expiation! Be at rest.—
> The past is Death's, the future is thine own;
> And love and joy can make the foulest breast
> A paradise of flowers, where peace might build her nest. (RI.VIII.xxii)

In Albion's fall, his Emanation Jerusalem (Forgiveness, Liberty, Love) is reduced to a wanderer, often condemned to work in the Satanic, Babylonian mills and dungeons created by the Reasoning Spectre. She laments that Albion, thinking of her as Sin and as a harlot, has cast her from him. In their life together in Eternity, however, they did not brood on evil:

> Wherefore hast thou [Albion] shut me into the winter of human life,
> And clos'd up the sweet regions of youth and virgin innocence
> Where we live forgetting error, not pondering on evil,
> Among my lambs & brooks of water, among my warbling birds:
> Where we delight in innocence before the face of the Lamb,
> Going in and out before him in his love and sweet affection? (J.20:5–10)

The Lamb, Jesus, represents love and forgiveness in contrast to the Abstract Philosophy that grows out of the Tree of Knowledge of Good and Evil. The child in "The Lamb" makes an exact equation between himself, the lamb and Jesus:

> I a child, & thou a lamb,
> We are called by his name. (p. 115)

And neither Jesus, the child nor the lamb—in Blake's view—is concerned with evil. They do not brood over past errors, but live totally in the present moment. Conversely, one of the most evil aspects of the Druids ("Natural Religion") is their attempt to make the remembrance of sin permanent:

> the Druids rear'd their Rocky Circles to make permanent
> Remembrance
> Of Sin, & the Tree of Good & Evil sprang from the Rocky Circle &
> Snake
> Of the Druid. (J.92:24–26)

Blake's Muses, the Daughters of Beulah, call upon the Divine Vision, Jesus, to remove the Druidical curse by which man binds himself to his sin:

> Come, O thou Lamb of God, and take away the remembrance of Sin.
> To Sin & to hide the Sin in sweet deceit is lovely!
> To Sin in the open face of day is cruel & pitiless! But
> To record the Sin for a reproach, to let the Sun go down
> In remembrance of the Sin, is a Woe & a Horror,
> A brooder of an Evil Day and a Sun rising in blood!
> Come then, O Lamb of God, and take away the remembrance of Sin. (J.50:24–30)

In order to make such forgetting and forgiving a viable process both for oneself and others, Blake solidifies evil into states that he variously terms Satan; Rahab and Tirzah; the Hermaphrodite; the Spectre, the Selfhood; Bacon, Newton, and Locke; the Druid Dragon; Mystery, the Harlot (Babylon); Ulro; Hand and Hyle, and many others. All these states, however, are aspects of the first evil or error—separation and restriction—created by Urizen. All individuals may be delivered from these states once the latter have been given definite form, for in the beginning after the fall, error is indefinite and unbounded (BL.4:30), like Urizen when he rises out of Eternity.

Because of Urizen's original formlessness when he separates himself from Eternity, Los has his work prepared for him. He must hammer Urizen into recognizable features in the early Prophetic Books (*The Book of Urizen, The Book of Los, The Four Zoas*). Los is "affrighted / At the formless, unmeasurable death" (BU.7:8–9) that Urizen becomes when he separates himself from Los and the other Eternals. Los binds him with the five senses, "till a Form / Was completed, a Human Illusion / In darkness and deep clouds involv'd" (BL.5:55–57). Thus infinite senses become reduced to five, and man, like Urizen, looks out from his caverned brain "to view a small portion & think that All" (FZ.7b.185). Blake describes this condition as follows in the words of Erin, an aspect of the true belief in forgiveness:

> Ah! shut in narrow doleful form!
> Creeping in reptile flesh upon the bosom of the ground!
> The Eye of Man, a little narrow orb, clos'd up & dark,
> Scarcely beholding the Great Light, conversing with the ground:
> The Ear, a little shell, in small volutions shutting out
> True Harmonies & comprehending great as very small:
> The Nostrils, bent down to the earth & clos'd with senseless flesh
> That odours cannot them expand, nor joy on them exult:
> The Tongue, a little moisture fills, a little food it cloys,
> A little sound it utters, & its cries are faintly heard. (J.49:32–41)

Like Urizen, Rahab—who represents Urizen's cruel religion of mystery, which suppresses energy—is also indefinite:

> And Rahab, like a dismal and indefinite hovering Cloud,
> Refus'd to take a definite form; she hover'd over all the Earth
> Calling the definite, sin, defacing every definite form
> Invisible or Visible, stretch'd out in length or spread in breadth
> Over the Temples, drinking groans of victims, weeping in pity
> And joying in the pity, howling over Jerusalem's walls. (J.80:51–56)

Such pity, of course, is the false, sadistic and hypocritical pity that Blake expresses in "The Human Abstract":

> Pity would be no more
> If we did not make somebody Poor;
> And Mercy no more could be
> If all were as happy as we. (p.217)

It is the same kind of pity that Mercury offers to the chained Prometheus (PU.I.410–411), and that Urizen talks of to the chained Orc (FZ.7a:110–129).

The indefinite comes into existence through Albion's fall in *The Four Zoas* and through Urizen's in *The Book of Urizen*. Most of Blake's characters are terrified of it. Urizen himself shrinks from indefinite space (FZ.2:20), and Ahania (Urizen's consort or Emanation), cast out by Urizen, wanders in fear of falling into it (FZ.3:208). The Reasoning Spectre—whom Los battles mightily throughout Plates 6, 7, 8, 9, and 10 of *Jerusalem*—attempts "to draw Los down / Into the Indefinite" (J.91:35–36). The Spectre himself is indefinite, identified with the "Rational Power" (J.64:5); and Los, in his attempt to bind Urizen, labors "Among indefinite Druid rocks & snows of doubt & reasoning (M.3:6–8). Conversely, truth is not formless, but definite and particular:

> He who would do good to another must do it in Minute Particulars:
> General Good is the plea of the scoundrel, hypocrite & flatterer,
> For Art & Science cannot exist but in minutely organized Particulars
> And not in generalizing Demonstrations of the Rational Power.
> The infinite alone resides in Definite & Determinate Identity. (J.55:60-64)[37]

Like truth, evil must also be given a "definite and determinate identity" as a permanent state so that it may be passed through.

Evil manifests itself in the natural world as accident, but "being formed / Into Substance & Principle by the cruelties of Demonstration":

> It became Opake & Indefinite, but the Divine Saviour
> Formed it into a Solid by Los's Mathematic Power.
> He named the Opake, Satan: he named the Solid, Adam. (M.29:35–39)

The more solid and definite the opaque state of Satan becomes (as in Bacon, Newton, and Locke or in Mystery, the Harlot), the nearer it approaches the possibility of being cast off by the individual who is in it. Edward J. Rose, in his article on the structure of Blake's *Jerusalem*, explains that the apocalyptic section of the poem, Chapter Four, "builds toward the epiphany of Jerusalem and the risen cosmic man by also building towards the epiphany of the Anti-Christ."[38] As in Blake's paradigm, the Revelation of St. John the Divine, evil reaches its highest intensity just at the point when it is destroyed.

Once the solidification of evil has taken place, there is hope of deliverance from it. "Man," states Blake,

> is born a Spectre or Satan & is altogether an Evil, & requires a New Selfhood continually, & must continually be changed into his direct Contrary. But your Greek Philosophy (which is a remnant of Druidism) teaches that Man is Righteous in his Vegetated Spectre. (J.52, p. 682)

The *state* of Spectre or Satan, however, into which man is born Blake distinguishes from the individual who is in it: "Evil is Created into a

State, that Men / May be delivered time after time, evermore" (J.49:70–71). Los forces the Spectre to work with him "Striving with Systems to deliver Individuals from those Systems" (J.11:5). Blake affirms that "the Spiritual States of the Soul are All Eternal." Thus, "Rahab is an Eternal State" (J.52, p. 681).

Blake cautions the Deists at the beginning of Chapter Three of *Jerusalem* to "distinguish between the man & his present State" (J.52, p. 681); "to distinguish the Eternal Human / . . . from those States or Worlds in which the Spirit travels." Such a distinction, Blake adds, "is the only means to Forgiveness of Enemies" (J.49:71;74–75), and his example is instructive: "Rousseau thought Men Good by Nature: he found them Evil & found no friend. Friendship cannot exist without Forgiveness of Sins continually" (J.52, p. 682). Both Moses and Abraham, for example, represent such states that man passes through (VLJ, p. 607). Moses signifies the restrictive moral code—the Decalogue—of Urizen and his religion of reason: "Moses beheld upon Mount Sinai forms of dark delusion" (SL.3:17); while "Abraham was called to succeed the Druidical age"—that is, he represents the cessation of the rite of human sacrifice, by which the Druids turned "allegoric and mental signification into corporeal command" (DC, p. 578). Sacrifice, like war and hunting, is a mental activity in Eternity: "Our wars are wars of life, & wounds of love / With intellectual spears, & long winged arrows of thought" (J.38:14–15). Abraham is thus a state higher on man's way to the true religion of forgiveness and love: Jesus, the Divine Vision, the Human Imagination. The churches before the flood (Adam and Noah were both Druids) "were fill'd with blood & fire & vapour [sic] of smoke; even till Abraham's time the vapor [sic] & heat was not extinguish'd" (VLJ, p. 606).

Man passes through these states "but States remain for Ever; he passes thro' them like a traveller who may as well suppose that the places he has passed thro' exist no more" (VLJ, p. 606). Since these states are permanent, man can "Foresee & Avoid / The terrors of Creation & Redemption & Judgment"—that is, he can avoid falling into the state of Satan (error)—only if he is able to see these states "in the Outward Spheres of Visionary Space and Time, / In the shadows of Possibility" and in "the Vision & in the Prophecy" (J.92:17–20).

This idea of a possibly impermanent apocalypse is almost precisely that of Shelley's in *Prometheus Unbound*. Although Prometheus overcomes evil and retires with Asia to his cave "paved with veined emerald" to watch "As the world ebbs and flows, ourselves unchanged" (PU.III.iii.13;24); although the Spirit of the Hour pours out the "lulled music" of his mystic shell "over the cities of mankind" (PU.III.iii.73–76), making man "Sceptreless, free, uncircumscribed" and "just, gentle, wise"; yet "chance, and death, and mutability" remain (PU.III.iv.194–201), and only through "Gentleness, Virtue, Wisdom, and Endurance" can man keep evil days at bay, since Eternity could "with infirm hand" release the serpent that attempts to encircle it (PU.IV.562–567). If this should happen, man may then *reassume* his control over evil through forgiveness, defiance of power, love, endurance and hope (PU.IV.570– 578). The notion of impermanence is more noticeable in *Prometheus Unbound* because humanity continues to exist in the utopian setting of the world itself, whereas in Blake's apocalypse the natural world is consumed and only Eternity remains.

In addition, this idea of impermanence (perhaps man will never achieve a spiritual stasis that cannot be disturbed) indicates the emphasis that both Blake and Shelley put upon movement, energy, activity, change, fluidity and similar qualities. These qualities belong to the nature of their perception and are characteristic of the Romantic consciousness. The Eternals in Blake's Eden, for example, blend in "thunders of intellect" and use "long, winged arrows of thought." Blake, in his "Mental Fight" to build Jerusalem "in England's green & pleasant land" calls for a bow of burning gold, arrows of desire, a spear, a Chariot of Fire and a sword (M.I.9–16). He turns the objects used for "corporeal" war into those of "mental" war, transmuting the former into energies to redeem mankind. It is noteworthy that in *Prometheus Unbound* only the gods retire to an unchanging state. Apparently, the regeneration of Prometheus creates an apocalypse for himself but only a precarious utopia for man.

Chapter Three

The Unascended Heaven

The loathsome mask has fallen, the man remains
Sceptreless, free, uncircumscribed, but man
Equal, unclassed, tribeless, and nationless,
Exempt from awe, worship, degree, the king
Over himself; just, gentle, wise: but man
Passionless?—no, yet free from guilt or pain,
Which were, for his will made or suffered them,
Nor yet exempt, though ruling them like slaves,
From chance, and death, and mutability,
The clogs of that which else might oversoar
The loftiest star of unascended heaven,
Pinnacled dim in the intense inane.

(PU.III.iv.193–204)

Blake's poetry sets forth his belief that the quality and kind of perception (that is, a vision developed through poetry and the other arts) can eradicate the evil of the world and bring about the apocalypse. In large part, Shelley shares this idea with Blake. For this evil, in Blake's view, is not radical or real but simply sin, error, or mistake—all easily forgiven and all appearances within the natural or unspiritual world that can be destroyed through fourfold vision, the perception of Eternity. To some extent, Shelley also shares this concept of evil as accident, and he certainly stresses the power of forgiveness in renovating the universe. Without forgiveness, Laon would never be worthy of the journey to the Temple of the Spirit, for like Urizen he himself remains bound very firmly by his mistakes until he finds the means of release. Similarly, Prometheus, without the forgiveness of Jupiter, would cry out forever from his rock in the Caucasus, since it is his own hatred and not Jupiter that binds him there to his torment. Indeed, the moment his hatred begins to lessen, the evil Furies, "Jove's tempest-walking hounds" (PU.I.331), lose their power over him and vanish. However, several major differences exist between Blake and Shelley. The most important lies in the way the younger poet qualifies his own apocalyptic and utopian vision.

Unlike Blake, Shelley tends to modify the view that *all* evils may be eradicated primarily because his skepticism always kept up a running battle with his belief in perfectibility. When he felt, he believed and hoped; when he reasoned, he doubted and sometimes despaired. Shelley's hope (as found in *Prometheus Unbound*) is that at least *most* of the evils in the world could be destroyed if man would only consent to love rather than to hate. Shelley was aware, however, that man is drawn now one way, now the other, between the forces of good and evil, just as he recognized that he himself was pessimistic or optimistic, skeptical or believing, by turns. Because he recognized this dichotomy, he fully realized his difficult poetic task of presenting the path of beauty and virtue in such a way that his readers would desire above all else to follow it.

One basic way toward a greater understanding of Shelley's view that all evils may not be eradicated lies in looking closely at a statement he made in 1811 to Elizabeth Hitchener: "I have considered it in every possible light & reason tells me that death is the boundary of the life of man. Yet I feel, I believe the direct contrary."[1] Although some critics have found it useful to trace Shelley's thought as developing from his early Godwinian beliefs in Necessity and Perfectibility (as in *Queen Mab*) into either Empiricism on the one hand or Platonism on the other,[2] it seems rather obvious that Shelley expresses in his mature years (as indicated in his early statement to Miss Hitchener) now one attitude of reasonable, reflective skepticism, now the other of intuitive, feeling belief. Newman Ivey White in his biography *Shelley* points out the differences between *Queen Mab* and *Prometheus Unbound*, the greatest difference being "the substitution of Love for Necessity."[3] But Shelley's belief in Necessity does not change so much as to become transmuted into the increasing depth of his insight. This depth, however, does not imply a total acceptance of "reason" or "belief" and "feeling," to use his own words.

In *Queen Mab*, Necessity is an absolute, pervading force in Nature, "an immense and uninterrupted chain of causes and effects," Shelley states in his notes to the poem, "no one of which could occupy any other place than it does occupy, or act in any other place than it does act" (p. 809). By the time he wrote *The Revolt of Islam* (five to six years after *Queen Mab*) Necessity had become, in Cythna's words, the power that binds evil with evil and good with good:

> In their own hearts the earnest of the hope
>> Which made them great, the good will ever find:
> And though some envious shades may interlope
>> Between the effect and it, One comes behind,
>> Who aye the future to the past will bind—
> Necessity, whose sightless strength for ever
>> Evil with evil, good with good must wind
> In bands of union, which no power may sever:
> They must bring forth their kind, and be divided never! (RI.IX.xxvii)

This binding and separation give the good something of a chance over its adversary, and leaves man with more desire to choose the good. Even though Necessity is an amoral ("sightless") power that does not distinguish between good and evil, if one creates good in the past Necessity will bind it to the future. This indicates that Shelley had come to accept far more free will in man than he was willing to concede in his notes to *Queen Mab:*

> The precise character and motives of any man on any occasion being given, the moral philosopher could predict his actions with as much certainty as the natural philosopher could predict the effects of the mixture of any particular chemical substance. (p. 810)

One or two years after *The Revolt of Islam*, in *Prometheus Unbound*, Shelley's power of insight—the imaginative power that in Coleridge's formula reconciles seemingly discordant opposites—not so much *substituted* Love for Necessity as it enabled him to collapse the two forces into one. The path through the forest that Asia and Panthea follow in order to reach Demogorgon's realm is filled with Spirits who are both attracted and impelled "by Demogorgon's mighty law" (PU.II.ii.43), while at the same time they "Believe their own swift wings and feet / The sweet desires within obey" (PU.II.55–56). The Spirits are *impelled* by their *inner* "sweet desires" of love, which are in reality the same as the *outer* force of Necessity which *compels* them. Necessity, acting from within the Spirits, is the highest freedom.[4] In *Prometheus Unbound*, also, Necessity becomes more than simply a force that *binds* evil with evil and good with good. Shelley has now realized a significant difference between the quality of good and that of evil. In the Third Act of *Prometheus Unbound*, in Bennett Weaver's words, "Evil is *caught* within its own nature and destroyed; Good is *released* through its own nature and triumphs."[5] Blake also sees evil (the chained Urizen, for example) as bound or as that which binds; and the true good (the intense and swiftly moving Los) as free or as that which frees. Because of this binding, evil (although it has great strength) is always limited: the eagle may win for a time but the snake is nourished in the breast of Love (which is eternal) until it gains enough energy to renew itself—as the good does in *Prometheus Unbound*. But in both *The Revolt of Islam* and *Prometheus Unbound* the triumph of the good is qualified. At the end of *The Revolt*, the Iberian priest wins the literal victory; and at the end of *Prometheus Unbound*, Jupiter is not destroyed but is only held in check.

Thus, whatever the causes (his education, innate mode of perception, or other factors), Shelley did not ever completely subdue his reason to imagination or feeling, as Blake could and did, although by the time Shelley wrote *Prometheus Unbound* he had moved very far from what he called his "early materialism."[6] Feeling led him toward Plato and the denial of evil as a reality; reason led him toward skepticism and the acceptance of evil as a reality. After the Third Act of *Prometheus Unbound,* in which the universe is purged of the evil in Man's mind, Shelley turned at once to the creation of a work dealing with radical—and in Asia's word "immedicable" evil—*The Cenci.* To complete the circle, after finishing *The Cenci* he wrote almost without pausing between them the final and intensely lyrical Fourth Act of *Prometheus Unbound. The Cenci* is what Shelley reasoned; *Prometheus Unbound* is what he felt or believed.

Though younger, Shelley was nevertheless much more of an inheritor of eighteenth-century rationalism than Blake, who had been born in its midst, ever was; and Shelley's works almost everywhere bear the stamp of an education, *a schooling,* of the sort that Blake considered himself fortunate to have escaped. Not that Shelley accepted all that he was taught. He was expelled from Oxford for writing a pamphlet on atheism, finally becoming an exile, banished from the society and the country that had no understanding of his genius. But he had to make his way painfully and with many doubts and hesitations toward that Temple of the Spirit which Blake intuitively built almost from his birth.

It should be remembered that even in the comparatively early *Revolt of Islam,* in which that Temple appears (a Temple often thought to be representative of Shelley's optimism about the eradication of evil), Laon and Cythna are burned to death by the Iberian priest in an attempt to propitiate a god who has brought down upon the earth, so the priest believes, plague, famine, and utter desolation.[7] Laon and Cythna thus escape by a fiery death a world in which—at least for their time—the revolution to overthrow tyrants has failed, and all the earth lies under sentence of death:

> The fish were poisoned in the streams; the birds
> In the green woods perished; the insect race
> Was withered up; the scattered flocks and herds
> Who had survived the wild beasts' hungry chase
> Died moaning, each upon the other's face
> In helpless agony gazing; round the City
> All night, the lean hyaenas their sad case
> Like starving infants wailed; a woeful ditty!
> And many a mother wept, pierced with unnatural pity. (RI.X.xv)

Even before this, Cythna has disclosed to Laon that they will not witness the passing of "the winter of the world" and the dawn of freedom and justice:

> O dearest love! we shall be dead and cold
> Before this morn may on the world arise;
> Wouldst thou the glory of its dawn behold?
> Alas! gaze not on me, but turn thine eyes
> On thine own heart—it is a paradise
> Which everlasting Spring has made its own. (RI.IX.xxvi.3694–3699)

Just as she places this paradise within the heart of Laon, so too does she place the hope for its achievement not in the overthrow of an outward tyrant (as Shelley tends to do in *Queen Mab*), but in men's hearts, in their unquenchable love for truth and liberty:

> In their own hearts the earnest of the hope
> Which made them great, the good will ever find. (RI.IX.xxvii.3703–3704)

Similarly, the later *Prometheus Unbound*, though an expression of Shelley's basic optimism, is qualified in its hope for the expulsion of all evils. Prometheus creates an apocalypse for himself, Asia, and their group, but only a utopia for mankind. Although Prometheus in some sense represents man and his will and ability to overcome evil, as a character within the drama itself Prometheus remains apart from the world he has regenerated. He and his troupe of immortals withdraw to their cave of "veined marble" to engage in artistic activity. "A simple dwelling," says Prometheus

> which shall be our own;
> Where we will sit and talk of time and change,
> As the world ebbs and flows, ourselves unchanged.
> What can hide man from mutability? (PU.III.iii.22–25)

Not even Prometheus possesses the power to destroy death and change. This passage may also indicate, insofar as Prometheus represents man, in the words of Carl Grabo, that "the social mind, mankind as a whole, is happy and eternal although the individual, the human mortal, is subject to the vicissitudes of change."[8] Earl Wasserman, in *Shelley's Prometheus Unbound,* states the belief that Prometheus represents the One Mind and that man is but a portion of that Mind. Therefore,

> Shelley's apocalypse and millennium are the forms of perfection at the two different levels of being: the timelessness of the One Mind and the nearest possible approximation to that condition in the human mind, which subsists as human mind by virtue of the illusions of diversity and change.[9]

Similarly, Milton Wilson, in *Shelley's Later Poetry,* remarks that Act Four of *Prometheus Unbound* is "basically a celebration of the millennium, not the final conquest of Time and Chaos."[10] In any case, whatever Prometheus is taken to represent, some type of evil still remains in Shelley's regenerated universe. At this point, however (the point at which the utopia is created), so much of the evil has been eliminated that both Prometheus and the world are prepared to engage happily in life-giving arts. Through these arts that express love, Prometheus will give that love to and receive that love from the "human mortal":

> And lovely apparitions . . .
> Shall visit us, the progeny immortal

Of Painting, Sculpture, and rapt Poesy,
And arts, though unimagined, yet to be.
The wandering voices and the shadows these
Of all that man becomes, the mediators
Of that best worship love, by him and us
Given and returned. (PU.III.iii.49;54–60)

Prometheus' "Painting, Sculpture, and rapt Poesy" are Shelley's version
of the "bright Sculptures of / Los's Halls" (J.16:61–62).

This concept of the apocalypse is quite different from Blake's, for
whom "All deities reside in the human breast" (MHH.11, p. 153). The
universe is human, contained in the mighty giant Albion, and there is no
difference between "Albion" and "man," no split between different
aspects of the mind. Blake defines evil as sin, error, mistake—negatives
that can be forgiven and destroyed. Death belongs to the "natural" or
"unspiritual" world that is consumed in the apocalyptic, regenerative
forces of love, understanding, and wisdom. When pressed, Blake would
not answer Crabb Robinson's question about "absolute evil." To Shelley,
however, absolute evil remains in some sense a reality. Prometheus
diminishes evil; Demogorgon *contains* Jupiter; but there are some absolutes that remain not only outside man's final control (though they
become his "slaves") but outside Prometheus' as well. In Demogorgon's
words, these absolutes are "Fate, Time, Occasion, Chance, and Change"
(PU.II.iv.119).

The Spirit of the Hour echoes Demogorgon at the end of the Third
Act by stating that man is not "exempt, though ruling them like slaves, /
From chance, and death, and mutability" (PU.III.iv.200–201). And in
Count Cenci the reader sees a totally unredeemable evil, an evil carried
to the very limits of human capacity. Significantly, however, in *Prometheus Unbound* Shelley places "eternal Love" beyond the power of
chance or change or death, and so his hope attends and limits his
propensity to doubt, much as Demogorgon does Jupiter.

Like Blake, Shelley tends to equate evil with the corruption of innocence that takes place in the education of the child. "I grieve at human
nature," he wrote to Elizabeth Hitchener, January 26, 1812,

> but am so far from despairing that I can readily trace all that is evil even in
> the youngest to the sophistications of society. It will not appear surprising
> that some original taint of our nature has been adopted as an opinion by
> the unthinking when they perceive how very early depraved dispositions
> are exhibited; but when it is considered what exhaustless pains are taken
> by nurses and Parents to make wrong impressions on the infant mind, I
> cannot be surprised at the earliest traits of evil and mistake.[11]

And yet—again like Blake—he occasionally comes very close to despair
when overwhelmed by the evils of the world. When two servants he had

dismissed spread malicious rumors about him, Shelley wrote (in a paraphrase of King Lear) to his friends John and Maria Gisborne (July 7, 1820): "An ounce of civet good apothecary to sweeten this dunghill of a world."[12] Accused by these same servants a year later of having Claire Clairmont as his mistress and of the crime of having abandoned his child by her, he wrote Mary Shelley (August 7, 1821) that he was not troubled by the former accusation (though to have had Claire as his mistress would have been a mistake):

> but that I have committed such unutterable crimes as destroying or abandoning a child—& that my own—imagine my despair of good—imagine how it is possible that one of so weak & sensitive a nature as mine can run further the gauntlet through this hellish society of men.[13]

To maintain himself in this hellish society, seeing "that the mass of mankind as things are arranged at present, are cruel deceitful & selfish," he wrote to Leigh Hunt: "I have taken suspicion to me as a cloak, & scorn as an impenetrable shield."[14] One may be permitted to wonder, however, how far Shelley's temperament allowed him to assume with success qualities that came quite naturally to his acquaintance Byron. For in a letter three months later, also to Hunt, Shelley asks his friend to cure him of his supposed misanthropy and suspicion (for such a cloak and a shield were no doubt more difficult for him to bear himself than they were obstacles to others) and indicates how very deeply he had been wounded by Byron's assertion of his superior worldly rank.[15] But Shelley's recurring, essential, basic spirit toward others, his ineradicable optimism, despite his efforts to graft onto his vulnerability an "impenetrable shield" of scorn, may be seen in all his outbursts throughout his short life against oppression and tyranny. "Oh, Irishmen!" he cries out in his youth on a note that never changed with his maturity, though it deepened with sadness, "I am interested in your cause; and it is not because you are Irishmen or Roman Catholics that I feel with you and feel for you; but because you are men and sufferers."[16]

These brief biographical references show that Shelley's view of evil in the world was far from superficial (though some readers have thought so),[17] that he could and did "despair of good." His reactions first to the Gisbornes and then to Hunt also reveal the battle between his skepticism and his belief, his reason and his feeling. For reason and the "facts" told him that men were cruel and deceitful, but in his feeling and hope, he believed that perhaps they did not have to remain so.

Demogorgon in *Prometheus Unbound* represents Shelley's hope that most of the evils—at least those that man inflicts upon man—can be eliminated. But he realized the difficult poetic task he had before him in presenting this idea as vividly as he could horror or injustice, for Shelley quite definitely recognized the difference between the world purged of evil that *could* be brought into existence and the world of evil that man actually inhabits.

To Panthea and Asia, Demogorgon is at first veiled, but even when the veil falls he reveals himself to Panthea only as a "mighty darkness," a "living Spirit," possessing "neither limb, / Nor form, nor outline." There is no indication that Asia sees more of Demogorgon than Panthea does, though Asia says only "The veil has fallen" and gives no description of him (PU.II.iv.2–6). Although Demogorgon says he can supply answers to all things that Asia demands, the "final" answer, the "deep truth" he gives to Asia's questions about the origin of evil, is as cryptic—and as equivocal—as he himself is. In this, Shelley differs greatly from Blake, for to Blake truth resides in definite, determinate outline, and it is error that lacks form and must be given one by the imagination before it can be cast off. Notwithstanding Demogorgon's similarities to Los, Urthona and Orc, his very characteristics—lack of form and outline—would have indicated, to Blake, his inability to reveal the truth to Asia.

To Asia's questions regarding who made the world, thought, passion, reason, will and imagination, Demogorgon answers, "God: Almighty God" and "Merciful God." But when she presses her questions about the origin of terror, madness, crime, remorse, hate, self-contempt, pain, and hell, he replies, "He reigns" three times (PU.II.iv.11;18;28;31). By this change from "God" to "He" Demogorgon apparently implies that the two are different beings and that the "He" is Jupiter. Asia, at the end of her long speech which follows, delineating in part how Jupiter now torments Prometheus for being man's benefactor, returns again to her original point: "but who rains down / Evil, the immedicable plague?" "Not Jove," she continues:

> while yet his frown shook Heaven, ay, when
> His adversary Prometheus from adamantine chains
> Cursed him, he trembled like a slave. Declare
> Who is his master? Is he too a slave?

To which Demogorgon replies: "All spirits are enslaved which serve things evil: / Thou knowest if Jupiter be such or no." This answer perhaps implies that Jupiter is a slave under the "Almighty God" Demogorgon has mentioned earlier, even though Jupiter "reigns" at the present time. Asia at this point strikes at the real crux when she asks, "Whom calledst thou God?" and "Who is the master of the slave?" And Demogorgon, with the opportunity to make clear a distinction between the "God" and the "He" he has mentioned earlier, fails to do so and tells Asia that "I spoke but as ye speak, / For Jove is the supreme of living things," which seems to collapse "God" and "Jupiter" into one. Further, he declares that the abysm cannot "vomit forth its secrets" because it has no voice—"the deep truth is imageless" (PU.II.iv.100–116).

The one idea that does become clear from Demogorgon's conversation with Asia is that Love exists eternally and is not subject to "Fate, Time, Occasion, Chance, and Change" (PU.II.iv.119–120), as all other things are, including Jupiter and the "immedicable plague" of evil. Even at this juncture in the poem, the destined hour that will bring about Jupiter's doom is already at hand. Thus, Jupiter cannot possibly be the "Almighty" or "Merciful" God that Demogorgon has spoken of previously. Moreover, Jupiter, judging by events in the poem, is a slave to evil and is subject to Fate and Change, which Demogorgon himself represents. Demogorgon slides very neatly away from Asia's questions because Shelley himself does not know who, if anything, rains down evil. It would have been surprising if he had known, for all the "answers" that can be given are ultimately unsatisfactory on one score or another. It is significant, however, and one cannot stress it too much, that Shelley places Love in the universe as the one element not subject to the changefulness and uncertainties of lesser deities. And if there is any "answer" to the problem of evil in *Prometheus Unbound* it lies in the unchanging and eternal nature—as he conceived it—of the deity Shelley worshipped. For only through its power does Prometheus become strong enough to break the hold of evil upon the world of men. This stirring of love within the soul of Prometheus: "I feel / Most vain all hope but love" (PU.I.807–808), unites him with one who is its personification: Asia. And it is she who then activates the dread, volcanic Demogorgon in order to destroy Jupiter's evil reign. Demogorgon, in his ambiguous and equivocal answer, states that the "abysm" of truth will not give up its secrets on the nature of evil or its origin, and he asserts this position despite the fact that he himself rises from that same abysm. What he does make clear, nevertheless, is that "all things" including evil (as represented by Jupiter) are temporary and dissoluble except Love. On this inner lamp, Shelley fastened all his hope for man's ultimate regeneration and triumph over evil. "Never joy illumed my brow," he addresses his Intellectual Beauty, "Unlinked with hope that thou wouldst free / This world from its dark slavery" ("Hymn to Intellectual Beauty," VI:68–70).

Prometheus is the god who symbolizes Love as an entity beyond man's power to destroy while at the same time he represents that Love as it exists within the human heart. When the outer fails, when all things are confounded to ill (as one of the Furies says); when the revolution for freedom hardens into an even more restrictive tyranny than the tyranny it overthrew; when the winter of the world decimates the earth with famine and plague, the wise must turn inward to seek the "everlasting spring," the hope of the future. Just before their death by fire, Cythna tells Laon:

Spring comes, though we must pass, who made
The promise of its birth,—even as the shade
Which from our death, as from a mountain, flings
The future, a broad sunrise; thus arrayed
As with the plumes of overshadowing wings,
From its dark gulf of chains, Earth like an eagle springs.
(RI.IX.xxv.3688–3693)

Shelley's point—often overlooked—is that regeneration will not come unless humanity works for it now. Even as early as "An Address to the Irish People" (1812) he had said: "Although we may see many things put in train during our life-time, we cannot hope to see the work of virtue and reason finished now; we can only lay the foundation for our posterity."[18] Through his poetry, he endeavors to lay that foundation and to make that spring arrive a bit earlier than it otherwise would. "The Nature of my Work is Visionary or Imaginative," states Blake, explaining his work in terms that exactly fit Shelley's statements in his Preface to *Prometheus Unbound.* "It is an Endeavour to Restore what the Ancients call'd the Golden Age" (VLJ, p. 605). Only through learning to love the good (so Shelley and Blake believed) not through precept and dogma but through *preference,* can man make that dawn a reality.[19] The unquenchable hope is that, "If Winter comes, can Spring be far behind?" (WW.V.70). Adonais, although seemingly at first buried under the frost and ice of death, at last breaks through the "dome of many-coloured glass" into "the white radiance of Eternity" (AD.III.462–463). Many of the evils of the world are not "immedicable" although they often appeared that way even to one of such an optimistic temperament as Shelley's.

As he states in his preface to *Prometheus Unbound,* Shelley was fully aware of his difficult poetic task in presenting "beautiful idealisms of moral excellence" (p. 207) to raise his readers' perception, to create a preference for the good:

> It requires a higher degree of skill in a poet to make beauty, virtue, and harmony poetical, that is, to give them an idealized and rhythmical analogy with the predominating emotions of his readers than to make injustice, deformity, and discord and horror poetical.[20]

In his dedication of *The Cenci* to Leigh Hunt, Shelley explicitly recognizes the difference between the visionary world that could be brought into existence by man and the world of evil that man actually inhabits, primarily because he lacks the impetus of will to change it. The distinction is that between feeling ("apprehensions") and reason ("sad reality"):

> Those writings which I have hitherto published, have been little else than visions which impersonate my own apprehensions of the beautiful and just. I can also perceive in them the literary defects incidental to youth

and impatience; they are dreams of what ought to be, or may be. The drama which I now present to you is a sad reality. I lay aside the presumptuous attitude of an instructor, and am content to paint, with such colours as my own heart furnishes, that which has been. (pp. 274–275)

However, Shelley clung tenaciously to what he calls "little else than visions," turning back to *Prometheus Unbound* after he had finished the "sad reality," *The Cenci*. In the same way, in the "Essay on Christianity," he states, "according to the indisputable facts of the case, some evil Spirit has dominion in this imperfect world," but adds at once and characteristically, "But there will come a time when the human mind shall be visited exclusively by the influences of the benignant power."[21]

Thus Shelley, far from being unaware of his dichotomies (in both belief and skepticism, pessimism and optimism), recognized the unresolved poles of his nature as readily as he did those in his friend Byron, who was troubled by them to an even greater extent than Shelley, as his *Cain* and *Don Juan* bear witness. One such polarity—the desire for solitude versus the desire for society—Shelley expressed in a letter to Thomas Jefferson Hogg, May 8, 1811:

> What strange being I am, how inconsistent, in spite of all my boasted hatred of self—this moment thinking I could so far overcome Natures law as to exist in complete seclusion, the next shrinking from a moment of solitude, starting from my own company as it were that of a fiend, seeking any thing rather than a continued communion with *self*—Unravel this mystery—but no. I tell you to find the clue which even the bewildered explorer of the cavern cannot reach.[22]

As we have seen, Blake burst open the cavern and its narrow chinks instead of exploring it, refusing to accept the separations and doubleness inherent in the Tree of Knowledge of Good and Evil. Blake's Mental Traveller is able to understand this double pattern of the fallen world because he is uninvolved in it:

> I travel'd thro' a Land of Men,
> A Land of Men & Women too,
> And heard & saw such dreadful things
> As cold Earth wanderers never knew. (p. 424)

The "wanderers" do not "know" how dreadful their situation is in the "unspiritual" world because they possess only single vision; they cannot "see" and "hear" as the traveller does who has fourfold vision. To travel, moreover, indicates purpose:

> Thus is the heaven a vortex pass'd already, and the earth
> A vortex not yet pass'd by the traveller thro' Eternity. (M.15:34–35)

To "wander" on the other hand is to be like Shelley's "bewildered explorer of the cavern." He does not have hold of Blake's golden string, which, wound into a ball, leads one into the gate of Jerusalem (J.77, p. 716).

Blake used the Tree of Knowledge of Good and Evil to symbolize man's fallen condition: his separation from an eternal state in which contraries were unified in the Tree of Life. Similarly, in Manicheism, Shelley found a name for this doubleness or dichotomy that all men experience within themselves:

> The Manichaean philosophy respecting the origin and government of the world, if not true, is at least an hypothesis comfortable to the experience of actual facts. To suppose that the world was created and is superintended by two spirits of a balanced power and opposite dispositions is simply a personification of the struggle which we experience within ourselves, and which we perceive in the operations of external things as they affect us, between good and evil.[23]

The struggle between the eagle and the snake in Canto One of *The Revolt of Islam* represents the battle of these psychic forces; though of course Shelley, like Byron, did not accept the idea as a consistent philosophical concept, but only as metaphor. The two forces are inextricably intertwined. In *Prometheus Unbound,* Jupiter, overcome by Demogorgon, says to the latter:

> We two will sink on the wide waves of ruin,
> Even as a vulture and a snake outspent
> Drop, twisted in inextricable fight,
> Into a shoreless sea. (PU.III.i.71–74)

Jupiter is not destroyed by Demogorgon; the most that Demogorgon can do is to contain and limit him; the two will "dwell together / Henceforth in darkness" (PU.III.i.55–56). In his "Essay on the Punishment of Death," Shelley speaks of "that intertexture of good and evil with which Nature seems to have clothed every form of individual existence."[24] Similarly, in the "Essay on Christianity" he states: "Good and evil subsist in so intimate an union that few situations of human affairs can be affirmed to contain either of the principles in an unconnected state."[25]

Blake, defining "Evil" as Energy (Hell) and "Good" as Reason (Heaven), "marries" these two contraries or qualities and so rises above the separative Tree of Knowledge of Good and Evil. Indeed, the four Zoas, regenerated, represent the perfect blend of *all* man's faculties. Shelley recognized a far greater difference between what he termed "apprehensions of the beautiful" and "sad reality," and both the early *Revolt of Islam* and the later *Prometheus Unbound* contain a limited apocalypse—if Laon and Cythna's arrival at the Temple of the Spirit may be called that. Because he thought some evils to be absolute (as the above discussion of *Prometheus Unbound* makes clear)—in contrast to Blake's sin, error, or mistake, which are evils easily forgiven—Shelley tended to see a battle between the forces of good and evil. Ultimately, good wins; but it remains, nevertheless, in a most precarious and tentative position. Thus, his terms *good* and *evil* and the idea of a struggle between them carry almost the full force of their traditional meanings. In this sense, to experience good and evil in their paradoxical "intimate union" (as Shelley says), and hence battle, is cause for dismay and suffering. Because Blake rejected absolute evil and viewed both Good and Evil as interacting contraries (until they are separated into the double Tree by Albion's fall), he sets forth a total apocalypse for man, in contrast to Shelley's utopia. In *The Cenci,* moreover, Shelley presents not utopia but the "sad reality" he spoke of to Leigh Hunt. In his tragedy, especially in the depiction of the Count, Shelley is most removed from Blake's view of evil.

Cenci exemplifies a most useful definition of Shelleyan evil—as in Blake's idea of evil as sin, error, or mistake based on the separative, single view of reason. The Count defines Shelley's idea of evil as "oppression" and "selfishness." These are expressed to their uttermost limit in Cenci, who is one of the most horrifying characters in English literature. For his evil permeates not only the society at large; he also turns his hatred, as one would say "unnaturally," upon the members of his own family, to riot, in Shelley's words, "in selfishness & antipathy."[26]

Shelley very early had occasion to recognize the havoc induced by a person who gives free rein to his selfish desires. Though a psychological study of Shelley's friend Thomas Jefferson Hogg might reveal some highly questionable and more interesting motives behind his "love" for most of the women in Shelley's life,[27] Shelley saw in Hogg's reactions to these situations what Blake termed the Selfhood. During one of Shelley's absences, Hogg had attempted (unsuccessfully) to seduce Shelley's wife Harriet; and the whole youthful affair—including Shelley's responses—makes an amusing incident for those of a more cynical bent. What is noteworthy, however, is Shelley's statement that his friend did not think of others first: "Certainly no desire either for Harriet's happiness or that of any other human being except *yourself,*" he wrote to Hogg, "has been the cause of all our present misery."[28] This same attitude is expressed just as forcefully in Shelley's prose and verse throughout the course of his life. Ten years after this incident, for example, in 1821, Shelley identified morality as love,

> or a going out of our own nature and an identification of ourselves with the beautiful which exists in thought, action, or person, not our own. A man, to be greatly good, must imagine intensely and comprehensively; he must put himself in the place of another and of many others; the pains and

pleasures of his species must become his own. The great instrument of
moral good is the imagination; and poetry administers to the effect by
acting upon the cause.[29]

Cenci has become incapable of going out of self. He is Blake's Pebble
personified. He "joys in another's loss of ease"—Cenci stresses such
unholy joy again and again—"And Builds a Hell in Heaven's despite."
He illustrates perfectly Shelley's contention (in the Preface to *Alastor*)
that "those who love not their fellow beings live unfruitful lives, and
prepare for their old age a miserable grave" (p. 15).

When the Second Fury says to Prometheus, "Dost imagine / We will
but laugh into thy lidless eyes?", Prometheus replies, "I weigh not what
ye do, but what ye suffer, / Being evil" (PU.I.479–481), and the entire
action of the poem bears the proposition out, for in Prometheus himself
Jupiter is the evil idea, which, for as long as Prometheus holds it, makes
him suffer. But in *The Cenci* the formula fails; or, more aptly, the
formula is not found in the drama at all. Camillo is confronted by the
open, joyful villainy of Cenci, who, like the Furies, feeds upon evil and
delights in others' agony. Cenci says:

> I love
> The sight of agony, and the sense of joy,
> When this shall be another's and that mine.
> And I have no remorse and little fear,
> Which are, I think, the checks of other men. (CE.I.i.81–85)

When Camillo asks, "Art thou not / Most miserable?"—as one should be
by the Promethean formula, and as Cenci no doubt is by Shelley's
highest standards, even though like the Furies he may be unconscious of
it—Cenci replies: "Why, miserable?— / No.—I am what your theologians
call / Hardened" (CE.I.i.92–94). His only regret is that he is getting old
and is therefore unable to act out all his evil thoughts. Just as the Furies,
in their wisdom, torment Prometheus not so much physically (a lesser
evil) but with the far greater psychic torment of attempting to make him
despair of the good and so destroy all hope and faith, so too has Cenci
largely given over the lesser, sensual, bodily lusts of his early manhood to
persevere in evil of far finer sophistication in his "dishonoured age"
(CE.I.i.53).

Shelley's creation of these two diverse characters—Prometheus and
Cenci—illustrates the depth of his perception into the nature of both
good and evil. In *Prometheus Unbound*, Mercury, the seemingly reluctant
messenger of Jove (Mercury exemplifies Blake's concept of the "cold
hypocrite")[30] shows a myopic misunderstanding of the tormented Prometheus when he tries to tempt him with "voluptuous joy" (PU.I.426).

The Furies, especially the one Fury who remains in Act One (line 576), after the others leave, have a better understanding of him. This remaining Fury attempts instead to play upon the highest feelings in Prometheus—his love for man and the desire for his freedom—in order to induce despair; for, as Iago understood, men are more easily ensnared through their virtues than through their vices. The Fury reveals Christ on the Cross:

> Behold an emblem: those who do endure
> Deep wrongs for man, and scorn, and chains, but heap
> Thousandfold torment on themselves and him. (PU.I.594–596)

He also shows Prometheus that men are weak, confused, and so filled with terror that they scarcely deserve Prometheus' concern:

> The good want power, but to weep barren tears.
> The powerful goodness want: worse need for them.
> The wise want love; and those who love want wisdom;
> And all best things are thus confused to ill. (PU.I.625–628)

Prometheus, however, is able to overcome this spiritual temptation to despair, for he pities, rather than hates, the evil: "Thy words are like a cloud of winged snakes; / And yet I pity those they torture not" (PU.I.632–633). Through this loving reaction, the power of the Fury is broken, and Prometheus is at once visited by "subtle and fair spirits / Whose homes are the dim caves of human thought" (PU.I.658–659), and these thoughts are hopeful ones of love, unselfishness, wisdom and immortality, contrary to what the Fury would have him believe.

Ironically, "voluptuous joy"—which Prometheus has no doubt never desired—has lost its appeal for Cenci; mere sensuality is no longer evil enough:

> When I was young I thought of nothing else
> But pleasure; and I fed on honey sweets:
> Men, by St. Thomas! cannot live like bees,
> And I grew tired:—yet, till I killed a foe,
> And heard his groans, and heard his children's groans,
> Knew I not what delight was else on earth,
> Which now delights me little. I the rather
> Look on such pangs as terror ill conceals,
> The dry fixed eyeball; the pale quivering lip,
> Which tell me that the spirit weeps within
> Tears bitterer than the bloody sweat of Christ.
> I rarely kill the body, which preserves,
> Like a strong prison, the soul within my power,
> Wherein I feed it with the breath of fear
> For hourly pain. (CE.I.i.103–117)

There is a progression in evil here and a subtle, skillful, and penetrating irony that reveal Shelley as anything but the superficial, young Godwinian dreamer (if he had ever been precisely that) that many readers have supposed him to be.

There have been three stages to Cenci's evil. The first involves his own sensual lust; the second his satisfaction in inflicting death and watching the physical results of torture upon his enemies. But he has passed through these stages and both have palled on him. Now in the third and final stage, he cares little about physical torment, rarely killing the body. Instead, he has reached the ultimate condition or state of evil in which he wants "the soul within my power," keeping the body alive, as Prometheus is kept alive, so that the soul may be tormented. Like all Shelley's tyrants, including Jupiter, Cenci is a portrait of the orthodox Christian God.[31] And a consummate irony is involved in Cenci's reason for giving over his first stage of evil: "men . . . cannot live like bees." That is, men can be satisfied neither with the natural pleasure nor, in the context, with the natural evil, but must perversely increase both. The lust for pleasure associated with the body gives way to the lust for power—power not over the body in this case either (since that pleasure has been left far behind), but over the soul and if possible its destiny.[32]

In Cenci, we can see the *idea* of evil taking precedence over any conception of it as utility. Thus, he is an interesting exception to the general rule that even when one performs evil, the evil itself is not the definite object.[33] This generalization fits Orsino, however, who sets out to "flatter the dark spirit" to achieve certain specific ends—in other words, for some good that he envisions for himself. To be sure, Cenci has a result in view, but it is not utilitarian or advantageous to him in any ordinary sense. In his hatred of Beatrice, he simply wishes to crush her soul: the pleasure of this evil itself is his object. Thus, he is conscious of his evil as evil, of its abstract idea, in his plans to rape his daughter:

> Come darkness! Yet, what is the day to me?
> And wherefore should I wish for night, who do
> A deed which shall confound both night and day? (CE.II.i.181–183)

And:

> 'Tis an awful thing
> To touch such mischief as I now conceive. (CE.II.i.124–125)

Through his attack on Beatrice's body, he wishes not to satisfy his lust, for that has passed with his youth, but to break her will, to bring her soul within his power, to make her acquiesce in the evil itself, perhaps even to enjoy it:

> No, 'tis her stubborn will
> Which by its own consent shall stoop as low
> As that which drags it down. (CE.IV.i.10–12)

When Lucretia informs him that Beatrice has heard a voice from heaven revealing his imminent death and calling upon him to confess his sins, Cenci realizes, however, that he has not succeeded in his "greater point, which was / To poison and corrupt her soul" (CE.IV.i.43–44).

In a happy state of society, Shelley had written in his youthful "Address to the Irish People," there would be no "thieves or murderers, because poverty would never drive men to take away comforts from another when he [sic] had enough for himself."[34] By the time he created Count Cenci, however, Shelley realized, as in the Underground Man's formulation, that economics might play only a small part, if any, in motivating crime:

> Now I ask you: what can be expected of man since he is a being endowed with such strange qualities? Shower upon him every earthly blessing, drown him in a sea of happiness, so that nothing but bubbles of bliss can be seen on the surface; give him economic prosperity, such that he should have nothing else to do but sleep, eat cakes and busy himself with the continuation of his species, and even then out of sheer ingratitude, sheer spite, man would play you some nasty trick.[35]

Cenci does not wish to deprive others of physical comforts that he requires for himself (he possesses all he desires in that way). He wishes, instead, to destroy his enemies' ease of soul, the "greater point."

While there is a good deal of truth in Shelley's portrait of a tyrant and a subtle and wholly admirable profundity in his delineation of that tyrant's progressive stages of evil, Cenci needs rounding out in order to be truly effective as a dramatic character. Cenci is quite a bit more, indeed, than a "sad reality": he is more consistently terrible than a person can ever be in reality. Since Shelley was capable of such a vision, the reader should not be surprised that the "loftiest star of unascended heaven" remains unclaimed by humanity at the end of *Prometheus Unbound*. Ironically, in his view of evil in *The Cenci*, Shelley in this precise failure in Cenci's characterization indicates more pessimism than either life or art will generally concede to us. For one thing, the reader sympathizes so little with Cenci—indeed, not at all—that his murder arouses a sense of satisfaction that almost destroys its terror; while, on the other hand, it should increase the awareness of Beatrice's "pernicious mistake" at the same time that one understands how she could make it. As it is, one entertains an almost abstract idea of Beatrice's guilt, as if she had crushed a monster ready to devour us all. As Robert F. Whitman has observed,

Beatrice is a tragic figure because she is human, and her story possesses in full measure that quality which is characteristic of most great tragedy, the tension created by a sense that an act can be at once understandable, and even forgivable, in strictly human terms, and at the same time be essentially evil, because it violates some basic moral principle of the universe.[36]

To a large extent, the reader feels that Cenci is not quite this human, but pretty much as Beatrice describes him: "a spirit of deep hell" (CE.IV.ii.7). Jupiter in *Prometheus Unbound* is properly a spirit, but Cenci is flesh and blood—or should be.[37] He is not less believable than Beatrice[38] simply because one cannot sufficiently explain his motives for evil, for one cannot do that, ultimately, with Iago either, whom most readers have considered nevertheless a fully believable character. Nor does this lack of motive—though readers rightly find it disturbing—make the Ancient Mariner less convincing in his killing of the Albatross: one is meant to be disturbed precisely by the lack of motive, and the Mariner himself does not know why he performs the "hellish" deed.

If Cenci had a sense of humor—although Beatrice speaks of "that wicked laughter round his eye" (CE.I.iii.37), the reader never sees it for himself—or if he were seen as having the residue, perhaps, of some fine qualities that had been debased or distorted (as, for example, we see in Macbeth), he might be one of the most impressive villains ever created for the stage. He might, for example, reveal that type of evil which springs from our ideals—such as saving humanity, pursuing knowledge, or creating perfection—when they are placed in a perverted inversion. Captain Ahab is a finely drawn dramatic and tragic character partly because he performs evil even while he attempts (as he believes) to destroy it. In his fiery hunt, he eventually loses all human compassion and becomes the thing he contemplates—in the Blakean and Shelleyan formula. In Conrad's Kurtz, we see what happens to Kurtz' ideal good when it is crushed against the limitations, paradoxes, and seemingly inescapable evil inherent in the actual and in himself. In his report to the International Society for the Suppression of Savage Customs, Kurtz reaches the heights in his expressions of a noble idealism. But his footnote, added later, "at the end of that moving appeal to every altruistic sentiment . . . blazed at you, luminous and terrifying, like a flash of lightning in a serene sky: 'Exterminate all the brutes!' "[39] As a dramatist, as a creator of human character, it seems to me that Shelley was misled by his tendency to portray unrelieved and unparadoxical evil.[40] Urizen oppresses his children because he desires only good— "good" as he sees it, of course, much like Dostoevski's Grand Inquisitor, who prefers bread and slavery to freedom because he wishes to lighten the burden of his people; because he believes, in T. S. Eliot's words, that men can't bear very much reality. For some reason, there is something more terrifying about such "good" than Cenci's out-and-out evil, for the mind boggles, in drama, at not having that mixture of good and evil that Shelley says clothes every form of individual existence.

But Shelley need not even have gone so far as to make Cenci a good man fallen. Accidentally, and in a quite fearful manner, Cenci might have been kind to Beatrice on occasion, in the way, perhaps, that the infamous Dr. Mengele of Auschwitz is said to have very carefully, gently, and hygienically delivered a baby before sending both mother and child to the ovens.[41] This example is instructive. The "indefatigable" doctor attempted to discover the cause of multiple births by performing autopsies on twins whom he had dispatched with chloroform shots directly into their hearts. In the course of his work his assistant, Dr. Nyiszli, happened to leave a grease spot on the "bright blue cover" of one of the files: "Dr. Mengele shot a withering glance at me [Nyiszli] and said, very seriously: 'How can you be so careless with these files, which I have compiled with so much love.' "[42] Shelley, to be sure, did not have anything approaching Auschwitz or Buchenwald for comparison, some of whose administrators and privileged prisoners took pride in reading Plato and Goethe,[43] but he did have very appropriate parallels in Shakespeare, whom he read avidly. Perhaps Cenci could have loved roses, as Goneril and Regan loved Edmund.

Despite his failings in the characterization of Cenci—though, as I have pointed out, these very failings suggest a far reaching doubt about man's ability to overcome evil—Shelley does come to grips in his drama with "immedicable" evil. As Peter Butter has pointed out, "the distinctive thing about [Shelley's] embodiments of evil is that they are almost always presented as dreams, visions, shadows cast by the human mind itself."[44] Butter's "almost" is significant, for though his statement is true of *The Revolt of Islam* and *Prometheus Unbound*, Count Cenci is a most substantial "embodiment of evil" and can hardly be said to come from the mind of the protagonist of that disturbing drama. Nor can she, even for a time, hold Cenci's evil in abeyance, as Demogorgon does Jupiter. Speaking of Mary Shelley's statement that Shelley believed man's will capable of overcoming evil, Butter asks, regarding *The Triumph of Life,* "But what if the will itself is corrupted, and a man becomes such that he is no longer capable of willing anything but evil?"[45] Blake, as we have seen, rejected the idea of "good will" in man, stating that will takes the form of persecution and selfishness. Instead, the achievement of the vision of Eternity lies in understanding, which is not natural, as will is, but must be acquired by "suffering & distress."

Although Prometheus does evil in cursing Jupiter, he never completely loses the will towards good, and the latter finally asserts itself above, indeed eradicates, his hatred of Jupiter. Carlos Baker states that *Prometheus Unbound* "is a drama of the inner mind, and evil is represented as a deformity of the mind. What is extirpated there can survive nowhere else in the universe."[46] In *The Revolt of Islam,* also, Shelley states that men's wills permit evil. Like Prometheus, they could cast the evil out of their minds if they but willed to do so:

> For they all pined in bondage; body and soul,
>   Tyrant and slave, victim and torturer, bent
> Before one Power, to which supreme control
>   Over their will by their own weakness lent,
>   Made all its many names omnipotent. (RI.II.viii.730–734)

Of this passage, Carl Grabo notes: "the will, though weak, is explicitly declared free in essence. Evil exists because men tolerate it."[47] Again, in *Julian and Maddalo,* speaking in the character of Julian, Shelley asserts this same freedom: "it is our will / That thus enchains us to permitted ill" (170–171). But in Cenci, the will itself does seem to be corrupted, so that even if Beatrice forgave him (as Shelley in the Preface states that she should), thereby assuring her own salvation (as Prometheus does), there would still be no redemption for Cenci himself, for he persists in evil to the end, without repentance.

I think, however, that, even for Cenci, Shelley would have found an answer to the problem of will (though not within the play itself, of course, for that would have destroyed whatever tragic effect it possesses). His answer is contained in his sonnet "Political Greatness":

> Man who man would be,
> Must rule the empire of himself; in it
> Must be supreme, establishing his throne
> On vanquished will, quelling the anarchy
> Of hopes and fears, being himself alone. (p. 642)

Cenci establishes his throne not on vanquished will but on its unlimited indulgence. He does not—despite appearance—really rule the empire of himself in the Shelleyan sense, and his final act of hatred spells his own destruction. Shelley's lines fit Prometheus, however, who does not need to vanquish his will so much as to bring it into harmony with the law of love: "Yet I am king over myself," Prometheus tells the Furies, "and rule / The torturing and conflicting throngs within" (PU.I.492–493).

Besides Cenci and his corrupted will, Shelley's handling of several other characters and scenes in *The Cenci* reveals his understanding of more ordinary types of men and their usual responses to evil. Such understanding, for example, is found in Camillo's reply to Cenci's blatant and horrifying statement of the nature of his evil—the statement quoted above in which Cenci delineates the three stages of his depravity. Camillo prefers simply to ignore Cenci's evil as "unbelievable," a mistake commonly made when the evil is of such gigantic proportions that the imagination can scarcely obtain a hold on it:

> Hell's most abandoned fiend
> Did never, in the drunkenness of guilt,
> Speak to his heart as now you speak to me;
> I thank my God that I believe you not. (CE.I.i.117–120)

Others prefer to wait until someone else takes action. When Beatrice begs the guests assembled at Cenci's banquet to rescue her from her father's despotism, even wishing to their faces that she were dead, each waits for the other to take the initiative:

> Camillo. A bitter wish for one so young and gentle;
> Can we do nothing?
> Colonna. Nothing that I see.
> Count Cenci were a dangerous enemy:
> Yet I would second any one.
> A Cardinal. And I. (CE.I.iii.140–144)

The will to good is ineffective and feeble (as the Fury in *Prometheus Unbound* points out), and because it is, Cenci not only can exist but flourish as well.

In Orsino, Shelley has added still another dimension to his depiction of the nature of evil. Orsino, a man who knows exactly what he is, has become reconciled to it and adept at treading a thin line between his conscience and "the depth of darkest purposes." Of the Cenci, he states:

> 'tis a trick of this same family
> To analyse their own and other minds.
> Such self-anatomy shall teach the will
> Dangerous secrets: for it tempts our powers,
> Knowing what must be thought, and may be done,
> Into the depth of darkest purposes:
> So Cenci fell into the pit; even I,
> Since Beatrice unveiled me to myself,
> And made me shrink from what I cannot shun,
> Show a poor figure to my own esteem,
> To which I grow half reconciled. I'll do
> As little mischief as I can; that thought
> Shall fee the accuser conscience. (CE.II.ii.108–119)

But Shelley's insight extends well beyond this. Orsino not only plans to maintain himself in perfect safety (as he thinks), resolving to do "as little mischief" as he can. He also realizes that the most effective and surest manner in which to accomplish his designs is not to attempt them himself, but to arouse the dormant evil within others:

> and he prospers best,
> Not who becomes the instrument of ill,
> But who can flatter the dark spirit, that makes
> Its empire and its prey of other hearts
> Till it become his slave . . . as I will do. (CE.II.ii.157–161)

As in Cythna's words calling upon Laon to turn his eyes inward to his own heart if he would see good, so too does evil make its empire in the hearts of those whose will is weak or corrupted and who do not seek eternal Love as the means by which it can be extirpated. In *The Triumph of Life* Shelley sees the latter as chained to the Chariot of Life, bound slaves to the dark spirit of evil, and therefore not ruling the empire of self. The nature of the evil in this last poem of Shelley's is quite similar to that of his early poems *Queen Mab* and *The Revolt of Islam:* the havoc wrought by the desire for power over others, the desire to carve out an empire in the outer world instead of developing an imaginative vision through which one could rule the empire of self. Othman, Jupiter, Cenci, and the rulers chained to the Car of Life in *The Triumph of Life* are all examples of a tyranny that Shelley fought throughout his life on his own poetic ground.

Shelley was working on *The Triumph of Life* at the time of his death, and in it he has given us a terrifying vision of the evils of the world that rivals that of the most thoroughgoing Christian, who would startle the reader into a recognition of his condition:

Methought I sate beside a public way

Thick strewn with summer dust, and a great stream
Of people there was hurrying to and fro,
Numerous as gnats upon the evening gleam,

All hastening onward, yet none seemed to know
Whither he went, or whence he came, or why
He made one of the multitude, and so

Was borne amid the crowd, as through the sky
One of the million leaves of summer's bier;
Old age and youth, manhood and infancy,

Mixed in one mighty torrent did appear,
Some flying from the thing they feared, and some
Seeking the object of another's fear;

And others, as with steps towards the tomb,
Pored on the trodden worms that crawled beneath,
And others mournfully within the gloom

Of their own shadow walked, and called it death;
And some fled from it as it were a ghost,
Half fainting in the affliction of vain breath:

But more, with motions which each other crossed,
Pursued or shunned the shadows the clouds threw,
Or birds within the noonday aether lost,

Upon that path where flowers never grew. (TL.41–65)

The believer stresses the utter horror of man's life without God, as Bunyan does or the seventeenth-century Moravian theologian John Amos Comenius,[48] in order to raise the reader's awareness above it to the Celestial City and to salvation. Although not stated in those terms, Shelley's purpose in most of his poetry (except when he deliberately laid aside his vatic mantle, as in *The Cenci*) was to somehow make men more loving of one another and thus advance the cause of brotherhood. *The Triumph of Life,* perhaps because it is unfinished, presents the horror of evil without any of the mitigation for all mankind that takes place at the end of *Prometheus Unbound.* Though *The Triumph* does present a bleak picture as it stands,[49] if Shelley had lived to finish it we would probably find it no more pessimistic than *Prometheus Unbound* or *The Revolt of Islam.* Even in its fragmentary form, the "sacred few"—the best spirits of the classical and the Judaic civilizations (who represent those in any age who have developed their capacity for love and wisdom)—manage to escape being chained to the Car of Life, much as Laon and Cythna rise above the chains of the Iberian priest. It is a measure of Shelley's enduring skepticism, perhaps, that neither Laon and Cythna nor the "sacred few" can effect salvation for the rest of mankind; and in *The Triumph* the reader understands more than ever Shelley's very deep doubts whether most men possessed sufficient will to rise above self in love. Nevertheless, by the side of the dusty road on which the Chariot (or Car) tramples them, humanity, as Donald H. Reiman has noted,[50] weary with their "vain toil" and "faint for thirst" (TL.66) could find fountains, breezes, grassy paths, caverns and violet banks, "but they / Pursued their serious folly as of old" (TL.73). But there is hope for some, at least, to escape the Car's influence, as the sacred few have been able to do and presumably all could do if they would give up the "serious folly" that chains them to the Car through their own will. The Car—or rather those who enforce its slavery—"upon the free / Had bound a yoke, which soon they stooped to bear" (TL.115–116). Shelley had already noted this freedom of the will many times in his poetry, as I have indicated in the discussion of *The Cenci.* Men are bound to the Chariot because they have misplaced their energies. Instead of seeking the fountains or violet banks of the imagination, they have, rather, sought what Blake called "Caesar's laurel crown" and what Shelley terms "Mitres and helms and crowns, or wreaths of light / Signs of thought's empire over thought." Thus, seeking power over others through Church, war, or intellect, they have had no chance "to know themselves; their might / Could not repress the mutiny[51] within / And for the morn of truth they feigned, deep night / Caught them ere evening" (TL.210–215). Like Cenci, they have not learned to rule the empire of self, but riot in their own selfishness. Rousseau himself, a captive to the Car, who has fallen by the wayside and recounts his story to the Poet, has been swept up into the multitude of the slaves of life through his vision of the "Shape all light"

(TL.352), an apprehension, ironically, as delusive as the "wreaths of light" that he says bind the other captives. Presumably, therefore, he too has not "known himself," and the Shape cannot possibly represent enlightenment, wisdom, understanding, or Shelley's eternal Love.

Initially depicted in terms of great beauty and desirability, so that one might think the Shape does indeed symbolize Shelley's concept of Intellectual Beauty,[52] her feet, nevertheless,

> seemed as they moved to blot
> The thoughts of him who gazed on them; and soon
>
> All that was, seemed as if it had been not;
> And all the gazer's mind was strewn beneath
> Her feet like embers; and she, thought by thought
>
> Trampled its sparks into the dust of death. (TL.383–388)

She comes from "the realm without a name" (TL.396) and when Rousseau drinks Nepenthe from her crystal cup, "suddenly my brain became as sand"

> Where the first wave had more than half erased
> The track of deer on desert Labrador;
> Whilst the wolf, from which they fled amazed,
>
> Leaves his stamp visibly upon the shore,
> Until the second bursts;—so on my sight
> Burst a new vision, never seen before. (TL.405–411)

This new vision is the Chariot of Life, whose slave Rousseau becomes. As Reiman has noted, *The Triumph of Life* does not contain the second wave that will wash away the evil, the wolf's track,[53] but if it did, the vision would have to be a higher one than that embodied in the Shape of light. Although Shelley calls Love "Nepenthe" in *Prometheus Unbound* (PU.III.iv.163), the potion that the Shape bears is apparently what makes Rousseau susceptible to the influence of the Chariot of Life: her Nepenthe is deadly, not life-giving like that in *Prometheus Unbound,* and Rousseau is swept up into the *danse macabre* behind the Chariot.

Though Shelley speaks of "the divine beauty of Rousseau's imagination,"[54] and compared him to Jesus in his dislike of "pusillanimity and sensuality,"[55] in *The Triumph of Life,* at least, he is what Newman Ivey White has noted him to be in Shelley's thought: "Rousseau was for Shelley always a splendid spiritual failure, never one of the few supremely great spirits."[56] Consequently, though thinking quite highly of Rousseau, Shelley placed him with Locke, Hume, Gibbon, and Voltaire as lesser moral influences on the world; whereas Dante, Petrarch, Boccaccio, Chaucer, Shakespeare, Calderon, Lord Bacon, and Milton have exerted such a strong influence that their absences would have made a great difference.[57]

The Shape Rousseau sees may be similar to or a parody of the "false Matilda" of Dante's *Purgatorio* (Cantos XXVIII–XXIX), as James Rieger and Harold Bloom believe, respectively;[58] or as Reiman thinks, "a distorted and limited . . . embodiment of the Ideal,"[59] but it is more likely an embodiment of *Rousseau's* ideal, as Shelley conceived it, a distortion that delivers him into the ranks of the Car's captives. Rousseau is not a member of the "sacred few" whom Shelley exempted from the Car's slavery. On the contrary, Rousseau's vision, like the Poet's in *Alastor*, is full of death, though paradoxically full of beauty as well. I believe the key to Shelley's depiction of Rousseau and his ideal may be found in a statement in his essay "Proposals for an Association of Philanthropists": "Rousseau gave license by his writings to passions that only incapacitate and contract the human heart."[60] Rousseau says of himself in *The Triumph of Life:* "if the spark with which Heaven lit my spirit / Had been with purer nutriment supplied, / Corruption would not now thus much inherit / Of what was once Rousseau" (TL.201–204). This "purer nutriment" Shelley delineated in Prometheus and Laon and also in his portrait of himself in *Epipsychidion*. We witness the corruption that Rousseau speaks of quite vividly in the Poet's description of their meeting. By the side of the road down which the ill-guided Car careens, Rousseau has become "an old root, which grew / To strange distortion" (TL.182–183)—a distortion repeated in his own Shape of light. But Rousseau did possess at least the spark, some idea of "divine beauty," even though it was corrupted. He separates himself from the "anarch chiefs" who "spread the plague of gold and blood." "Their power was given / But to destroy," he tells the Poet-Narrator. "I / Am one of those who have created, even / If it be but a world of agony" (TL.285–295). Similarly, he states that "if I have been extinguished, yet there rise / A thousand beacons from the spark I bore" (TL.206–207). Judging by the statements about Rousseau that Shelley made elsewhere, and judging also by Rousseau's own Shape of light, which is very beautiful (though it leads to his ruin), there is no reason to doubt that these words of Rousseau's come fairly close to Shelley's own manner of looking at him.

Thus, the answer to the question, "Then what is life?" (TL.544), which the Poet asks at the end of this fragment, could not have been and would not have been supplied by Rousseau.[61] His Shape has very little in common even with Shelley's most playful vision of his ideal goddess of love, the Witch of Atlas,[62] who, while she is amusingly prankish, really hurts no one:

> Friends who, by practice of some envious skill,
>   Were torn apart—a wide wound, mind from mind!—
> She did unite again with visions clear
> Of deep affection and of truth sincere. (WA.LXXVII.661–664)

Moreover, she has a most salutary affect on the beings around her:

> The brinded lioness led forth her young,
>   That she might teach them how they should forego
> Their inborn thirst of death; the pard unstrung
>   His sinews at her feet, and sought to know
> With looks whose motions spoke without a tongue
>   How he might be as gentle as the doe.
> The magic circle of her voice and eyes
> All savage natures did imparadise. (WA.VII)

Rousseau's Shape, on the contrary, is his undoing, though she seems to him "a light of heaven" (TL.430).

Of the concluding verses of *Hellas*, Shelley wrote in his notes to the poem:

> The concluding verses indicate a progressive state of more or less exalted existence, according to the degree of perfection which every distinct intelligence may have attained. Let it not be supposed that I mean to dogmatise upon a subject, concerning which all men are equally ignorant, or that I think the Gordian knot of the origin of evil can be disentangled by that or any similar assertions. . . . That there is a true solution of the riddle, and that in our present state that solution is unattainable by us, are propositions which may be regarded as equally certain: meanwhile, as it is the province of the poet to attach himself to those ideas which exalt and ennoble humanity, let him be permitted to have conjectured the condition of that futurity towards which we are all impelled by an inextinguishable thirst for immortality. (p. 478)

This statement as much as any other sums up Shelley's general attitude toward the problem of evil. *The Cenci* is his attempt (and it is at least successful on this point) not to "dogmatise upon a subject, concerning which all men are equally ignorant." *Prometheus Unbound* reaches toward "a true solution of the riddle" even though a final answer is "unattainable," revealing (as Shelley hoped and may have been mistaken in) "those ideas which exalt and ennoble humanity." Though the attitude toward evil within his work may reveal more about his own nature, worth, and spiritual possibilities than it ever can about men in general; and though it is true in the words of Milton Wilson that he "remains, to a considerable extent, tentative and even skeptical in his thinking about ultimate problems,"[63] yet I think it would be wise, in order to come to a just appraisal of Shelley's idea concerning evil, to remember that he created Prometheus as well as Cenci, and that the former should be as acceptable to us as the latter. That he may not be perhaps reveals more about us than it does about Shelley's vision itself. That is, Shelley's vision of the eradication of the evil *may* lie in the will of man, who accepts evil too readily, who believes in it as a stronger force than the good. As

Newman Ivey White maintains: "Surely the faith that there is an inextinguishable spark within the human spirit is intellectually as respectable as the contrary belief, when neither is capable of absolute proof by the ordinary laws of reason."[64] Shelley's hope and faith are that man will not always remain in his "present state" of ignorance. As he evolves toward a higher state, the solution to evil, now unattainable, may rise on the horizon with that new dawn of man's regeneration. The "loftiest star of unascended heaven" may then be within reach. Meanwhile, in Cythna's words,

> In their own hearts the earnest of the hope
> Which made them great, the good will ever find.

Chapter Four

The Shattered Visage

I met a traveller from an antique land
Who said: Two vast and trunkless legs of stone
Stand in the desert . . . Near them, on the sand,
Half sunk, a shattered visage lies. . . .

("Ozymandias")

Blake's and Shelley's ideas of the selfhood are strikingly similar. This selfhood or selfishness originates and manifests in the oppressive father, the hypocritical priest, the malicious king and the tyrannical God. In the poetry of both poets, the selfhood is created by a fall within the mind of man in which thought or reason (depicted as cold and icy) becomes divorced from affection or love (delineated in terms of fire and heat). The cruelty, torture, and death consequent upon this separation, especially employed by the tyrant ruler, the poets convey through images involving iron, brass, caves, chains, silence, coldness, and concealment, just as they oppose the ice of reason to the fire of affection. To this selfhood, Blake and Shelley oppose their notions of the real God: the personal Divine Humanity (Blake), and the impersonal Spirit of the Universe (Shelley). On this point the poets show more divergence than they do in their equally vociferous and equally strong denigrations of the orthodox Christian deity and his earthly counterpart, the king, and representative, the priest.

Before considering the origin of the tyrant within man's mind, it is necessary to show why Blake and Shelley turned from their early emphasis on revolutions in the outer world and finally came to the position of placing all their stress on the change *within* the mind itself. For it is from this inner world, the poets came to believe, that the tyrant arises, rather than from evil institutions.

Blake had hopes that both the American and the French revolutions heralded the new day when men would turn from the tyrants of rationalism, Deism, and empire. His early Prophecies (*The French Revolution, America, Europe*) turned outward to these immense upheavals on the American and European continents.[1] But, as Northrop Frye points out, their spirit was not truly Losian and therefore any outward revolution could only be of brief duration.[2] "When it became painfully clear to

[Blake] that the revolutionaries were not revolting in the name of humanity but in their own," states Peter F. Fisher,

> and that they were not transforming the political state but appropriating it, the subject of his verse became less revolutionary and more prophetic. Politically, he hated priests and kings to the end of his life, but these were not the priests and kings of the political arena but their originals in the substances of human life and thought.[3]

Finally disillusioned with the course of outer events, though never forsaking his vision, Blake, as Shelley did in *Prometheus Unbound*, turned inward in *The Four Zoas* and *Jerusalem* to consider more and more the mind and heart of man. Only if these could be changed was there hope that the outer world could be. "That mankind, or the will of man personified in Prometheus, refuses allegiance to the god of its creating," states Carl Grabo, "is the sole hope of ultimate deliverance."[4] When the empire of the self was regenerated—an inner, Promethean and Losian spiritual endeavor—then all earthly empires in the outer world would fall. The visage of the tyrant, his wrinkled lip and sneer of cold command, would then lie, like that of Ozymandias, shattered within the decay of the colossal wreck of his kingdom. His evil power would have no effect without the consent it finds within the divided and unloving hearts of other men. Thus, at the end of *The Four Zoas* all tyranny is overthrown because Albion is at one with himself; his Zoas act in harmony instead of discord:

> Let the slave, grinding at the mill, run out into the field;
> Let him look up into the heavens & laugh in the bright air.
> Let the inchained soul, shut up in darkness & in sighing,
> Whose face has never seen a smile in thirty weary years,
> Rise & look out: his chains are loose, his dungeon doors are open;
> And let his wife & children return from the opressor's scourge.
> (FZ.9:670–676)

Similarly, as *Prometheus Unbound* closes, the Spirit of the Hour brings word to Prometheus and his party of immortals that man now reigns supreme over himself, having conquered hate and fear, so that the outer tyrant does not have to be overthrown; he is simply disregarded:

> The loathsome mask has fallen, the man remains
> Sceptreless, free, uncircumscribed, but man
> Equal, unclassed, tribeless, and nationless,
> Exempt from awe, worship, degree, the king
> Over himself. (PU.III.iv.194–197)

If one considers *Queen Mab* in relation to *Prometheus Unbound*, he can see that Shelley, like Blake, had come to place far greater emphasis on the mind (Prometheus) that creates the evil tyrant. The traditional Christian (and heathen) God whom Shelley discusses and reviles in *Queen Mab* emerges in full-dress regalia in his portrait of the cruel and malicious Jupiter in *Prometheus Unbound* and in the God who is satisfied with nothing less than the fiery deaths of his opponents in *The Revolt of Islam*. The same tyrant is visible in the paternal despot Cenci and in those rulers (such as Napoleon) who are chained to the Car of Life in *The Triumph of Life*. In *Queen Mab*, the Fairy Mab rolls back the scroll of history to reveal to Ianthe that "Beside the eternal Nile . . . / an inhuman and uncultured race / Howled hideous praises to their Demon-God"—a God who supported war, "the trade of blood" (QM.II.126;148–150;157). Those who have most to gain by inculcating this concept of the deity are kings, priests and statesmen, "Whose safety is man's deep unbettered woe, / Whose grandeur his debasement. Let the axe / Strike at the root, the poison-tree will fall" (QM.IV.80–82).

Although in *Queen Mab* the twenty-year-old Shelley tends to place the blame rather simply on kings and priests themselves, in later works such as *Prometheus Unbound, The Cenci,* and *The Triumph of Life* he asserts that the root that nourishes the poison tree of tyranny grows within man himself. The tree is nourished by selfishness, hypocrisy, deceit, and hate—all close very early over the head of the maturing child, who, instead of singing with the skylark, must, like Blake's school boy,

> go to school in a summer morn,
> O! it drives all joy away;
> Under a cruel eye outworn,
> The little ones spend the day
> In sighing and dismay. (p. 124)

Under this "cruel eye" the child, as he matures to manhood, learns how to produce the apple of the tree (as in Blake's "A Poison Tree") by which he destroys his foe. Later, the tree grows into a tough, heavy-fibered, and tight-rooted organism that generates all the evils of religion, tyrannical government, and systems of oppressive morality. "Tyranny is seldom (in the long run, never) imposed on people from without," Northrop Frye asserts. "It is a projection of their own pusillanimity."[5] Wherever Urizen sits, who is the priest of Blake's myth, the tree of his mystery religion shoots up from under his foot, proliferating so rapidly into many other trees that Urizen himself very nearly becomes enclosed in their thickness (FZ.7a.31–40). After he separates himself from the other Eternals,

> he sat on a rock
> Barren: a rock which himself
> From redounding fancies had petrified.
> Many tears fell on the rock,

Many sparks of vegetation.
Soon shot the pained root
Of Mystery under his heel:

It grew a thick tree: he wrote
In silence his book of iron,
Till the horrid plant bending its boughs
Grew to roots when it felt the earth,
And again sprung to many a tree. (BA.3:56–67)

Thus, both Shelley (in works after *Queen Mab*) and Blake find within the self, not in institutions, the origin of the evil God, tyrant, priest, and king. In language that is strikingly similar, they assert that all aspects of tyranny are reflections of man's selfishness or selfhood, a shade cast by and through his own mind. In this process of thought, man's mind becomes turned in upon itself, thought is divorced from feeling, affection, or love, and that limited self image is then projected upon all outer things. Such an image Blake terms the "Ratio," and associates it with Urizen, the reason and single vision: "He who sees the Infinite in all things, sees God [i.e., the Divine Humanity]. He who sees the Ratio, sees himself only" (NR, p. 98). When man sees only the Ratio, the tyrant rules supreme: the father in the family, the priest in the church, the king in the country, and God in heaven. In all these, the selfhood is reflected, just as each type of tyranny reflects the other: the pattern below mirrors the one above. Thus, Shelley states that monarchy is the "prototype" of the "empire of terror which is established by Religion";[6] Blake terms the orthodox God "an Allegory of Kings & nothing Else" (pp. 788–789).[7]

In the words of Cythna to the mariners who rescue her from her cave by the sea, Shelley indicates how the tyrant of selfishness comes into being:

What is that Power? Some moon-struck sophist stood
  Watching the shade from his own soul upthrown
Fill Heaven and darken Earth, and in such mood
  The Form he saw and worshipped was his own,
  The likeness in the world's vast mirror shown;
And 'twere an innocent dream, but that a faith
  Nursed by fear's dew of poison, grows thereon,
And that men say, that Power has chosen Death
On all who scorn its laws, to wreak immortal wrath. (RI.VIII.vi)

When Blake recounts the fall of Albion (in *The Four Zoas*) and that of Urizen (in *The Book of Urizen*) he uses most of Shelley's terms, and the idea remains essentially the same. In Shelley's version, the sophist stands worshipping his own form or likeness in the mirror of the world. This form is a shade that darkens the earth. The Power (or God) that rises from the shade institutes laws and if these laws are broken, the Power is

filled with wrath. Similarly, in *The Four Zoas,* Albion "Turning his Eyes
outward to Self" (FZ.2:2) and to the natural or unspiritual world,
worships a Shadow that rises from his own "wearied intellect." For
Shelley's "vast mirror" Blake uses "a wat'ry vision" that functions exactly
like a mirror. All the evils of man's selfhood—what Cythna terms the
"dark idolatry of self" (RI.VIII.xxii.3390)—are reflected in it. Albion is
"mourning" because the Zoas who represent his four spiritual powers
have separated from him and from one another; but the fall is still
incomplete at this point:

> Then Man ascended mourning into the splendors of his palace,
> Above him rose a Shadow from his wearied intellect
> Of living gold, pure, perfect, holy, in white linen pure he
>   hover'd,
> A sweet entrancing self delusion, a wat'ry vision of Man
> Soft exulting in existence, all the Man absorbing.
>
> Man fell upon his face prostrate before the wat'ry shadow,
> Saying, O Lord, whence is this change? thou knowest I am
>   nothing.
> And Vala trembled & cover'd her face, & her locks were spread
>   on the pavement. (FZ.3:49–56)

Vala, the feminine consort of the Zoa Luvah (the affective faculty) is the
character in Blake's myth who represents the natural world (what Blake
often refers to as the "goddess nature") and its changefulness—its
ungraspable, fleeting characteristic—like a "veil" hiding the Eternal. She
supplies Albion with the "soft deluding slumber" (FZ.3:45) that makes
him susceptible to the lower, "wat'ry vision" of himself, the unspiritual
world created by the separative reason. Though a Shadow, this vision is
clothed in gold (Urizen's metal in Eternity) and white (generally associated with Urizen's aged aspect) and Albion sees it as pure, perfect, and
holy: all three are Urizenic qualities[8] and Blake uses them ironically and
pejoratively throughout his work. Urizen's quest for purity, perfection,
and holiness leads to a solid without fluctuation, to the dead world of
Ulro, to rigid moral and religious laws, to sin, guilt, error, mistake, to
pain, punishment, disappointment, and contention, and finally to slavery both for those whom he binds and for himself. The more he
restricts, the more restricted he becomes. Except for this, his stranglehold on futurity (FZ.6:233) might well become Albion's undoing. For
Urizen finally sinks to a scaly dragon form on the brink of Non-Entity
(he becomes what he beholds and creates), and he sees that unless he
capitulates he will be destroyed (FZ.9:145–157).

When Albion falls "Idolatrous to his own Shadow" (FZ.3:59)—that is,
to his selfhood—futurity (formerly contained in the present, eternal
moment in Eden) appears before him "Like a dark lamp" (FZ.3:75), and

it is this future time that his reason will henceforth attempt to grasp and bind: Urizen "Traces the wonders of Futurity in horrible fear of the future" (FZ.7a.86). In addition, the "Eternal Brotherhood" enjoyed by the Eternals (Albion with his infinite senses contracted) exists no longer (FZ.3:76), and Albion is delivered into the hands of his selfhood or Spectre. "Humanity shall be no more," he asserts, "but war & princedom & victory!" (J.4:32). Such is the origin of the tyrant in all his manifestations. Los must now battle this terrific opponent, the Spectre of selfishness and self-righteousness, for although in Albion's fall all his Zoas fall with him, the imagination is still able to keep its ties with the eternal world of Eden, to keep the Divine Vision in time of trouble (J.95:20). In this alone lies hope for the overthrow of the internal tyrant who assumes dominance in the fall, what Blake terms variously—among many other names—the selfhood, Satan, the Spectre, rational demonstration, Bacon, Newton, and Locke, Deism, and Mystery the Harlot.

In Blake's myth, Urizen, who is primarily responsible for the fall of Albion, represents both the orthodox, traditional God and the power of thought or reason within man (Albion) that creates that God. Similarly, in *Prometheus Unbound,* Jupiter symbolizes this same God while at the same time he is a distortion within the mind of Prometheus created by and permitted to exist through Prometheus' hatred—for hatred is based on thought or reason when it exists in isolation from love or affection (Asia). When this power of thought acts in isolation from Albion's other faculties it creates a frozen world of hatred and despair; and Urizen, the "primeval Priest" (BU.2:1) and ruler of this world is a remote, cloudy, indefinite, and inaccessible deity of thunder and darkness—that is, in Blake's terminology, *inhuman.* For the Divine Humanity (the real God) possesses the exact opposites of these characteristics: personified (often as Jesus), he is definite (J.55:64), near at hand within the breast of each man (J.4:18–19), and loving and merciful (J.96:23–28). Indeed, to Blake, Christianity is nothing more and nothing less than "Forgiveness of Sins" (EG. p. 757).

In *Jerusalem,* Los's Spectre (the reasoning faculty) describes his God:

> For he is Righteous, he is not a Being of Pity and Compassion,
> He cannot feel Distress, he feeds on Sacrifice & Offering,
> Delighting in cries & tears & clothed in holiness & solitude. (J.10:47–49)

But the Divine Humanity does feel distress, pity, and compassion, as indicated in the last stanza of "On Another's Sorrow" (here, the Divine Humanity is synonymous with Jesus):

> O! he gives to us his joy
> That our grief he may destroy;
> Till our grief is fled & gone
> He doth sit by us and moan. (p. 123)

Moreover, Jesus, the "only God,"[9] like Los, possesses great imaginative energy—enough to shatter the Urizenic God's Decalogue into a thousand fragments. "I tell you, no virtue could exist without breaking these ten commandments," states one of the Devils in *The Marriage of Heaven and Hell*. "Jesus was all virtue, and acted from impulse, not from rules" (MHH.22–24, p. 158).

When thought or reason creates a God, however, he is not the articulate and energetic Divine Humanity, but the silent and cold "Nobodaddy":[10]

> Why art thou silent & invisible,
> Father of Jealousy?
> Why dost thou hide thyself in clouds
> From every searching Eye?
>
> Why darkness & obscurity
> In all they words and laws,
> That none dare eat the fruit but from
> The wily serpents jaws?
> Or is it because Secresy gains females'
>   loud applause? (p. 171)

The quality of secrecy is characteristic of the feminine (Vala) in separation from the masculine (as noted above in the discussion of Albion's fall from Eternity); for Urizen provides the "wat'ry vision" of the material man, while Vala supplies the desire to sink down into it. Once Albion does so, the feminine world of nature is veiled to him, flees outward from him, and tortures him with its mystery and elusiveness. Beside Dr. Thornton's statement in his "New Translation of the Lord's Prayer": "Dim at best are the conceptions we have of the Supreme Being, who, as it were, keeps the human race in suspense, neither discovering, nor hiding Himself," Blake wrote: "a Female God!" (p. 788). In Eternity, the androgynous Albion is at one with his feminine counterpart, his Emanation.[11] In his fall, this unity (among many others) is broken, and the Emanation—Jerusalem—separates from Albion to take on the form of Vala (the natural world), a form that Albion no longer recognizes as his own and which is "veiled," hidden, secret and dark (the "Shadowy Female" is another term applied to Vala). Vala constricts even further into the two females Rahab and Tirzah, who are responsible for carrying out the human sacrifice demanded by Urizen's mystery religion and for maintaining his strict laws of morality and chastity. Thus, the feminine aspect of Albion, in conjunction with reason, acts in a highly restrictive manner that would keep him forever on the treadmill of self, repeating the same dull round over again, were it not for the imagination and its constantly renewed efforts to break through the barrier, the "veil" of the outer, and to reveal the truth of Eternity.

Like Shelley's "moon-struck sophist" worshipping the shade cast by his own soul, or like Albion himself, Urizen rises (as he thinks) out of Eternity in order to create a void or vacuum in which he can become "Self-clos'd" and "self-contemplating" (BU.3:3;21). In this, he reveals what Shelley calls "the sordid lust of self" (QM.V.90), the "turned in" spiritual position that both poets find so pernicious. As Hazard Adams notes, in this position of reason dominant, Urizen's thoughts revolve "over and over again the same intellectual rubbish."[12] When he creates, his world is like the one that other tyrant Jupiter forces Prometheus to endure (PU.I.31–43), or like the "winter of the world" that Cythna describes to Laon, a winter brought about by the tyrant Othman and his bloodlust: a world of coldness and darkness, or of snow, hail, and ice, but in either case always one of pain and constriction in which his children base their pursuits, in Shelley's words, on "the grovelling hope of interest and gold" (QM.V.91):

> His cold horrors silent, dark Urizen
> Prepar'd; his ten thousands of thunders
> Rang'd in gloom'd array, stretch out across
> The dread world; & the rolling of wheels,
> As of swelling seas, sound in his clouds,
> In his hills of stor'd snows, in his mountains
> Of hail & ice; voices of terror
> Are heard, like thunders of autumn
> When the cloud blazes over the harvests. (BU.3:27–35)

Urizen has this effect on everything around him. When Los finishes the gigantic task of binding the indefinite Urizen into recognizable features in order to keep the cosmos from further fragmentation, the fire on his anvil goes out:

> Infected, Mad, [Los] danc'd on his mountains high & dark as heaven,
> Now fix'd into one stedfast bulk his features stonify,
> From his mouth curses, & from his eyes sparks of blighting,
> Beside the anvil cold he danc'd with the hammer of Urthona,
> Terrific pale. (FZ.5:1–5)

One of Urizen's reasons for pursuing his selfhood, for creating separation, is to escape the eternal fire of self-sacrifice for others, a mutual annihilation of the selfhood (M.38:35–36) that burns in Eden—a "Universal Brotherhood" (FZ.1:10) that Urizen wishes to deny:

> Why will you die, O Eternals?
> Why live in unquenchable burnings? (BU.4:12–13)

The Eternals—that is, Man or Albion with his infinite senses contracted to perceive multitude (J.38:17–18)—must continually give themselves, "die," one for another, for when one sins or falls into error in Eden, he is forgiven by his Brother, "which is Self Annihilation" (J.98:23). Urizen refuses this death to self, a spiritual act that must be repeated again and again in "unquenchable burnings," as he says. In Eden,

> As the breath of the Almighty such are the words of man to man
> In the great Wars of Eternity, in fury of Poetic Inspiration,
> To build the Universe stupendous, Mental forms Creating. (M.30:18–20)

"Our wars are wars of life, & wounds of love" the Savior tells Albion after his fall, "with intellectual spears, & long winged arrows of thought" (J.38:14–15). But Urizen desires to escape the fire of Eden, its continual flux, fluidity and intense creativity. He prefers his wide world of solid obstruction (BU.4:23), composed of snow, hail and ice. The Shape who drives the Car of Life in Shelley's *The Triumph of Life* is, like Urizen, cold, icy, concealed and "Crouching within the shadow of a tomb" (TL.90). As Donald H. Reiman has noted, "the cold, fascinating light of the moon-like car suggests mere reason."[13] From Shelley's description, Urizen could easily be the driver of the Car. The Shape, like Urizen, constricts its followers and represents their binding to their own selfhood, as clearly seen in the conquerors like Napoleon who are chained to the Car. Only the "sacred few," it may be presumed, have held to the vision of oneness that poured down upon the Poet from the burning fountain in *Adonais,* for they "touched the world with living flame" (TL.130).

Thus, both poets associate fire with the life of the spirit, cold and ice with the selfhood. When Albion makes his movement toward his outward self, "losing the Divine Vision" (FZ.2:2), he turns "from Universal Love, petrific as he went, / His cold against the warmth of Eden rag'd with loud / Thunders of deadly war" (J.38:7–9). The coldness (Urizen) associated with the selfhood can be overcome by the warmth of the affections (Luvah), or by imagination (Los), or by loving another enough to give up self for him. Laon, for example, attempts to sacrifice himself for Cythna; he gives himself up to the tyrant's priests on condition that Cythna go free (RI.XI.xxiv.xxv). But Cythna chooses to die with him (RI.XII.xv). In this way, although on a physical as well as spiritual level, they illustrate Blake's concept of "Mutual Sacrifice" (J.61:23) or mutual annihilation (M.38:35–36).

This destruction of the selfhood, however, is a spiritual, not a physical act in Blake's poetry, for to perform it literally is, like the Druids, "to turn allegoric and mental signification into corporeal command" (DC, p. 578). Therefore, the creation of a God who demands human sacrifice, atonement, expiation, is one of the greatest evils engendered by the fall, for if one decides that *another* shall be sacrificed, he evinces his own selfhood, but in Eternity or Eden it is precisely this selfhood that is given up *for* another. The outcome of the fall is "From willing sacrifice of Self, to sacrifice of (miscall'd) Enemies / For Atonement" (J.28:20–21). In Eden, this self-annihilation is an inner, perpetual, centrifugal movement of the spirit in forgiving others. Otherwise, Eden could not exist at all (FZ.1:9–10). Blake told Crabb Robinson that the Atonement was a "horrible doctrine," adding, "if another pay your debt I do not forgive it."[14] Likewise, Shelley in discussing the sacrifice of Jesus as satisfying "eternal justice" wrote in his essay "A Refutation of Deism":

> But it is no less inconsistent with justice and subversive of morality that millions should be responsible for a crime which they had no share in committing than that, if they had really committed it, the crucifixion of an innocent being could absolve them from moral turpitude.

To Shelley, this was the "irrefragable logic of tyranny."[15]

Many of Blake's characters perform an act in which they give up their selfhood, most of them for Albion, since he must be awakened out of his deadly Ulro sleep if the universe is to be regenerated. London, for example, personified as a "Human awful wonder of God," gives himself for Albion (J.38:29–39). Los, though terrified that he will forget Eternity, must stay by Albion until the latter awakens: "O Albion, my brother! / Corruptability appears upon thy limbs, and never more / Can I arise and leave thy side, but labour here incessant / Till thy awaking: yet alas, I shall forget Eternity!" (J.82:84;83:1–3). Albion himself, once roused from his sleep of error, casts himself into the furnaces of affliction for his "Friend Divine" Jesus (J.96:30–31;35). Similarly, Milton, in Blake's poem of that name, must give himself to redeem his Emanation, Ololon (M.2:18–20), the spiritual representation of his three wives and three daughters.

At the beginning of the poem Milton is in heaven, but he cannot be happy until he has become one with the feminine aspect of himself that his restrictive Puritanism has denied. Significantly, two of his wives or daughters (or perhaps one of each—Blake does not specify) are called Rahab and Tirzah (M.17:10–11). Moved by the Bard's (i.e., Blake's) song, Milton descends "to self annihilation and eternal death, / Lest the Last Judgment come & find me unannihilate / And I be siez'd & giv'n into the hands of my own Selfhood" (M.14:22–24). Previously, Milton, another Iberian priest as in Shelley's *The Revolt of Islam*, has possessed the same kind of selfhood that called for the cruelties of human sacrifice, offered up in "expiation" to a deity drunk with power and blood, the deity of *Paradise Lost*:

> And [Milton] appear'd the Wicker Man of Scandinavia, in whom
> Jerusalem's children consume in flames among the Stars. (M.37:11–12)

In this Druidic method of sacrifice, the wicker limbs of a huge human figure were filled with the victims, raised aloft, then set on fire.[16]

Through the influence of the Bard's song, however, Milton abjures rational demonstration, Bacon, Locke, and Newton (M.41:3–5), and gives himself for his Spectre (Satan), the personification of his error:

> Such are the Laws of Eternity, that each shall mutually
> Annihilate himself for others' good, as I for thee. (M.38:35–36)

Though Shelley tended to view the act of sacrifice in what Blake termed its "corporeal" sense, he agreed with Blake that it is an act that one can decide only for himself. One cannot—that is, he should not—make a decision in which another is sacrificed. Indeed, he should give up his own life for another, even for his enemy if need be. One of the "subtle and fair spirits / Whose homes are the dim caves of human thought" (PU.I.658–659) that the Earth calls up to comfort Prometheus after his ordeal with Jove's Furies, reveals that it comes from a terrific storm at sea, where it has seen the ultimate act of selflessness:

>   I alit
> On a great ship lightning-split
> And speeded hither on the sigh
> Of one who gave an enemy
> His plank, then plunged aside to die. (PU.I.718–722)

This giving up of the selfhood, in Blake's view, remains impossible so long as man holds to the view of a "righteous" deity of reason remote from his life who demands adherence to dimly perceived "iron laws" that no flesh nor spirit can really abide by (BU.23:24–25). If he does hold to this concept, man remains constantly with the burden of a sin or mistake, for any law carries its own inherent transgression within it. But, if these laws are broken, the deity is full of wrath. Consequently, Blake said "To God":

> If you have form'd a Circle to go into,
> Go into it yourself & see how you would do. (p. 557)

For this reason, as in several of his annotations to Swedenborg's *Divine Love and Divine Wisdom*, Blake stresses the necessity of perceiving God as Man, as the Divine Humanity or Poetic Genius, a perception based not on the reason with its laws of prudence but on the affections, represented by the Zoa Luvah. "Think of a white cloud as being holy [here, Blake uses *holy* as he does at the end of *The Marriage of Heaven and Hell:* "For every thing that lives is Holy" (MHH.25–27, p.160)], you cannot love it," he writes.

> But think of a holy man within the cloud, love springs up in your thoughts,
> for to think of holiness distinct from man is impossible to the affections.
> Thought alone can make monsters, but the affections cannot.

He adds: "Thought without affection makes a distinction between Love & wisdom, as it does between body & Spirit" (p. 90).

Thus, wherever Urizen travels his "thought alone" or "thought without affection" creates monsters and divisiveness. He burns Luvah in a furnace of affliction (FZ.2:80). He sees myriads of "Ruin'd Spirits, once his Children and the Children of Luvah":

> The horrid shapes & sights of torment in burning dungeons & in
> Fetters of red hot iron; some with crowns of serpents & some
> With monsters girding round their bosoms; some lying on beds
>   of sulphur,
> On racks & wheels. (FZ.6:103–106)

He also beholds the "forms of tygers & of Lions, dishumaniz'd men" (FZ.6:116). When he attempts to speak to both the human and the animal forms, his voice is "but an inarticulate thunder":

> for their Ears
> Were heavy & dull, & their eyes & nostrils closed up.
> Oft he stood by a howling victim Questioning in words
> Soothing or Furious; no one answer'd; every one wrap'd up
> In his own sorrow howl'd regardless of his words, nor voice
> Of sweet response could he obtain, tho' oft assay'd with tears.
> He knew they were his Children ruin'd in his ruin'd world. (FZ.6:124–130)

This is but one of many similar passages in *The Four Zoas*, all indicating the nature of the tyrant God created by reason and the quality and condition of that God's world: a "closed up" dark cave. In his discussion of *The Book of Urizen*, Foster Damon notes Urizen's differences from the "conventional devil" (for of course he is the conventional God), and the self deception inherent in his tears for his children. "In fact," Damon observes,

> Urizen's only fault is his lack of Imagination. He has not enough intuitive insight to realize that "One Law for the Lion & Ox is Oppression," that the Eternals may prefer their various modes of life to his; nor does he realize that the sufferings around him are really caused by himself alone.[17]

Urizen weeps and wails over his children, but the pain and binding they experience arise directly out of his religious and moral precepts written in his books of iron and brass or drawn behind him in the web or net which grows from his own soul. Blake depicts him as cold, selfish, proud, white, and aged—a traveller through darkness:

> For Urizen lamented over [his children] in a selfish lamentation
> Till a white woof cover'd his cold limbs from head to feet,
> Hair white as snow cover'd him in flaky locks terrific
> Overspreading his limbs; in pride he wander'd weeping,
> Travelling thro' darkness, & wherever he travel'd a dire Web

Follow'd behind him, as the Web of a Spider, dusky & cold,
Shivering across from Vortex to Vortex, drawn out from his
    mantle of years:
A living Mantle adjoined to his life & growing from his soul.
And the Web of Urizen stre[t]ch'd direful, shivering in clouds,
And uttering such woes, such burstings, such thunderings. (FZ.6:239–248)

In *The Revolt of Islam* one form that evil takes is "Fear, Hatred, Faith, and Tyranny, who spread / Those subtle nets which snare the living and the dead" (RI.I.xxix.386–387). When one is caught in Urizen's web, he is forced into what Shelley terms "religion's labyrinth caves" (RI.VIII.xi.3292), for no matter what thread of the web or path of the cave one follows, he goes ever deeper into error. Thought alone creates only enclosed, argumentative mazes: the cave, the net, the trap, the web, the prison, the chain, the dungeon.[18]

Thus, when Albion accepts Urizenic religion, he becomes the "cavern'd Man" (E.III.1) closed in by his bony skull, who looks out from the narrow chinks (the senses) of this cavern with the single vision of the reason. The Angel in *The Marriage of Heaven and Hell* who leads Blake successively through a stable, a church, the church vault and a mill, finally reaches a cave where "a void boundless as a nether sky appear'd beneath us, & we held by the roots of trees and hung over this immensity" (MHH.17–20, p. 155). This immense void—a cave with no definite bottom—is a creation of the separative faculty of thought (BU.3:3–6). Within its Satanic mill just above the cave Blake finds "Aristotle's Analytics," and he tells the Angel "it is but lost time to converse with you whose works are only Analytics" (MHH.17–20, p. 157). He sees in the analytical Angel "a confident insolence sprouting from systematic reasoning" (MHH.21–22, p. 157). In *The Four Zoas,* Urizen explores his dens—the same ones that the Angel shows Blake in *The Marriage of Heaven and Hell*—in an attempt to discover the force (Orc) "That shakes my cavern with strong shudders." Orc, as the son of Los (and the fallen aspect of Luvah: revolutionary energy), must be feared by Urizen, because Orc has the potential ability—the fire—to destroy Urizen's cavern. Even Urizen realizes that "When Thought is clos'd in Caves Then love shall shew its root in deepest Hell" (FZ.5:239–241).

In *Prometheus Unbound,* Jupiter represents "thought alone" creating monsters. All things in the earth, including mankind, are his slaves, and for their "knee-worship, prayer, and praise" their reward is "fear and self-contempt and barren hope" (PU.I.6–8). Like Urizen's rule, Jupiter's is based on "falsehood" and "force" (PU.I.127), and at the beginning of *Prometheus Unbound* the entire world lies groaning and frozen in its chains of terror and despair. Just as Urizen cannot obtain a "voice of sweet response" because every form is closed within its own pain, so too in *Prometheus Unbound* all the former singing and articulate voices of the earth have been constricted or silenced. "Hideous monsters" of iron and brass spring from Urizen's thought to obstruct his exploration of the fallen Zoas' territories (FZ.6:75–76); they attack Urizen himself (FZ.6:138–140). In the same way, the Furies rise from the "all-miscreative brain of Jove" (PU.I.448). The same monstrous thought without affection is revealed by Othman in *The Revolt of Islam* (whose tortures are similar to those instituted by Urizen) when he takes revenge on his enemies. he "bade the torturing wheel / Be brought, and fire, and pincers, and the hook, / And scorpions; that his soul on its revenge might look" (RI.X.viii.3862–3864). Similarly, near the end of *The Four Zoas* when Urizen feels his hold on the other Zoas loosening, the only way he thinks he can keep the universe in subjection is by using "his Engines of deceit":

> that linked chains might run
> Thro' ranks of war spontaneous: & that hooks and boring screws
> Might act according to their form by innate cruelty. (FZ.8:132–134)

The monster Blake refers to most often in connection with Urizenic thought is the serpent. It is "serpent reasonings" that entice us—as Urizen entices Albion—to divide all things into categories of "Good" and "Evil," a division into abstraction and generalization symbolized by the Tree of Knowledge of Good and Evil. "Reasonings like vast Serpents / Infold around my limbs," the Poet says in *Jerusalem*, "bruising my minute articulations" (J.15:12–13). The serpent, therefore, Blake associates (until the apocalyptic regeneration) with the fall of Albion into the world of Generation—the natural or unspiritual world of the five senses. After the fall, the form of nature itself rolls apart from Eternity and appears like a vast serpent (FZ.3:97). The coiled, wreathed or folded serpent— the Ouroboros—is particularly pernicious because it represents the "closed up" position of the selfhood, its Satanic dissimulation (p. 386) and craftiness ("To Nobodaddy," p. 171). This "self-contemplating" posture inevitably leads to wars instigated by the "Prester Serpent" who calls upon the warriors to store the "Seven Diseases of Man" (sin in all its forms) "in secret places that I will tell thee of" (FZ.7b.118–121). One of these secret places is Urizen's serpent temple, for "thought chang'd the infinite to a serpent" (E.10:16); that is, after the fall thought or reason becomes the ratio and in effect stands still, "unable to do other than repeat the same dull round over again" (NR, p. 97):

> Then was the serpent temple form'd, image of infinite
> Shut up in finite revolutions, and Man became an Angel,
> Heaven a mighty circle turning, God a tyrant crown'd. (E.10:21–23)

Here, Blake uses "angel" in the sense of "self-righteous" or "systematic reasoner" as he does in *The Marriage of Heaven and Hell.*

Urizen's rules and laws based on thought (or reason) without affection (or energy)—exemplified in his instruments of torture and his serpent temple—are contained in his books of iron and brass. In the book of iron (as he writes it, his tree of mystery grows under his foot), one can read the laws of his secret mystery religion; in the book of brass his rigid, hypocritical moral code of conduct specifying "One command, one joy, one desire, / One curse, one weight, one measure, / One King, One God, one Law" (BU.4:38–40). The book of brass "Kings & Priests had copied on Earth" (E.11:3–4). Urizen takes pleasure in torturing the bound Orc (Los's son and thus an aspect of energy and imagination) by reading out of the book of brass:

> Compell the poor to live upon a Crust of bread, by soft mild arts.
> Smile when they frown, frown when they smile; & when a man looks pale
> With labour & abstinence, say he looks healthy & happy.
> ....
> With pomp give every crust of bread you give; with gracious cunning
> Magnify small gifts; reduce the man to want a gift, & then give with pomp.
> Say he smiles if you hear him sigh. If pale, say he is ruddy.
> Preach temperance: say he is overgorg'd & drowns his wit
> In strong drink, tho' you know that bread & water are all
> He can afford. Flatter his wife, pity his children, till we can
> Reduce all to our will, as spaniels are taught with art. (FZ.7a.117–119;123–129)

Orc calls this "Cold hypocrisy" (FZ.7a.135), and Shelley "cold sophistry" (QM.V.108). In almost the exact words of Urizen, Shelley wrote from Ireland to Elizabeth Hitchener: "The rich *grind* the poor into abjectness & then complain that they are abject.—They goad them to famine and hang them if they steal a loaf."[19] Shelley describes Urizen and his brazen hypocrisy exactly in the following lines from *Queen Mab:*

>   grave and hoary-headed hypocrites
> Without a hope, a passion, or a love,
> Who, through a life of luxury and lies,
> Have crept by flattery to the seats of power,
> Support the system whence their honours flow. (QM.IV.203–207)

Likewise, some of the priests who burn Laon and Cythna rush through the ranks of the people "counterfeiting / The rage they did inspire" (RI.X.xlv.4189–4190). More subtly in *Prometheus Unbound* Shelley stresses that Jupiter's power is built on "falsehood" (PU.I.127), "eldest faith, and hell's coeval, fear" (PU.III.i.10). All the great of the earth chained to the Car of Life in *The Triumph of Life, feign* "the morn of truth" but "deep night / Caught them ere evening" (TL.214–215).

Urizen not only writes his codes in an iron book, he also uses an iron pen. In his unending exploration of the fallen worlds of the Zoas, he

> threw his flight
> Onward, tho' falling, thro' the waste of night & ending in death
> And in another resurrection to sorrow & weary travel.
> But still his books he bore in his strong hands, & his iron pen.
> ....
>   for such a journey none but iron pens
> Can write And adamantine leaves recieve, nor can the man who
>   goes
> The journey obstinate refuse to write time after time. (FZ.6:164–167;173–175)

But Shelley and Blake's point is that one does not have to go this "journey obstinate" mapped out by the tyrant reason within and the tyrant king and priest without. In *The Revolt of Islam*, Cythna, speaking of this same "iron pen," tells the mariners:

> Look on your mind—it is the book of fate—
> Ah! it is dark with many a blazoned name
> Of misery—all are mirrors of the same;
> But the dark fiend who with his iron pen
> Dipped in scorn's fiery poison, makes his fame
> Enduring there, would o'er the heads of men
> Pass harmless, if they scorned to make their hearts his den. (RI.VIII.xx.3372–3378)

Thus, Blake announced to his contemporaries that the caverned world of Bacon, Newton, and Locke created by reason and bounded by the five senses was an iron hindrance, a "Ratio" of man's selfhood and not creative action (VLJ, p. 617), and so it passed harmlessly over his head. "O Divine Spirit, sustain me on thy wings," he cries out for inspiration in *Jerusalem*, "That I may wake Albion from his long & cold repose; / For Bacon & Newton sheath'd in dismal steel, their terrors hang / Like iron scourges over Albion" (J.15:9–12). Similarly, Shelley felt during the oppressive reign (1760–1820) of the insane George III (which very nearly spanned the lifetimes of both Shelley and Blake), that liberty had died in England, murdered by the iron scourge of the tyrant. In "An Address to the People on the Death of the Princess Charlotte," in which he criticizes his countrymen for weeping only for the princess when all around them the poor barely existed or died in wretchedness, he wrote: "Fetters heavier than iron weigh upon us, because they bind our souls. We move about in a dungeon more pestilential than damp and narrow walls because the earth is its floor and the heaven its roof."[20] Shelley wrote his essay in 1817, a year in which the Tory government, among other restrictions, suspended the Act of Habeas Corpus. Many years before in 1794, when Shelley was two years old, at the height of the Reign of Terror and just before the rise of a different, European tyrant—Napoleon—Blake wrote in *Europe:*

> Every house a den, every man bound: the shadows are fill'd
> With spectres, and the windows wove over with curses of iron;

Over the doors "Thou shalt not," & over the chimneys "Fear" is
   written:
With bands of iron round their necks fasten'd into the walls
The citizens, in leaden gyves the inhabitants of suburbs
Walk heavy; soft and bent are the bones of villagers. (E.12:26–31)

"The shadows are fill'd / With spectres"—that is, with men's objectified selfhoods, "hideously multiplied" like those which dance round Laon, all in his own likeness (RI.III.xxiii.1314). The fetters of iron and the curses of iron, in government and religion and within and without his mind, man forges by accepting his selfhood as a reality, by refusing to recognize that as he binds so he becomes bound.

Both Shelley and Blake hold the idea that the tyrant himself is a slave, for he exercises his selfhood to an even greater extent than the ordinary person in forcing his will upon others and thus becomes what he does or contemplates. Queen Mab reveals to Ianthe a vision of a king who is "Grasping an iron sceptre, and immured within a splendid prison" (QM.III.90–91)—that is, he is within his palace chained to his selfhood. Similarly, Cythna, in her sermon to the mariners in The Revolt of Islam, indicates that what binds the tyrant emanates from him in the first place: "for none of Woman born, / Can choose but drain the bitter dregs of woe, / Which ever from the oppressed to the oppressors flow" (RI.VIII.xv.3331–3333). The pernicious circle of oppression returns ultimately to chain the tyrant spiritually to his throne, which then becomes his "splendid prison." Like the oxymoron "serious folly" that Shelley applies to the captives of the Car of Life in The Triumph of Life, the splendid prison of the tyrant asserts that the appearance is likely to be deceptive; that Caesar's laurel crown appears a serious, splendid object to be desired but is actually a fool's dream that leads to a spiritual prison—the selfhood; that what flows from man's heart into the outer, both good and evil, makes a circle, coming back like bread cast upon the water. If one grows a chain out of his own mind, as Urizen does, thinking to remain free while he oppresses others, he will find that chain closing ever tighter round his own soul. In other words, the condition of evil is its own punishment; and that being who can approximate the good, no matter how he suffers or in what poverty he must live, pities the evil, as Prometheus does, regardless of its splendid outer trappings, its powers, or its "voluptuous joy." Although one who follows the good may be involved in disaster—as we see in the deaths of Laon and Cythna—while those who follow evil often prosper, there is no comparison between their spiritual condition, and on this point the full poetic force of Prometheus Unbound and Jerusalem ultimately falls. St. Augustine has stated this difference between good and evil in the following way:

Lying involves the will to speak falsely; thus we find many who wish to lie, but no one who wishes to be deceived. Since a man lies knowingly but suffers deception unwittingly, it is obvious that in a given instance a man who is deceived is better than a man who lies, because it is better to suffer iniquity than to perform it.[21]

For this reason, Prometheus tells Mercury to "Pity the self-despising slaves of Heaven, / Not me, within whose mind sits peace serene, / As light in the sun, throned" (PU.I.429–431).

The tyrant Othman in *The Revolt of Islam*, like Jupiter, is a self-despising slave to evil. For a moment when he first sees Cythna, "to great Nature's sacred power / He bent," but when he rapes her, "then he bore / Again his load of slavery, and became / A king, a heartless beast, a pageant and a name" (RI.VII.v.2867–2868;2872–2874). Similarly, when Albion's sons torture Luvah on the Druid Altar, they themselves bear a "load of slavery": "Sudden they become like what they behold, in howlings & deadly pain" (J.65:75). In *Prometheus Unbound*, Prometheus states that all men are the slaves of Jupiter, yet Prometheus calls Jupiter "a prostrate slave" (PU.I.52), for as Demogorgon asserts, "All spirits are enslaved which serve things evil" (PU.II.iv.110). Just like the hypocritical Mercury—though Mercury is a willing tool of Jupiter—Prometheus, through his hatred, is also a slave to the tyrant. This chaining to evil on all these levels—man, Prometheus, Jupiter—can be broken only by that being who is able to go out of his selfhood and pity the evil, as Prometheus ultimately does. This leap or thrust of imaginative energy places one beyond his self in the realm of freedom: hate is centripetal; love is centrifugal. Los too reaches the point where he no longer hates but loves his "enemy" Urizen (FZ.7a:496–498).

In *The Triumph of Life* Shelley parades before the reader the "great" men and women of the past such as Frederick, Paul, Catherine, Leopold, Napoleon, who, in forcing their wills on others, have now reached the condition of slavery themselves. "Every image, every phrase, almost every word," asserts Donald H. Reiman, "carries the paradoxical relationship of power and virtue—that one cannot extend his power over the wills of other men and still remain free himself."[22] "Who is he with chin / Upon his breast, and hands crossed on his chain?" the Poet asks. "The child of a fierce hour," Rousseau replies, "he sought to win

> The world, and lost all that it did contain
> Of greatness, in its hope destroyed; and more
> Of fame and peace than virtue's self can gain
>
> Without the opportunity which bore
> Him on its eagle pinions to the peak
> From which a thousand climbers have before
>
> Fallen, as Napoleon fell. (TL.215–224)

The so-called "great" people of the past are not truly great as Blake and Shelley define the term. For them, greatness lies not in self-aggrandizement but in selflessness. "A Lord Chancellor's opinions," avows Blake (in a statement that Shelley would have had reason to respect considering his own problems with a Lord Chancellor), are "as different from Christ['s] as those of Caiphas or Pilate or Herod: what such Men call Great is indeed detestable" (p. 407). When Bacon asserted in his essay "Of Ceremonies and Respect": "small matters win great commendation, because they are continually in use and in note," Blake wrote in his copy: "Small matters—What are they? Caesar seems to me a Very Small Matter & so he seem'd to Jesus: is the devil Great? Consider" (p. 410). In striving for Caesar's laurel crown the persons chained to Shelley's Car of Life are deluded by "phantoms": all desires for empire, religious and political, are evil. These phantoms

> made a cradle of the ermined capes
>
> Of kingly mantles; some across the tiar
> Of pointiffs sate like vultures; others played
> Under the crown which girt with empire
>
> A baby's or an idiot's brow, and made
> Their nests in it. (TL.495–500)

Even without the desire for empire, Prometheus fears that, in looking on the "execrable shapes" of Jove's Furies, he may become like them (PU.I.449–450). Los, who has the necessary task of binding Urizen after the fall to keep him from total disintegration, discovers that in limiting Urizen he has inevitably limited and enslaved himself. Again, Blake uses iron and brass as symbols of this limitation:

> And thus began the binding of Urizen; day & night in fear
> Circling round the dark Demon, with howlings, dismay & sharp
>   blightings,
> The Prophet of Eternity beat on his iron links & links of brass;
> And as he beat round the hurtling Demon, terrified at the Shapes
> Enslav'd humanity put on, he became what he beheld. (FZ.4:119–203)

One cannot kill or harm another even in the most noble cause without becoming a slave to evil and to his selfhood. When Laon and Cythna are first set upon by the tyrant's men in *The Revolt of Islam,* Cythna beseeches Laon to remember that the men who bear her away are simply slaves who are taking her to her appointed task: to spread the word of freedom among the people. But Cythna's words fall on Laon's "unheeding ear," and

> so I drew
> My knife, and with one impulse, suddenly
> All unaware three of their number slew,
> And grasped a fourth by the throat, and with loud cry
> My countrymen invoked to death or liberty! (RI.III.x.1193–1197)

The tyrant's men chain Laon to a grate of brass (that is, he is bound to his sin) high in a tower overlooking the sea and there for four days (until released by the old hermit) he suffers all the torments of his restrictive selfhood, including the appearance of his *doppelgänger,* "hideously multiplied" (RI.III.xxiii.1314).

Although to a lesser degree, Cythna herself experiences this chaining to self. Imprisoned and raped by Othman, she, like Laon, fails to meet the inner demand of love under all circumstances and descends into madness (RI.VII.vii). Confined by Othman within a cave by the sea, she gradually renews her mind not only through loving the child that is born to her but also through the outward movement away from self by which all creatures in the earth could be regenerated. She shields a nautilus from the eagle who brings her food, not by violence and hatred toward the eagle, but by offering it her own food. The eagle is then transformed. "The eager plumes subsided on his throat— / He came where that bright child of sea did swim, / And o'er it cast in peace his shadow broad and dim" (RI.VII.xxvii.3070–3072). In the same way, when Albion casts off his selfhood, "The spider, The bat burst from the harden'd slime, crying / To one another: 'What are we, & whence is our joy & delight?' " (FZ.9:608–609).

In *The Cenci* we witness a much stronger binding than Cythna's to the selfhood, not only in Cenci himself but in Beatrice, for neither of the major characters in Shelley's drama manages to transcend the self as Laon and Cythna do in their "mutual sacrifice" and consequent flight to the Temple of the Spirit. Beatrice's chaining to self comes about because she convinces herself that she can be the judge and executioner of Cenci. Like Dostoevski's Raskolnikov, though for a different reason, she believes she has the right to decide that another human being shall live or die, and when one decides that another shall die or be sacrificed, he makes manifest his selfhood.

In Act I, Scene iii, when Cenci reveals the deaths of his sons, Beatrice, supporting the half-fainting Lucretia, cries out: "Dear lady, pray look up / Had it been true, there is a God in Heaven, / He would not live to boast of such a boon" (CE.I.iii.51–53). But it is true, and Cenci does live to boast and to do more evil: no just God strikes him down for his evil acts. It is Beatrice herself who must finally do that, for she at last realizes

> In this mortal world
> There is no vindication and no law
> Which can adjudge and execute the doom
> Of that through which I suffer. (CE.III.i.134–137)

Therefore, she becomes the instrument through which this doom can be executed, not because of revenge[23] but because Cenci's murder seems the only way in which she can rid herself of more evil yet to come. In taking such a step, in Melvin R. Watson's words, "she does not consider herself principally a daughter intent on revenge for an outrage to her body, but the agent of divine justice who believes herself permitted by God to remedy a flaw in the scheme of things." And it is this hubris, as Watson points out, that corrupts her character,[24] far more than the motive of revenge would have done, considering the kind of person she is. For in becoming a judge of Cenci rather than forgiving him she takes on an attribute (the unmerciful judge) of that God whom Shelley called a "demon,"[25] the anthropomorphic God of the Old Testament and in all major respects the God that Cenci worships. Even though Beatrice could not have done otherwise than commit the murder and remain the tragic figure required by the play, it is obvious, not only from Shelley's Preface to the play (where he calls her act a "pernicious mistake") but from most of his other works, that he believes forgiveness and love should always hold the dominant position in man's mind. Indeed, "eternal Love"—the spirit of oneness in the universe—is the only deity that Shelley ultimately recognizes in his finest and most representative poems: *Adonais* and *Prometheus Unbound*. To the end of his life, he continued to denigrate the concept of an arbitrary, personal, wrathful God who judged and then saved or condemned the creatures that he had himself created to fall. Hence, the God of Beatrice, however just under the particular circumstances, is no less evil than Cenci's God. In the Shelleyan formula, Beatrice becomes like that which she contemplates or creates.

In a much stronger, more evil, and more arrogant fashion, Cenci is also bound to his selfhood. Newman Ivey White speaks of Cenci's "peculiarly horrible piety,"[26] which would be a paradox except for the fact that Cenci has created his God in the image of his own selfhood. Therefore, he can be thoroughly evil and at the same time thoroughly pious, just as the Iberian priest shows piety when he burns Laon and Cythna. What is striking about Count Cenci and very Shelleyan (in that it reveals Shelley's exact concept of both the earthly and the heavenly tyrant) is the reliance that Cenci places upon God throughout the drama, a reliance that is completely divorced from any idea of truth or goodness. " 'Tis plain," he says, "I have been favored from above, / For when I cursed my sons they died" (CE.IV.i.39–40). In his attempt to force Beatrice to come to him of her own will (in order to achieve his "greater point" of destroying her soul), he states that he will curse her if she fails to comply, just as God calls down evil on the world when it displeases him:

With what but a father's curse doth God
Panic-strike armed victory and make pale
Cities in their prosperity? The world's Father
Must grant a parent's prayer against his child,
Be he who asks even what men call me. (CE.IV.i.104–108)

When Lucretia warns him that the granting of such a prayer may involve his own punishment, Cenci makes the ultimate correlation between himself and the "world's father" he images—a correlation indicating the arbitrary nature of their power: "He does His will, I mine!" (CE.IV.i.138).

As Donald H. Reiman has noted in his study of *The Triumph of Life*, Shelley's Car of Life "symbolizes arbitrary power"—the same sort of power that Cenci wields and that he attributes to his God. "But to Shelley there could be no truly divine power that did not conform to some law of justice," Reiman continues, "and no exhibition of omnipotence could make right an arbitrary decision; the will of man or God, to be righteous, must be obedient to the law of love."[27] Cenci's "laws" (his own will) and those of his God are contained in Urizen's books of brass and iron, in which all affection has been left out and thought riots in its own antipathy. Such laws have nothing to do with real truth or real error. Shelley distinguishes between what is really right and wrong, for example, and what a particular society agrees to consider "right" and "wrong," for which a law is then made. "The origin of law . . . was the origin of crime, although the ideas of right and wrong must have subsisted from the moment that one human being could sympathize in the pains and pleasure of another. Every law supposes the criminality of its own infraction."[28] In words quite similar to Shelley's, Blake maintains that

> All Penal Laws court Transgression & therefore are cruelty & Murder. The laws of the Jews were (both ceremonial & real) the basest & most oppressive of human codes, & being like all other codes given under pretence of divine command were what Christ pronounced them, The Abomination that maketh desolate, i.e., State Religion, which is the source of all Cruelty. (p. 393)

In *The Cenci* Beatrice is well aware of the cruelty of such laws that give all to her father while her petitions are denied. She believes that no one at the banquet will assist her in her effort to escape the tyranny of her father because she has cried out from her heart, not through "some form / Of scrupulous law" (CE.I.iii.135–136). All evil is based upon a law which upholds it: "Prisons are built with stones of Law, Brothels with bricks of Religion" (MHH.8:1). Jesus came to destroy the laws of state religion through forgiveness of both the sinner and his sin. In *Jerusalem*, the Poet sees the Urizenic "Wheel of [State] Religion" and is told by "a Watcher & a Holy-One": "Jesus died because he strove / Against the current of this Wheel" (J.77:12–17). The Watcher tells the Poet to do likewise, and not to curse but to pity evil (as Prometheus finally learns to do). Only in this way can the wheel and its intricate, stultifying laws be broken:

Pity the evil, for thou are not sent
To smite with terror & with punishments
Those that are sick, like to the Pharisees
Crucifying & encompassing sea & land
For proselytes to tyranny & wrath;
But to the Publicans & Harlots go,
Teach them True Happiness, but let no curse
Go forth out of thy mouth to blight their peace;
For Hell is open'd to Heaven: thine eyes beheld
The dungeons burst & the Prisoners set free. (J.77:26–35)

"Hell is open'd to Heaven" only through forgiveness, and "by forgiveness." Northrop Frye remarks,

> Blake means a release of imaginative power, the creating of conditions
> which make it possible for a harlot to "go and sin no more," as opposed to
> the miserable futility of the Pharisaic attempt to destroy harlotry by killing
> harlots.[29]

To the tyrannical God of thought (Urizen, Jupiter) both Blake and
Shelley juxtapose a God (or in Shelley's term a Spirit) of love. To Blake,
this loving God is synonymous with the Divine Humanity, Poetic Genius,
Jesus, Albion, the Eternals and the Human Imagination. As indicated in
"The Divine Image," God and Man are one:

For Mercy, Pity, Peace, and Love
Is God, our father dear,
And Mercy, Pity, Peace, and Love
Is Man, his child and care. (p. 117)

Or, stated prosaically, "Human nature is the image of God" (p. 83).
Blake underlined Johann Caspar Lavater's aphorism, "He who adores
an impersonal God, has none," writing beside it, "Most superlatively
beautiful & most affectionately Holy and pure; would to God that all
men would consider it" (p. 82). Thus, in Blake's illustrations to the Book
of Job, one of the last works he completed before his death, Job and his
God are mirror images; and as Joseph Wicksteed notes, "in the ninth
illustration, where Eliphaz is speaking of *his* vision of God, the Deity
bears the same kind of facial likeness to the speaker as he does elsewhere
to Job."[30]

In *The Everlasting Gospel* Blake humorously asserts that his God is like
himself:

The vision of Christ that thou dost see
Is my Vision's Greatest Enemy;
Thine has a great hook nose like thine;
Mine has a snub nose like to mine. (EG.a.1–4)

If one looks into the mirror supplied by his reason, as Albion does in the fall, he sees the tyrant God who is the reflection of his own selfhood; if he looks into the mirror supplied by the affections, as Albion does in his regeneration, he sees the merciful Son or the loving Father, both identifiable with Albion himself, the Divine Humanity. As Blake's definitive statement of his credo—*Jerusalem*—draws to a close in Chapter Four, the Four Zoas "arose into / Albion's Bosom" (that is, he is now restored to his original unity of sight and being); and when Albion calls on his Emanation, Jerusalem, to "Awake and overspread all Nations as in Ancient Time" (for the highest aspect of the Emanation—unlike Vala, Rahab and Tirzah—is liberty, joy, fulfillment, forgiveness)—when Albion calls on his Emanation, the words are those of the "Universal Father" speaking *within* Albion (J.96:41–42;97:2,5–6).

Examples of Blake's belief that the regenerated Man is also God could be multiplied almost indefinitely, since nearly every page of *Jerusalem* and *The Four Zoas* contains some reference to his idea of the real God. Blake never denigrated the concept of God as a loving father. What he does revile, as Northrop Frye points out, is God as Nobodaddy—the Urizenic God-tyrant who oppresses his children down into the Ratio of self. Failure to distinguish these two as separate aspects of the father in Blake's work has led some to think, in Frye's words, "that [Blake] was inspired by an obscure psychological compulsion to attack the Fatherhood of God." Blake, however,

> is merely insisting that man cannot approach the superhuman aspect of God except through Christ, the God who is Man. If man attempts to approach the Father directly, as Milton, for instance, does in a few unlucky passages in *Paradise Lost,* all he will ever get is Nobodaddy.[31]

As much as he revered Milton, therefore, Blake wrote an entire Prophetic Book in part to correct Milton's false notion of the deity.

The false father-tyrant-God whom Blake called Nobodaddy appears very early in his work; for example, in the aged Tiriel (1789), and in the father who sells his child to be a chimney sweeper in the *Songs of Innocence* (1789) and the *Songs of Experience* (1794). And it is primarily against this cruel father-tyrant that Shelley protests in his delineation of Count Cenci. Nothing is more sinister than Cenci in his capacity as father or the father aspect of the God he worships and with whom he so closely identifies. Beatrice calls upon God as father many times in the play—"I have knelt down through the long sleepless nights / And lifted up to God, the Father of all, / Passionate prayers" (CE.I.iii.117–119). However, as Joan Rees points out, there is no response to Beatrice's prayers; but this God always answers when Cenci prays,[32] even when he asks for the deaths of his sons. For this reason, the Father-God invoked by both Beatrice and Cenci takes on a most malign quality: helpful to evil, ignoring the good. When a guest at Cenci's banquet asks Cenci to reveal the cause of the celebration, the "desired event" that has brought them together, Cenci replies:

> It is indeed a most desired event.
> If, when a parent from a parent's heart
> Lifts from this earth to the great Father of all
> A prayer, both when he lays him down to sleep,
> And when he rises up from dreaming it;
> One supplication, one desire, one hope,
> That he would grant a wish for his two sons,
> Even all that he demands in their regard—
> And suddenly beyond his dearest hope
> It is accomplished, he should then rejoice,
> And call his friends and kinsmen to a feast,
> And task their love to grace his merriment,—
> Then honour me thus far—for I am he. (CE.I.iii.21–33)

Within the next few lines, we learn how Cenci's prayer for his sons has been answered:

>   God!
> I thank thee! In one night didst thou perform,
> By ways inscrutable, the thing I sought.
> My disobedient and rebellious sons
> Are dead! (CE.I.iii.40–44)

In fact, Cenci insists that "Heaven has special care of me" (CE.I.iii.65), for the Father-God in heaven is the mirror image of the tyrant-father on earth, and the latter's curses may even "Climb with swift wings after their children's souls / And drag them from the very throne of Heaven" (CE.I.iii.85–86). Thus, when Beatrice asks: "Thou, great God, / Whose image upon earth a father is, / Dost thou indeed abandon me?" (CE.II.i.16–18), the answer must be most emphatically yes: for if this God's image is reflected in Cenci (as Shelley indicates) then neither father can have any love for his children. Similarly, the "Holy Father" (CE.II.i.24), the Pope, tells Camillo, when Camillo urges him to check Cenci:

> Children are disobedient, and they sting
> Their fathers' hearts to madness and despair,
> Requiting years of care with contumely.
> I pity the Count Cenci from my heart;
> His outraged love perhaps awakened hate,
> And thus he is exasperated to ill.
> In the great war between the old and young
> I, who have white hairs and a tottering body,
> Will keep at least blameless neutrality. (CE.II.ii.32–40)

Therefore, the Pope refuses to take action on Beatrice's behalf, fearing, as Camillo says, "to weaken the paternal power, / Being, as 'twere, the shadow of his own" (CE.II.ii.55–56).

In addition, the Pope's reference to "white hairs" reminds one that Cenci himself is old, like Tiriel and Urizen, and that the mysterious Shape who drives Shelley's Chariot of Life "So sate within, as one whom years deform" (TL.88). Giacomo in *The Cenci*, waiting for news of his father's murder, muses on the possibility that "when my hairs are white, / My son will then perhaps be waiting thus, / Tortured between just hate and vain remorse; / Chiding the tardy messenger of news / Like those which I expect" (CE.III.ii.25–29). As I have pointed out elsewhere, Blake and Shelley contrast age to youth because one needs a childlike quality of perception to overcome what Blake calls Abstract Philosophy (the divisiveness of the Tree of Knowledge of Good and Evil which creates the unloving tyrant); or, in Shelleyan terms, "To burst the chains which life forever flings / On the entangled soul's aspiring wings" (RI.II.xxxiii.958–959). However, as soon as the child is taught "the crucifying cruelties of Demonstration" (J.24:55), which grow from reason without affection, like Giacomo, he then turns the hatred he has learned back upon his tyrannical father: "My son! My son! Thou treatest me / But as I have instructed thee" (GP, p. 771)—these words of Blake's might well be the epigraph of *The Cenci*. Like the circle of hatred that flows from oppressor to oppressed and back again which binds them both, the next generation—because the cycle of hatred remains unbroken—repeats the same pattern. Thus, Giacomo foresees or fears his own death by *his* son in that of his father, when his "hairs are white" like Cenci's and the Pope's. This fear causes the paternal authority to harden even further, and widens the gulf between the generations, the "great war between the old and young." Partly for this reason, both Blake and Shelley completely discount the judgemental, authoritative, arbitrary, tyrannical concept of God—what Blake called "Our Father Augustus Ceasar [sic]" (p. 788), since the God in heaven is an allegory of the king on earth.

Though Shelley posits the same loving God that Blake does, to the younger poet God *is* impersonal, another name for the universal, one Spirit that pervades the entire world, making all things one, not through Urizen's one law and one command but through the plastic, fluid power of love.[33] This Power acts as the firm foundation that sustains the world from beneath, while at the same time it is the volatile, fiery force that sweeps down from above to kindle the "dull dense world" into forms of beauty (AD.XLIII.382). "I should doubt the existence of a God," Shelley wrote to Elizabeth Hitchener, "who if he cannot command our reverence by Love, surely can have no demand upon it from Virtue on the score of terror."[34] This God whom Shelley doubts is thus not the "eternal

Love" he reveres in *Prometheus Unbound,* or the "one Spirit" in *Adonais* whose breath drives his bark toward "the inmost veil of Heaven" (AD.LV.493), but the debased, terrifying image of the Father that Blake called Nobodaddy. Accordingly, in the Preface to *The Revolt of Islam,* Shelley contends that in his poem he does not speak against the idea of a "Supreme Being itself," but only against "the erroneous and degrading idea which men have conceived" of it, for love is "the sole law"—or should be—in men's concepts of the "moral world" (p. 37).

Such a debased image as Nobodaddy, acceptable to both the orthodox Protestant and the orthodox Catholic, Shelley, like Blake, thought stultifying and repressive in its effects upon the one who held it. In the Preface to *The Cenci,* while seeming at first to explain to the "Protestant apprehension" that there is "something unnatural in the earnest and perpetual sentiment of the relations between God and men which pervade the tragedy," Shelley nevertheless scorns the Protestant apprehension of God as well. "Protestants," he states,

> will especially be startled at the combination of an undoubting persuasion of the truth of the popular religion with a cool and determined persever-ance in enormous guilt. But religion in Italy is not, as in Protestant countries, a cloak to be worn on particular days; or a passport which those who do not wish to be railed at carry with them to exhibit; or a gloomy passion for penetrating the impenetrable mysteries of our being, which terrifies its possessor at the darkness of the abyss to the brink of which it has conducted him.

On the contrary, religion in Italy "is adoration, faith, submission, peni-tence, blind admiration; not a rule of moral conduct" (p. 277). To Shelley, both these concepts of religion—as a "cloak," a "passport," "gloomy passion," "terror," or "submission," "penitence," "blind admira-tion"—were anathema. The "Spirit of the Universe" cannot possess human characteristics, and therefore all "ceremonies, or confessions, or burials, or processions, or wonders"[35] have nothing to do with a true perception of that Spirit and its relation to men. "Moral qualities are such as only a human being can possess," Shelley states in his essay "A Letter to Lord Ellenborough":

> To attribute them to the Spirit of the Universe, or to suppose that it is capable of altering them, is to degrade God into man and to annex to this incomprehensible being qualities incompatible with any *possible* definition of its nature. It may be here objected—ought not the Creator to possess the perfection of the creature? No. To attribute to God the moral qualities of man is to suppose him susceptible of passions which, arising out of corporeal organization, it is plain that a pure spirit cannot possess.[36]

The orthodox God, who, "resembling men in the moral attributes of His nature, having called us out of non-existence, and after inflicting on us the misery of the commission of error, should superadd that of the punishment and the privations consequent upon it" was "inexplicable and incredible" to Shelley (p. 478).

On the contrary, the "pure spirit" that Shelley conceived was not like Jupiter, Venus, Vulcan, Proteus or Pan, but "the ruling Power of the universe," the "collective energy of the moral and material world." This Power surrounds us "like the atmosphere in which some motionless lyre is suspended, which visits with its breath our silent chords at will."[37] Thus, Shelley asks the West Wind, who both destroys and preserves— the Power in its most intense and tumultuous creative aspect—to "make me thy lyre" (WW.V.57) so that it may speak through the Poet the prophecy of the "new birth" (WW.V.64) to all mankind, of that Spring to which the earth rises "like an eagle" in *The Revolt of Islam* (RI.IX.xxv.3693).

Jean L. De Palacio speaks of Love and Music as the emanations of Shelley's unseen Spirit or Power: "As such, Love and Music may be set down as the two major components of Shelley's spiritual world, which perhaps there is no severing, on account of their common origin."[38] Certainly, much of the energy the reader feels pouring out of the lines of *Prometheus Unbound* comes from those lyrics (for example, "My Soul is an Enchanted Boat") in which love seems to ride the long, swelling wave of music—what Shelley terms the "stream of sound" (PU.IV.504;506).[39] One of the two Fauns whose home is the forest through which Asia and Panthea pass on their way to Demogorgon's realm tells the other that the spirits "which make such delicate music in the woods" live inside the bubbles which the sun sucks from the flowers that grow on the bottoms of lakes and pools. When the bubbles rise and burst, the spirits within ride on the air the bubbles formerly contained "and rein their headlong speed, / And bow their burning crests, and glide in fire / Under the waters of the earth again"(PU.II.ii.65;71–82).[40] As I have previously noted, Blake associates the selflessness of Eden with "unquenchable burnings"—those which Urizen will not endure—and with the fiery motion of loving creativity. So too, the spirits in *Prometheus Unbound* who engage in the art of music "bow the burning crests" of the airy steeds they ride "and glide in fire." The Earth tells Asia that her torchbearer— who rises in the form of a winged child—"let his lamp out in old time with gazing / On eyes from which he kindled it anew / With love, which is as fire" (PU.III.iii.149–151). Love, fire, music, and motion—that is, intense creativity based on feeling and affection—are aspects and ema- nations of both Shelley's unseen Power and Blake's Poetic Genius or Human Imagination. Blake sets forth his final great poem *Jerusalem* under the aspect of fire and love in the hope that the reader, through these tranfiguring forces, can share in his own perceptions of oneness: "I also hope the Reader will be with me, wholly One in Jesus our Lord, who is the God of Fire and Lord of Love" (J.3, p. 621). In other words, God becomes a name for the flowing of regenerative energy into all things, "as each mass may bear." And to the imaginative eye, even the "particle of dust" contains this energy. "Then tell me, what is the material world, and is it dead?" Blake asks the Fairy in *Europe*, whom he catches within a "streak'd tulip" and takes home in his hat—a delightfully small creature who sits upon Blake's table and dictates that poem to the Poet:

> He, laughing, answer'd: "I will write a book on leaves of flowers,
> If you will feed me on love-thoughts & give me now and then
> A cup of sparkling poetic fancies; so, when I am tipsie,
> I'll sing to you to this soft lute, and shew you all alive
> The world, where every particle of dust breathes forth its joy." (E.III.14–18)

Music, love, poetry and song to both Blake and Shelley are conditions for seeing "all alive / The world."[41]

"In the long run men hit only what they aim at," states Thoreau in *Walden*. "Therefore, though they should fail immediately, they had better aim at something high." In attempting to eradicate the evil selfhood within themselves and so destroy the inner seed out of which the tyrant sprouts in all his forms (for both poets tried to live by the conduct they stressed in their poetry), Shelley and Blake aimed at something high. And though they did sometimes fail, this should not, as Reiman points out in connection with Shelley, "blind one to either the nobility of the attempt or the considerable measure of his success."[42] In getting rid of the selfhood, one must forgive his own past sins as he does those of others, to keep from being bound to them; and ultimately he must also free himself from the collective chains: mankind's past of bloodshed and death. Only then will he be able to aid in the creation of the apocalyptic future. The final Chorus of *Hellas*, in which Shelley hazards the exercise of his bardic prophetic faculty, looks forward to such a time:

> Oh, cease! must hate and death return?
>   Cease! must men kill and die?
> Cease! drain not to its dregs the urn
>   Of bitter prophecy.
> The world is weary of the past,
> Oh, might it die or rest at last! (*Hellas*, 1096–1101)

Blake early donned his vatic mantle—a light lyric one:

> In futurity
> I prophetic see
> That the earth from sleep
> (Grave the sentence deep)

Shall arise and seek
For her maker meek;
And the desart wild
Become a garden mild (p. 112)

—that later lengthened into the sonorous rhythms of *Jerusalem:*

Awake, Awake, Jerusalem! O lovely Emanation of Albion,
Awake and overspread all Nations as in Ancient Time;
For lo! the Night of Death is past and the Eternal Day
Appears upon our Hills. Awake, Jerusalem, and come away! (J.97:1–4)

Chapter Five
The Golden Chalice

and yet I feel
Most vain all hope but love; and thou art far,
Asia! who, when my being overflowed,
Wert like a golden chalice to bright wine
Which else had sunk into the thirsty dust.
(PU.I.807–811)

Blake and Shelley's similar ideas of the selfhood as revealed in the tyrant father, priest, king, and God are striking, but the two poets reveal an even greater affinity in their concepts of sexual love, its function and meaning, and the quality of the relationship that should, they believe, obtain between the sexes.

Blake sees Woman in her highest aspect as the Emanation of Man. That is, in Eternity Albion is androgynous and his perfectly blended feminine portion, Jerusalem, *emanates* from him as his artistic creations, his mental "children," and the unfallen form of what is called "Nature" in the world of Generation—the fallen world man sees with his caverned five senses. In Albion's fall Jerusalem takes on the form of Vala, the natural world. Sexual selfhood (i.e., evil) is revealed in the fact that this outer world becomes "veiled" to Albion (hence Vala's name), closed off from him through virginity and secrecy—the "female Will" created through the separation of Albion's masculine and feminine components which were one in Eternity. Vala then constricts further into Rahab and Tirzah.

Shelley's idea of the epipsyche, the feminine aspect of the male psyche, is very much like Blake's Emanation. She is man's "ideal proto-type" of excellence. She appears in Cythna in *The Revolt of Islam*, Emily in *Epipsychidion* and Asia in *Prometheus Unbound*. There are many points of comparison between the Emanation and the epipsyche, as well as dissim-ilarities, for Shelley's notions of woman often differ radically from Blake's. Unlike Cythna and Asia, Emilia Viviani, the epipsyche of *Epipsychidion,* was a real woman as well as a manifestation of the epi-psyche; therefore, it is very nearly impossible to discuss *Epipsychidion* without reference to Shelley's biography. However, I have relegated most of these references to footnotes in which the curious reader may follow up almost endless discussions among Shelley's critics regarding the intricate symbolism of the poem (the comet, the moon, the sun, for example)—an aspect of the poem and its biographical meaning that I have chosen to ignore for this reason.

"In Eternity," states Blake, "Woman is the Emanation of Man; she has No Will of her own. There is no such thing in Eternity as a Female Will" (VLJ, p. 613). The Emanation's duty is to delight, love, soothe, inspire, and otherwise gratify the "Male Genius," giving him her handmaidens as freely as she does herself, for in man's unfallen condition love knows nothing of possessiveness, jealousy, or secrecy. The Emanations (they too become plural when Albion chooses to behold multitude) live only for their male consorts and have no separate lives of their own. Blake often depicts them as residing "separately" in their land of Beulah, which surrounds Eden, where they can repose away from the strong intellectuality of Eden. However, Beulah and Eden are never closed to each other. In *Milton* the Emanations state that they cannot endure the "great Wars of Eternity"—that is, its intense, mental, artistic activity—and beg their fathers and brothers in Eden to create for them a "Temporal Habitation," Beulah, where they can obey the words of Man as Man obeys Jesus—a most Miltonic idea despite Blake's other "corrections" of Milton. Though the Emanations say they are "but for a time & . . . pass away in winter" (M.30:19–31), yet "they revive in spring with music and songs" (FZ.1:67), and Beulah "is evermore Created around Eternity, appearing / To the Inhabitants of Eden around them on all sides." Beulah, to those inside, appears "As the beloved infant in his mother's bosom round incircled / With arms of love & pity & sweet compassion." Since this love is one of the primary functions of Beulah, the Sons of Eden find it, when they tire of their thunderous intellectual wars in Eden, "a mild & pleasant Rest" (M.30:8–14).

To Blake, "the female life lives from the light of the male" (p. 82). Therefore, Beulah is always associated with the soft moon and its somewhat delusive, though lovely, borrowed light (J.17:27), in contrast to the blazing, strong, well-defined, masculine sun of creativity in Eden. Beulah possesses "moony shades & hills" (M.30:5), and "moony habitations" (M.30:13). It is "Pure, mild and Gentle" (FZ.1:96), "merciful" (J.17:28), "shadowy" (J.48:19), and filled with flowers (FZ.7a:239) and soft couches for repose (FZ.9:558;M.34:10). In Beulah,

> every Female delights to give her maiden to her husband:
> The Female searches sea & land for gratifications to the
> Male Genius, who in return clothes her in gems & gold
> And feeds her with the food of Eden; hence all her beauty beams.
> She Creates at her will a little moony night & silence
> With Spaces of sweet gardens & a tent of elegant beauty,
> Closed in by a sandy desart & a night of stars shining

And a little tender moon & hovering angels on the wing;
And the Male gives a Time & Revolution to her Space
Till the time of love is passed in ever varying delights. (J.69:15–24).[1]

Beulah, as the world immediately below and around Eden, is in this way sexually (emotionally) organized through threefold vision. On the other hand, Eden is humanly (imaginatively) organized through four-fold vision (p. 818). Though in Beulah "Contrarieties [Male and Female] are equally True" (M.30:1), Blake considers that a separation nevertheless exists between them. When Albion perceives with fourfold vision—or when one of the Sons of Eden ascends from Beulah back into Eden—his Emanation is completely at one with him: the sexual is consumed into the human. Jerusalem asks Vala (one of the fallen forms of Jerusalem herself) why she separates the masculine from the feminine, "hardening against the heavens / To devour the Human! Why dost thou weep, upon the wind among / These cruel Druid Temples? O Vala! Humanity is far above / Sexual organization & the visions of the Night of Beulah" (J.79:71–74).

Blake often depicts Albion under the form of the "Eternals" or the "Sons of Eden" (when Albion chooses to contract his infinite senses, he sees multitude), and so there are many Emanations in Eden—all, of course, Jerusalem multiplied. They "emanate" from the deepest, innermost soul of the Sons of Eden, as Beulah itself does, and they and their children in one sense represent the loving, affective, artistic creations of masculine intellect. Only through the feminine Emanation, through love, can one man be joined to another:

When in Eternity Man converses with Man, they enter
Into each other's bosom (which are Universes of delight)
In mutual interchange, and first their Emanations meet
Surrounded by their Children; if they embrace & comingle,
The Human Four-Fold Forms mingle also in thunders of Intellect:
But if the Emanations mingle not, with storms & agitations
Of earthquakes & consuming fires they roll apart in fear. (J.88:2–8)

If the feminine Emanations embrace with affection, masculine "thunders of Intellect" can take place, for "Man is adjoin'd to Man by his Emanative portion / Who is Jerusalem in every individual Man" (J.44:38–39). In other words, affection or love is the foundation for true creation, perception, or wholeness. This perfect blend of the masculine-feminine Blake calls "androgynous"; the imperfect, evil combination he terms "hermaphroditic," for the latter implies opposites existing in one form or being but unreconciled and inharmonious. For example, Satan (the name of any error or sin), is "hermaphroditic" (FZ.8:103–105;251). Thus, the androgynous feminine and masculine quality is simply an aspect of Albion himself. Like Good and Evil, the male and female principles are not separate entities, and if separated (as they are in the fall), they war hermaphroditically against each other and against Albion:

> The Feminine separates from the Masculine & both from Man,
> Ceasing to be His Emanations, Life to Themselves assuming. (J.90:1–2)

When Albion becomes divided from his Emanation, he becomes a "dark Spectre" (J.53:25)—that is, he is ruled entirely by reason and the selfhood. Thus, Los must admonish his Spectre not to reason against the "dear approach" of his children, "Nor them obstruct with thy temptations of doubt & despair." He states that he breaks the "brazen fetters" of Shame, for to the Spectre, Los's children—the fiery creations of the imagination—are "Sins." Instead, the Spectre wishes to offer Los's children on the altar of the Urizenic God (J.10:37–39). In "A Vision of the Last Judgment" (only drawings remain of this lost or destroyed painting), Blake depicted "Jesus . . . surrounded by Beams of Glory in which are seen all around him Infants emanating from him; these represent the Eternal Births of Intellect from the divine Humanity" (VLJ, p. 613). Such "Eternal births" the Spectre attempts to destroy.

On many occasions, Albion, under the influence of the Reasoning Spectre, also sees his children as "sins" (an idea that Los must combat within Albion as well as for himself), but Jerusalem takes their part. She tells Albion, "all thy little ones are holy; / They are of Faith & not of Demonstration" (J.31:45–46). These "little ones" represent any imaginative, energetic, passionate creation of beauty in the arts; any adornment or grace of the soul; any "mental gift" of genius existing in another (MHH.22–24, p.158); inspiration or vision (DC, p. 579); and "Gifts of the Spirit" (VLJ, p. 613). Blake states that the "Gifts of the Gospel" are "Mental Gifts," that "to Labour in Knowledge is to Build up Jerusalem. . . . He who despises & mocks a Mental Gift in another, calling it pride & selfishness & sin [as the Spectre does] mocks Jesus the giver of every Mental Gift" (J.77, p. 717). Religion and art are one in the Tree of Life, the unified Tree that in the regeneration of Albion supplants the double Tree of Knowledge of Good and Evil. Thus, genius is the "Holy Ghost in Man" (J.91:10).[2] In his separation from his Emanation, however, Albion says: "All these ornaments are crimes, they are made by the labours / Of loves, of unnatural consanguinities and friendships / Horrid to think of when enquired deeply into" (J.28:6–8). The former fiery blendings through love and through the Emanations that occur among the Sons of Eden creating "Thunders of Intellect" Albion now looks on as "unnatural" and "horrid." Consequently, "cold snows drifted around him: ice cover'd his loins around" (J.28:13). The energy contained in the loins is the same energy that pours out into artistic creation, into "children," "sons," "daughters," and "infants."

This correlation between the sex act that creates children and the mental act that creates art is no accident in Blake's poetry. He had few objections to Lavater's *Aphorisms on Man*, which he annotated, but he pointed out Lavater's mistake in not realizing that virtue consists in act, that evil is whatever hinders another (such as murder or theft). The "origin of this mistake in Lavater and his cotemporaries is, They suppose that Woman's Love is Sin; in consequence all the Loves & Graces with them are Sin" (p. 88). Enion, the Emanation of the Zoa Tharmas (who represents sensation) in the fall and separation of the Zoas from Albion, finds that in destroying Tharmas' "loves and Graces" she has in reality destroyed her own children:

> I thought Tharmas a sinner & I murder'd his Emanations,
> His secret loves and Graces. Ah me wretched! What have I done?
> For now I find that all those Emanations were my Children's souls. (FZ.1.163–165)

Therefore, despite their lower position, the Emanations are vitally necessary to maintain Eden and their male consorts in a state of unity. Without them, the Sons of Eden (or Albion) would be unable to create the "children" of the imagination, to build up Jerusalem, or to possess any loves and graces, any mental gifts. In the fall, of course, the Emanations themselves—as Enion indicates—also tend to view these creations as sinful.

In Blake's myth, Jerusalem—both a city and a woman—is the feminine Emanation, consort or counterpart of Albion (as Beulah, where the females live, is the Emanations of the masculine land of Eden). Blake specifically identifies Jerusalem with light, liberty, and forgiveness. In Eternity, the divine forms are masculine (when considered as Albion or Jesus, of course, they are one rather than many), and each form is surrounded by his Emanation, a garment of light:

> In Great Eternity every particular Form gives forth or Emanates
> Its own peculiar Light, & the Form is the Divine Vision
> And the Light is his Garment. This is Jerusalem in every Man,
> A Tent & Tabernacle of Mutual Forgiveness, Male & Female Clothings.
> And Jerusalem is called Liberty among the Children of Albion. (J.54:1–5)

In Albion's fall from Eternity, Jerusalem separates from him—one of the many divisions that occur as a result of Albion's acceptance of Urizen's "wat'ry vision" of himself. In Los's words, this division constitutes spiritual death: "Albion is dead! his Emanation is divided from him!" (J.12:6). As Good and Evil divide from their eternal state as "contraries" (a division symbolized by the Tree of Knowledge of Good and Evil) and then harden into abstractions and generalizations, so too the feminine portion, Jerusalem, of the formerly androgynous Man separates from him to become not liberty, joy, love, inspiration, rest, renewal, light, and forgiveness (as she was in Eternity), but a cruel Female Will who torments him with jealousy, possessiveness, chastity, and secrecy: the selfhood in its sexual aspect. In Eden, there are no sexes, no division; there is nothing but the Human, the Divine Humanity, of which the Emanations are a part. "Sexes must vanish & cease / To be when Albion arises from his dread repose," states Los (J.92:13–14). In Albion's fall, however, "Jerusalem came down in a dire ruin over all the Earth" (FZ.2:45) as Vala or fallen Nature. Because of his consequent restriction to the caverned five senses with their single vision, Albion can no longer see this outer form as his inner one; it rolls before him like a huge polypus or serpent that refuses his control (J.29:80).

At times after his fall, Albion realizes what has happened to him, what it means to be without the loving Emanation who formerly made his life a paradise:

> O Jerusalem, Jerusalem, I have forsaken thy Courts,
> Thy Pillars of ivory & gold, thy Curtains of silk & fine
> Linen, thy Pavements of precious stones, thy Walls of pearls
> And gold, thy Gates of Thanksgiving, thy Windows of Praise,
> Thy Clouds of Blessing, thy Cherubims of Tender-mercy
> Stretching their Wings sublime over the Little-ones of Albion!
> O Human Imagination, O Divine Body I have Crucified,
> I have turned my back upon thee into the Wastes of Moral Law. (J.24:17–24)

This "Moral Law" is that found in Urizen's book of brass, and in giving consent to its precepts, Albion crucifies both the Divine Body and his Emanation, who cannot exist except in freedom. Jerusalem is both a city and an Emanation or Woman. (FZ.9:222), and such a city can be built only by imaginative effort emanating from Man, the Divine Humanity. In the fall, Babylon, the city of Vala, takes the place of Jerusalem.[3] Instead of praise, blessing and mercy, Albion now experiences groans, miseries, and destruction:

> But Albion is cast forth to the Potter, his Children to the Builders
> To build Babylon because they have forsaken Jerusalem.
> The Walls of Babylon are Souls of Men, her Gates the Groans
> Of Nations, her Towers are the Miseries of once happy Families,
> Her streets are paved with Destruction, her Houses built with Death. (J.24:29–33)

The Sons or Children of Albion acquiesce in this work: they combine into "three Immense Wheels turning upon one-another,"[4] crying out to cast forth Jerusalem "Our Father Albion's sin and shame" and instead "To build / Babylon the City of Vala, the Goddess Virgin-Mother. She is our Mother! Nature!" (J.18:13;28–30). Jerusalem is then forced to labor in the Satanic Mills, the dungeons of Babylon:

She sat at the Mills, her hair unbound, her feet naked
Cut with the flints, her tears run down, her reason grows like
The Wheel of Hand incessant turning day & night without rest,
Insane she raves upon the winds, hoarse, inarticulate. (J.60:41–44)

"Round my limbs," Jerusalem says to Vala, "I feel the iron threads of love & jealousy & despair" (J.31:48–49). Near the end of *The Four Zoas,* Vala in the form of Rahab has so far triumphed that Jerusalem has become her "Willing Captive, by delusive arts impell'd / To worship Urizen's Dragon form, to offer her own Children / Upon the bloody Altar" (FZ.8:598–600). Blake specifically associates Urizen's religion with Deism or natural religion, which he calls "Babylon again in Infancy" (FZ.8:620). However, at this very lowest point, hope arises for the release of Jerusalem and her reunion with Albion. For Urizen becomes a dragon form through his embrace of Rahab (false religion), the scarlet Whore spoken of by St. John the Divine, Blake's paradigm; and when error is solidified into its very lowest form, it can then be cast off. Urizen embraces "the shadowy Female" in the form of Rahab; at once scales cover his forehead, neck, bosom, hands, and feet, "And his immense tail lash'd the Abyss" (FZ.8:428). He no longer "bore the human form erect" (FZ.8:458). Only when he falls to this condition does Urizen realize that he has not derived his powers from himself, as he thought, but only from the Divine Humanity, and that he must repent, give up his selfhood, his books of brass and iron, and his attempt to control futurity. Only then can he reassume his human form (FZ.9:191–193).

As I have noted, the Emanation, Jerusalem, joins man to man in Eden. But when Albion falls, Vala, the "shadow" of Jerusalem "builded by the Reasoning power in Man" (J.44:40), by Urizen, takes her place and overspreads all the earth as Nature and as Babylon, the false religions Druidism and Deism (or "natural religion"). Thus Blake identifies Vala,[5] as a false religion, with the scarlet Whore of the Book of Revelation, who comes riding on the beast with seven heads, and "with whom the Kings of the earth have committed fornication" (Revelation 17:2):

Vala, drawn down into a Vegetated body, now triumphant.
The Synagogue of Satan Clothed her with Scarlet robes & Gems,
And on her forehead was her name written in blood, "Mystery."
When view'd remote she is One, when view'd near she divides
To multitude, as it is in Eden, so permitted because
It was best possible in the State called Satan to save
From Death Eternal & to put off Satan Eternally.
The Synagogue Created her from Fruit of Urizen's tree
By devilish arts, abominable, unlawful, unutterable,
Perpetually vegetating in destestable births
Of female forms, beautiful thro' poisons hidden in secret
Which give a tincture to false beauty; then was hidden within
The bosom of Satan The false Female, as in an ark & veil

Which Christ must rend & her reveal. Her daughters are call'd
Tirzah; She is named Rahab. (FZ.8:280–294)

If Vala solidifies into the Whore of Babylon, she can be seen as sin, error,
or mistake and be cast off. Vala is the fruit that grows on Urizen's tree of
mystery, the false religion instituted by the same kings of the earth that
St. John speaks of, a tree that shoots up from under Urizen's heel
wherever he sits or a net or web he draws behind him. The precepts of
this religion he writes down in his books of brass and iron. And, as we
have seen in the previous chapter, both Urizen and Vala operate in
concert to bring about Albion's fall from Eternity. Vala is indeed "built"
by Urizen. She is the "false female" because her Babylonian, Druidic
religion preaches the separation of the female (virginity) from the male
"as in an ark & veil." To Blake, this constitutes her "whoredom": her
Urizenic purity. The secret, constricted, cruel, selfish, possessive, jealous
qualities associated with Vala are "virgin" ones. They are "false" female
qualities because they are unknown to the Emanations in Beulah, who
delight in openness and freedom. It is important to keep this distinction
in mind; otherwise one might think Blake was excoriating woman
herself or the female principle as an attribute of the universal man
Albion. On the contrary, the Sons of Eden themselves cannot blend in
masculine, brotherly, and intellectual love unless their Emanations and
their children first blend in feminine, maternal, and emotional love.

In the fallen world, however, Jerusalem as Vala hides herself in an
"ark" or "veil" of virginity, the sexual selfhood. Erin, a character in
Jerusalem who represents imagination, states that such "veiling" is one of
the greatest evils, for in its selfishness it murders the Divine Humanity:

> By Laws of Chastity & Abhorrence I am wither'd up:
> Striving to Create a Heaven in which all shall be pure & holy
> In their Own Selfhoods: in Natural Selfish Chastity to banish
>   Pity
> And dear Mutual Forgiveness, & to become One Great Satan
> Inslav'd to the most powerful Selfhood: to murder the Divine
>   Humanity. (J.49:26–30)

Vala, however, strives for just such Urizenic purity and holiness. Like
Urizen, she is constantly prying after sin or the double Tree. She tells
Jerusalem:

> we have found thy sins; & hence we turn thee forth
> For all to avoid thee, to be astonish'd at thee for thy sins,
> Because thou art the impurity & the harlot, & thy children,
> Children of whoredoms, born for Sacrifice, for the meat & drink
> Offering, to sustain the glorious combat & the battle & war,
> That Man may be purified by the death of thy delusions. (J.31:61–66)

Man cannot be purified (in the true sense) by sacrifice for sin, but only by forgiveness of sin, the religion of Jesus. While Albion slumbers on his oozy rock, the "Druids demanded Chastity from Woman & all was lost." But Los knows they are wrong:

> How can the Female be Chaste, O thou stupid Druid, Cried Los,
> Without the Forgiveness of Sins in the merciful clouds of Jehovah
> And without the Baptism of Repentance to wash away Calumnies and
> The Accusations of Sin, that each may be Pure in their Neighbours'
>   sight? (J.63:26–29)

Thus, Blake uses virginity to symbolize whatever is hidden, constricted, or selfish—qualities the female acquires in the Fall and only in the Fall. Vala's veil is the same as that "which Satan puts between Eve & Adam, / By which the Princess of the Dead enslave their Votaries / Teaching them to form the Serpent of precious stones & gold" (J.55:11–13). This is, of course, the same Urizenic "serpent religion" I have discussed in the preceding chapter. Such a religion could not exist except for the veil—the separation—between Eve and Adam, between Albion's Emanation and himself and between man and woman. Urizen and Vala thus derive the energy for their engines of torment from the suppression of libidinous energy. When this energy flows into "children" (art), Urizen, Vala and their various manifestations consider it one of the greatest sins. Before Milton can become whole—before he can become a true creator—his Emanation Ololon must put aside her virginity: the Satanic veil. Only then can she be united to him (M.42:3–6).

This veil cast over truth must be rent; the error of Urizen and Vala must be exposed; the temple of the Divine Humanity must be revealed. Circumcision represents this freeing of energy, an opening, a revelation, a masculine cutting away of the evils of a feminine secrecy: "Establishment of Truth depends on destruction of Falsehood continually, / On Circumcision, not on Virginity" (J.55:65–66). When Vala hears Jerusalem's lamentation from her Babylonian dungeon,

> she triumphs in pride of holiness
> To see Jerusalem deface her lineaments with bitter blows
> Of despair, while the Satanic Holiness triumph'd in Vala
> In a religion of Chastity & Uncircumcised Selfishness. (J.60:45–48)

"Since 'Outward Ceremony' is Antichrist," observes Edward J. Rose, "Blake reconceives the physical act or religious rite of circumcision as a mental or esthetic act of art or vision. An 'Uncircumcised' anything is, therefore, anything from which an 'Incrustation' or 'false Body' has not been 'put off & annihilated.' "[6] Specifically, in the present context, the "false Body" is Vala and her mystery religion based on virginity or female secrecy. Such a "Satan"—as Blake often terms it (i.e., a state of error)—must be "circumcised," revealed for what it really is by the masculine imagination, through artistic endeavor, through giving up the selfhood, through any action based on the perception of oneness rather than division, and so replacing the double Tree with the unified Tree. The imaginative Erin, who sees the forthcoming regeneration when the false body will be put off, speaks of the "cruel holiness . . . of Chastity & Uncircumcision" (J.49:64). The Warriors in *Jerusalem* who are "drunk with unsatiated love" because "the Virgin has frown'd and refus'd" (J.68:62–63), speak of Vala's "tabernacle & . . . ark & secret place" (J.68:15). They are torn in opposite directions, much as man is when he eats of the Tree of Knowledge of Good and Evil: "Sometimes I curse & sometimes bless thy fascinating beauty," the Warriors say of Vala (J.68:64). In "The Sick Rose" the worm destroys the rose with its "dark secret love" (p. 213), just as in the closed ark behind the veil in the serpent temples of the Urizenic mystery religion the "pompous High Priest" enters by "a Secret Place." In Eden, there is no secrecy, and "Embraces are Cominglings from the Head even to the Feet" (J.69:43–44).

This relation of sex to what he called false religion is not gratuitous in Blake's poetry. Only by circumscribing sexual energy can Urizen, Vala, Rahab, and Tirzah maintain their religion at all. This is amply demonstrated in Urizen's use of engines of torment and the Stone of Trial on which Luvah is sacrificed. Those who follow this religion's rules and suppress their energies turn out to be warriors and sadists. Blake, in showing the necessary connection between the suppression of libidinous energy and its rise into either war or sadomasochism, reveals a psychological insight, based on intuition, whose time had not yet generally come. Freud, of course, has given us most of our terminology, but this connection has been expressed with great simplicity and clarity by Erich Fromm:

It would seem that the amount of destructiveness to be found in individuals is proportionate to the amount to which expansiveness of life is curtailed. By this we do not refer to individual frustrations of this or that instinctive desire but to the thwarting of the whole of life, the blockage of spontaneity of the growth and expression of man's sensuous, emotional, and intellectual capacities. Life has an inner dynamism of its own; it tends to grow, to be expressed, to be lived. It seems that if this tendency is thwarted the energy directed toward life undergoes a process of decomposition and changes into energies directed toward destrucion. In other words: the drive for life and the drive for destruction are not mutually independent factors but are in a reversed interdependence. The more the drive toward life is thwarted, the stronger is the drive toward destruction; the more life is realized, the less is the strength of destructiveness. *Destructiveness is the outcome of unlived life.*[7]

In a similar manner, Wilhelm Reich describes the "armored organism" and the distortion of blocked biological energies:

The armored organism is essentially different from the unarmored one in that a rigid wall is erected between its biological core, from which all natural impulses stem, and the world in which it lives and works. As a result every natural impulse, particularly the natural function of and capacity for love, is impeded. The living core of the armored organism has retained its impulses, but they can no longer find free expression. *In the desperate attempt "to express itself," every natural impulse is forced to penetrate or break through the wall of the armoring. The impulse must use force to reach the surface and the goal.* While the impulse is trying to overcome the armoring by force, it is transformed into a destructive rage, regardless of its original nature. It does not matter what happens to this secondary rage reaction later, after passing through the armor; whether it spends itself or is inhibited, whether it turns into morbid self-pity or reaches its goal as undisguised sadism: *the core of the process is the transformation of all love impulses into destructiveness while passing through the armor.* To repeat: it is the effort to express itself naturally and reach its goal that converts every basic biological impulse into destructiveness. In the process, the total being of the armored person acquires a characteristic that can only be described as hardness or disharmony.[8]

Because of such blocking and suppression, torture and suffering are two primary characteristics of both Blake's poetry and designs—an emphasis that was not understood in his own day. Blake maintains that in the world of Generation, the caverned world we ordinarily see, "Holy Love" (i.e., Urizenic "love") is nothing more than "Envy, Revenge & *Cruelty*" (my emphasis), and these qualities are partly responsible for Albion's fall: they "separated the stars from the mountains, the mountains from Man, / And left Man, a little grovelling Root outside of Himself" (J.17:30–32).

From the seemingly impregnable stronghold of her suppressed energy, the female torments man (or men, depending on the context) with a chaste unattainability, with revenge and cruelty. She attempts to curb the male's energy, which poses a threat to her supremacy. The "Females of Amalek," for example—Tirzah, Noah, Malah, Milcah and Hogla—bind the males down on stones of torture. These five sisters were the daughters of Zelophehad in the Old Testament (Numbers 26:33;27:1–7). Because Zelophehad left no male heir, the daughters were given his inheritance. Thus, as S. Foster Damon notes, the sisters symbolize to Blake the Female Will,[9] especially Tirzah, who is the speaker here:

Go, Noah, fetch the girdle of strong brass, heat it red hot,
Press it around the loins of this expanding cruelty.
Shriek not so, my only love.
Bind him down, sisters, bind him down on Ebal, mount of cursing.

Malah, come forth from Lebanon, & Hoglah from Mount Sinai,
Come circumscribe this tongue of sweets, & with a screw of iron
Fasten this Ear into the Rock. Milcah, the task is thine.
Weep not so, sisters, weep not so; our life depends on this.
Or mercy & truth are fled away from Shechem & Mount Gilead,
Unless my beloved is bound upon the stems of Vegetation. (FZ.8:312–321)

The sisters use the Urizenic metals iron and brass for this binding; and like Urizen himself they believe they are doing what is necessary not only for their own preservation (for one "dies" in fire when he gives up the selfhood in Eden) but so that "mercy and truth" may obtain. Here as elsewhere, Blake reveals his subtlety in having all his Urizenic characters—and especially Urizen himself—desire only the good. Such a desire, of course, can lead to far greater evil than a simple live-and-let-live attitude of self-indulgence, as I noted when considering Shelley's Count Cenci. In this, as in so much else, Blake shows the powers of several modern psychologists combined. Rather than burning in the fire of his own self-annihilation (the unquenchable burnings of the Eternals), one who believes he is "right" burns others instead—he becomes what Blake calls the Wicker Man of Scandinavia. And Vala, Rahab and Tirzah and their various manifestations or representatives all believe in their own righteousness.

In addition, Tirzah addresses the male she is torturing as "my only love," which recalls Urizen's search for one law, one command, one joy, resulting in "One law for the lion and ox is oppression." In Blake's view, cruelty seems to be the inevitable result of restriction, and especially any restriction placed upon an energy that flows freely in its eternal, unconditional state. Oothoon in *Visions of the Daughters of Albion,* a Blakean woman of the highest type, asks, "How can one joy absorb another? are not different joys / Holy, eternal, infinite?" (VDA.5:5–6). Los points out that in the fall "the affectionate touch of the tongue is clos'd in by deadly teeth, / And the soft smile of friendship, & the open dawn of benevolence / Become a net & a trap, & every energy render'd cruel" (J.43:24–26). Sexual energy, creative energy is rendered especially cruel since it is most restricted: the more Rahab and Tirzah attempt to bind it, the more violently it rises into their forms of torture on the Druid Stone. For, as Fromm has noted, if energy is thwarted in its attempt to expand, "it undergoes a process of decomposition and changes into energies directed toward destruction." But Tirzah and her sisters do not understand this connection and believe that they are *preserving* life and truth: the virgin refuses and the warriors rush to war.

According to Los this false Female Will as seen in Vala, Rahab, and Tirzah (the fallen form of Jerusalem) usurps the throne in Man that should be occupied by the Divine Humanity. One should note Los's contention that Albion himself is responsible for the creation of this will (in his fall) and, further, that Los is not speaking of the true Emanation but of her fallen manifestation:

> There is a Throne in every Man, it is the Throne of God;
> This, Woman has claim'd as her own, & Man is no more!
> Albion is the Tabernacle of Vala & her Temple,
> And not the Tabernacle & Temple of the Most High.
> O Albion, why wilt thou Create a Female Will?
> To hide the most evident God in a hidden covert, even
> In the shadows of a Woman & a secluded Holy Place,
> That we may pry after him as after a stolen treasure . . .
>
> Is this the Female Will, O ye lovely Daughters of Albion, To
> Converse concerning Weight & Distance in the Wilds of Newton &
>   Locke? (J.34:27–34;39–40)

The fallen Female Will can be eradicated (Vala can be raised to Jerusalem) by the various efforts of Losian creativity. She can also be overcome much as Albion finally asserts his will over Urizen with the threat of the latter's destruction (FZ.9:151–157). For example, the "Divine Voice" in *Milton* declares that when he first married the "Daughter of Babylon" (who was Jerusalem in Eternity), she was "lovely, mild & gentle" but has since become jealous and "cut off my loves in fury till I have no love left for thee" (M.33:4–7). Therefore, the male may make the Emanation give up her possessiveness by ceasing to love *her* as well as all other females (for this is where her jealousy arises, since the Emanation does not understand that if she restricts her consort he will not love her either). This is how Milton convinces his sixfold Emanation Ololon to relent and abjure her selfishness, for if she does not she herself cannot exist:

> When the Sixfold Female percieves that Milton annihilates
> Himself, that seeing all his loves by her cut off, he leaves
> Her also, entirely abstracting himself from Female loves
> She shall relent in fear of death; She shall begin to give
> Her maidens to her husband, delighting in his delight. (M.33:14–18)

Blake's concept of the Emanation, who functions both as Jerusalem and Vala, has much in common with Shelley's idea of the epipsyche, the "soul of my soul," as James A. Notopoulous translates Shelley's title "Epipsychidion."[10] In his "Essay on Love" Shelley defines the epipsyche in the following way:

> We dimly see within our intellectual nature a miniature as it were of our entire self, yet deprived of all that we condemn or despise, the ideal prototype of every thing excellent or lovely that we are capable of conceiving as belonging to the nature of man. Not only the portrait of our

external being but an assemblage of the minutest particles of which our nature is composed; a mirror whose surface reflects only the forms of purity and brightness; a soul within our soul that describes a circle around its proper paradise which pain, and sorrow, and evil dare not overleap.[11]

Like the Emanations in Beulah, Emily, the epipsyche of the Poet in *Epipsychidion*, is "a beloved light / A Solitude, a Refuge, a Delight" (EPI.64–65). The epipsyche differs from the Emanation, however, in that the former reflects only the best and highest in her male counterpart, whereas the Emanation reflects the highest in her unfallen form only—Jerusalem. In the fall, the Emanation becomes Vala (fallen Nature) and Rahab and Tirzah (mystery religion and restrictive moral law), and far from describing a circle that shuts out pain, sorrow, and evil, she actively creates these in her quest for domination (a "Female Will"). Cythna in *The Revolt of Islam*, Emily in *Epipsychidion*, and Asia in *Prometheus Unbound* are examples of the Shelleyan epipsyche in her highest form. Each one is "the ideal prototype of every thing excellent or lovely that we are capable of conceiving as belonging to the nature of man."

Cythna in *The Revolt of Islam*—though Shelley does not use the term *epipsyche* itself—functions as Laon's "second self" or "shadow" (RI.II.xxiv.874–875), although, unlike the Emanation, she is equal to Laon in all respects. Cythna's thoughts are the same as Laon's (RI.II.xxxi.940): he sees his own mind in hers (RI.II.xxxii.948), and she refers to him as the "brother of my soul" (RI.II.xlvii.1083). When Laon looks into a pool of water after his great spiritual suffering (lasting seven years) for having killed three of the tyrant's men, he still sees Cythna's image in the reflection of his lined and hollow face (RI.IV.xxx). It is this inner image that seems to shed a light round his path as he sets forth again on his mission of peace (RI.IV.xxxiv). In the same way, Jerusalem clothes the masculine forms in Eden with a garment of light. Without such a beacon, Laon could not accomplish his purpose; union with Cythna is of the utmost importance.

Cythna ingeniously indicates this close identity in her feeling about the child she has borne Othman. To her, the child looks like Laon (RI.VII.xviii), for Laon is the spiritual father. Shelley's description of Laon and Cythna's physical and spiritual union also illustrates their oneness. In their union their blood mingles "like fire" (RI.VI.xxxiv.2636); their spirits leap up in unison from the earth (RI.VI.xxxiv.2640); their entire beings blend into one "unutterable power" (RI.VI.xxxv.2643); their "restless frames" combine "in one reposing soul" (RI.VI.xxxvi.2658); and over their "blind mortality" they feel the shadow of "divine darkness" (RI.VI.xxxvii.2660–2661).

In the opening of *Europe* Blake indicates that the sense of touch, sex, is less restricted than the other senses, for the others are confined to the "cavern" of the head and thus closed in and unexpansive. Because the

sense of touch is still distributed over the entire body, it can become a
means of perception that is denied to the other senses in their fallen
condition. It can become centrifugal on its highest level: love. We have
been taught, however, that sight and hearing are the higher senses. But
Blake states in *The Marriage of Heaven and Hell* that the cherub who
guards the Tree of Life with his flaming sword can be commanded to
leave his post so that all things can "appear infinite and holy." Such a
command "will come to pass by an improvement of sensual enjoyment"
(MHH.14, p. 154). This "improvement" is essentially what Laon and
Cythna experience. The Fairy in *Europe* states that man could "pass out"
through this cleansed door of perception (MHH.14, p. 154), "but he will
not, / For stolen joys are sweet & bread eaten in secret pleasant"
(E.III.4–5). That is, man possesses the Urizenic notion of sex as "sin,"
something to be concealed (as Albion conceals his Emanation, his loves
and graces) and indulged in covertly (as in prostitution), if at all. Once
Urizen effectively suppresses this energy, he can use it for his wars and
for the tortures and blood sacrifice of his mystery religion, aided, of
course, by Rahab and Tirzah. Blake maintains that in Eden, however,
love is a commingling from head to feet (J.69:43), and Shelley defines
love as a communion "of our whole nature, intellectual imaginative, and
sensitive,"[12] a definition quite similar to Erich Fromm's statement that
man's full powers, "sensuous, emotional and intellectual," are necessarily
all related. Love connects man not only to his Emanation or epipsyche
but to other creatures as well. Through the power of love, man realizes
his oneness with all creation. Because Urizen suppresses this power, he
sees all things separated and no articulate voice comes to him from his
howling and constricted world. To Shelley, also, love is "the bond and
the sanction which connects not only man with man [as in Blake's Eden,
for example] but with everything which exists."[13]

   This is the total union that Laon and Cythna achieve[14] and that Shelley
desired to have with Emilia Viviani,[15] his "ideal prototype" in *Epipsychidion.* Despite Shelley's injunction to Emily (as he Anglicized her name) to
remain a "vestal sister" to his "dull mortality" (EPI.389–390), the final
section of the poem depicts a union on all levels as intense as that of
Laon and Cythna's:

> Our breath shall intermix, our bosoms bound,
> And our veins beat together; and our lips
> With other eloquence than words, eclipse
> The soul that burns between them, and the wells
> Which boil under our being's inmost cells,
> The fountains of our deepest life, shall be
> Confused in Passion's golden purity,
> As mountain-springs under the morning sun.
> We shall become the same, we shall be one
> Spirit within two frames. (EPI.565–574)

Because Emily is an actual woman as well as representative of the epipsyche, and because Shelley seems to be caught between his "Platonism" and his flesh, the poem causes some difficulties in interpretation. David Perkins, for example, finds such a combination, a "seeking to know mortality and eternity in one presence . . . highly unstable," and that the poem presents "a disunity almost grotesque."[16] Carlos Baker, however, maintains that *Epipsychidion* is not "an invitation to adulterous elopement," but that Emily is, "mainly, one more metaphor of the Shelleyan epipsyche."[17] Newman Ivey White contends that the love depicted in *Epipsychidion* is Platonic,[18] and Glenn O'Malley stresses it as a "spiritual union which represents the limit of [Shelley's] personal aspiration toward the ideal."[19] Joseph Barrell, on the other hand, sees *Epipsychidion* as "a poem of romantic love" and as an "idealization of passion" that is "medieval and romantic, not Platonic and Hellenic."[20] This confusion arises, as Peter Butter notes, because the poem exists on two levels: the personal—Shelley's relationship to the real Emily—and the generalized story of the lover's search for his epipsyche. "In so far as it was about Shelley and Emilia," Mr. Butter states,

> he wanted to say—what was quite true—that his relations with her were "Platonic," and that he did not intend them to be otherwise; on the other hand, in so far as it was about the lover's finding of his epipsyche, it was appropriate that he should be completely and in every way united with her.[21]

From the Blakean viewpoint, this explanation, though it resolves the dichotomy in Shelley's poem perhaps better than any other, constitutes another Urizenic division. As we have seen, Shelley had greater difficulty in resolving the problem of evil than Blake did because Shelley based much of his thought on reasoned discourse. So too, he apparently experienced greater difficulty, not so much in *seeing* the eternal within the finite and immortal love within the mortal frame, but in *maintaining*[22] his view once he had seen it. His struggle and disillusionment are evident from most of his late lyrics, many of them addressed to Jane Williams—perhaps another love that had been thwarted. In "Lines: When the Lamp is Shattered" he sees the human heart as a place where love is born and where it also dies, for the mortal vessel cannot sustain it:

> O Love! who bewailest
> The frailty of all things here,
>   Why choose you the frailest
> For your cradle, your home, and your
>   bier? (p. 668)

He records the indifference and lack of sympathy that he often received even from those with whom he was most intimate:

Away, away, from men and towns,
To the wild wood and the downs—
To the silent wilderness
Where the soul need not repress
Its music lest it should not find
An echo in another's mind. ("To Jane: The Invitation," p. 668)

He longed for "some world far from ours, / Where music and moonlight
and feeling / Are one" ("To Jane: The Keen Stars Were Twinkling,"
p. 673).

I think, however, despite the split in *Epipsychidion* between Emily the
real person he loved, and her aspect as the ideal prototype, the epipsyche—a split in which his relationship with the real woman was
"platonic" and his relationship to the epipsyche was total union—in the
final section of the poem all "levels" of love disappear, and Shelley's
description of the union of the psyche and the epipsyche is as universal-
ized as that of Laon and Cythna's or Prometheus and Asia's. For man is
not passionless at the end of Shelley's utopia in *Prometheus Unbound* (the
poem I take to be his definitive statement). As in *Epipsychidion*, passions
are refined into a "golden purity" along with the other faculties of soul.
But because of this discrepancy in *Epipsychidion* between the ideal and
the actual, Cythna is a more successful embodiment of the epipsyche
than Emilia.

In the original version (called *Laon and Cythna*) of *The Revolt of Islam*,
which Shelley withdrew at the request of his publisher, Laon and Cythna
were brother and sister as well as lovers. This was unacceptable to
Shelley's publisher and probably would have been to most of his readers.
In myth, however, it is simply a means by which the notion of oneness is
intensified. As Carl Grabo notes, incest is "a relationship expressive of
the Platonic conception of affinities, the two parts, masculine and feminine, of the integrated soul."[23] In Shelley's own words, incest was simply
"a very poetical circumstance."[24] Blake reveals the same propensity in his
myth by creating a variety of relationships between Albion and Jerusalem and her various forms: Vala, Brittannia (the personification of
England), and Rahab and Tirzah. Jerusalem is Albion's daughter
(J.22:19;48:22) and sister (J.23:11), the bride of the Lamb (J.27:6–
7;46:28), the sister and daughter of Vala (J.20:19). England is Brittannia
(J.94:20), Jerusalem and Vala (J.36:28). Vala herself is Albion's bride
and wife (J.33:39;63:7). And at least once Blake speaks of Brittannia as
the wife of Albion and Jerusalem as their daughter (VLJ, p. 609). The
females of this group descend further from Vala, who is Rahab (J.78:15–
16), into Tirzah, whose mother is Rahab (M.13:41;19:54). Vala (the
natural world) is the shadow of Jerusalem (J.44:39–40). In other words,
all these names represent the various ways in which Albion perceives his
Emanation. Her highest eternal form is Jerusalem, and to indicate her

oneness with Albion, she is daughter, wife and sister. Personified as England's "green & pleasant Land" (M.I.15), in which the Poet tried to build Jerusalem—his works of genius, his loves and graces—Blake calls her Brittannia. In the fall, she takes on the veiled form of Vala or Nature (hence, "natural" or false religion). Constricting further, she becomes Rahab and then Tirzah, her very lowest forms. These two are responsible for carrying out the dictates of Urizen's mystery religion based on "holiness," cruelty and the selfhood. Blake, however, does not mention any sexual acts of incest as such between his characters. Though Urizen may embrace Rahab, for example, one sees at once that such an action is not viewed in the usual sexual sense by Blake: it means that Urizen has become more restricted, more rational, more solidified. The various relationships between Albion and Jerusalem, Vala, Brittannia, Rahab and Tirzah are all aspects of Albion himself. Literal human relationships are used as symbols of Albion's integrity.

In addition to this symbolic use, incest preoccupied the Romantics for other reasons, as well. For example, in Shelley's *The Cenci* it indicates the *excess* of hate and selfishness, "that cynical rage which confounding the good & bad in existing opinions breaks through them for the purpose of rioting in selfishness & antipathy."[25] In Chauteaubriand's *René*, as well as in the Byronic hero, the forbidden proclivity toward incest removes him from lesser endowed mortals, for it intensifies his suffering and his already exquisitely refined sensibilities. "Il vaut mieux, mon cher René," his sister writes to him, "ressembler un peu plus au commun des hommes et avoir un peu moins de malheur." ("It is better, dear René, to resemble ordinary men a little more and be a little less unhappy.") Although this *mal du siècle* is one of the more striking aspects of Romanticism, Shelley's use of the theme in *Laon and Cythna*, as well as Blake's multirelated characters in the Prophetic Books, is, again, not Romantic "perversity" but an attempt to indicate the blended masculine-feminine character of the universe they perceived. A blood relationship compounded by a sexual one is the closest tie possible among human beings and thus came to stand for the essential oneness of the universe. In myth, such ties are the rule rather than the exception. In most primitive myths, the primordial male and female, the Sky-Father and the Earth-Mother, are almost always brother and sister (often mother and son) as well as husband and wife.[26] The Egyptian pair Osiris-Isis and the Greek Zeus-Hera are perhaps better known brother and sister, husband and wife combinations. Many gods were themselves bisexual (like Albion), for, as Mircea Eliade notes, "bisexuality was a mark of divinity for the primitive; it represented a formula (approximative, like most mythological formulae) of *totality*, of the *integration of opposites*, of the *coincidentia oppositorum*."[27] In Hinduism, the integration of the personality is symbolized by the union of the male god Shiva and his feminine counterpart Shakti. Through yoga, these two contrary principles are united within the body.[28] In the Kabbalah, the first hypostasis, Kether, of the En-Soph (God) is male-female. This female principle is termed the "Shekinah" and spoken of as daughter, mother, and sister, as well.[29] Instances could be multiplied almost indefinitely. Shelley's publisher, in his rejection of Shelley's first version of *The Revolt of Islam,* turned what Blake called allegoric and mental signification into the corporeal, although it must be admitted that Shelley had embodied the concept in two characters who are also literal human beings, unlike Blake's titanic characters. The fact remains, however, that Shelley's public would not have understood his use of incest in the original version of *The Revolt of Islam,* and for this reason: "When the mind is no longer capable of perceiving the metaphysical significance of a symbol," states Mircea Eliade, "it is understood at levels which become increasingly coarse."[30]

Like Emilia in *Epipsychidion* and Cythna in *The Revolt of Islam,* Asia in *Prometheus Unbound* may be considered a form of the Shelleyan epipsyche. Like Blake's Emanation, she cannot exist except in freedom and unselfishness, and Prometheus' curse on Jupiter, as in Albion's fall, has resulted in her separation from Prometheus. Carl Grabo notes: "evil is symbolized in the separation of the mind of man [Prometheus] from nature [Asia] with consequences disastrous to both."[31] In Blake's myth, nature as inwardly perceived (Jerusalem) becomes nature as outwardly perceived (Vala), and certainly with dire consequences. Asia has been exiled by Prometheus' "fall" to a "desolate and frozen" vale in the Indian Caucasus, which her "transforming presence" has turned into a paradise (PU.I.826–833). There, with no diminishing of her original loveliness, she awaits the word from her sister Oceanid, Panthea, that Prometheus has revoked his curse on Jupiter. Unlike the Blakean Emanation, Asia experiences no reduction from her highest state. It is interesting to note, however, that only the lesser manifestations of love, her sisters Panthea and Ione, can remain with Prometheus in his suffering. His curse seems to remove him from the highest form of his epipsyche, though Ione and Panthea, unlike Rahab and Tirzah, are his comforters, not tormentors. The Echoes who re-sound the words of Panthea's message to Asia from Prometheus—"Follow! Follow!"—explicitly recognize Asia's superiority: they tell Asia that she alone can awaken Demogorgon and so overthrow the evil power of Jupiter:

> In the world unknown
>   Sleeps a voice unspoken;
> By thy step alone
>   Can its rest be broken;
>   Child of Ocean! (PU.II.i.190–194)

Shelley makes no distinction between Asia's sexual relationship to Prometheus and her power to illumine the world with brotherly love: Eros and Agape blend. "There are no categories or levels of love in the poem," states Earl R. Wasserman; "the Platonic distinction between the heavenly and earthly Venuses customary in discussions of Shelley seem to me quite beside the point."[32] In this sense, *Prometheus Unbound* succeeds where *Epipsychidion* fails, and brings Shelley closer to Blake's vision in *Jerusalem*, in which Jerusalem is both Albion's Emanation and the bride of the Lamb. These divisions are all aspects of the Divine Humanity. Prometheus himself recognizes the sanctity on all "levels" of his relationship to Asia. Tied down on his frozen rock, he begins his movement of regeneration that will awaken and revive the entire earth, recalling that Asia,

> when my being overflowed,
> Wert like a golden chalice to bright wine
> Which else had sunk into the thirsty dust. (PU.I.809–811)

Wasserman notes that this passage is "implicitly sexual" but with "eucharistic overtones."[33] No other image, perhaps, could so tellingly reveal Shelley's attitude that ultimately all divisions are arbitrary. Like Jerusalem and Albion, Prometheus and Asia are necessary to each other: Asia must be reunited to Prometheus before the Spirit of the Hour can pour the music of the mystic shell down upon the earth. Panthea remarks that Asia's being would fade if it were not mingled with Prometheus' (PU.I.832–833). Similarly, Jerusalem is the lover of Albion, yet within each man (as his emanative portion) she represents the force in Eden by which the males themselves can be joined together.

Thus, though love may be expressed in different ways, as in the maternal and sexual love of Beulah or in the brotherhood of Eden (which is the highest type because within it the sexual becomes perfectly blended into the Human), all love is one. When Asia is transfigured through her love for Prometheus (a transfiguration that is dependent on Prometheus, for he must first cast off his hatred for Jupiter), and is about to be reunited to him, Panthea cannot endure the radiance of her beauty. And Panthea reveals that when Asia was born out of the sea, like Venus, and stood within her "veined shell,"

> love, like the atmosphere
> Of the sun's fire filling the living world,
> Burst from thee, and illumined earth and heaven
> And the deep ocean and the sunless caves
> And all that dwells within them. (PU.II.v.23;26–30)

When this love again flows out from Asia in her reunion with Prometheus, Panthea feels that not she alone seeks closeness to Asia, but
that "the whole world" has become one in sympathy with her: "Hearest
thou not sounds i' the air which speak the love / Of all articulate beings?
Feelest thou not / The inanimate winds enamoured of thee?"
(PU.II.v.34–37). Similarly, as *Jerusalem* closes all the living creatures of
the earth "Humanize" (J.98:44) and become articulate, "even Tree,
Metal, Earth & Stone," and Jerusalem flows outward from "All Human
Forms" as their Emanation (J.99:1–5), overspreading "all Nations as in
Ancient Time" (J.97:2). In the words of Demogorgon, Love rises like a
huge bird off the steep crag of agony and "folds over the world its
healing wings" (PU.IV.561).

This mystical blending of the universal male and female principles
indicates, in the words of Carl Grabo, the "union of man and nature."[34]
Both Jerusalem and Asia thus represent the outer, feminine form
(nature) of an inner masculine mind. Jerusalem emanates from Albion
as every beautiful form—his loves and graces—that he can conceive or
create; and as soon as Asia blends with Prometheus—as soon as she
activates Demogorgon and becomes the golden chalice in which the
bright wine of Prometheus' being can be contained so that his creativity
cannot be lost—the universe is transformed.

Chapter Six
Love Makes All Things Equal

I know
That Love makes all things equal: I have heard
By mine own heart this joyous truth averred:
The spirit of the worm beneath the sod
In love and worship, blends itself with God.
(EPI.125–129)

The Blakean Emanation and the Shelleyan epipsyche, despite certain differences, possess remarkable similarities, especially in their aspects as an outer, feminine nature (or receptacle) to which an inner, masculine mind of creativity stands in a complementary relationship. But neither Blake nor Shelley pauses on that height. Both have very definite, practical—often psychological—ideas about what should be the true relationship between the sexes. If woman's love is viewed as sinful (a notion that both poets oppose) and forced underground, a restrictive possessiveness takes hold of men in which marriage—and chastity for those who are unmarried—leads to prostitution and passion turns into lust. Such possessiveness is a form of the selfhood. Lust exists, in Blake's view, because man separates his body and soul, the physical and the spiritual, the "higher" and the "lower," instead of "marrying" them. Blake's and Shelley's views of sex differ not in their attempt to blend the soul and the body but in the fact that Shelley, unlike Blake, stresses the equality of women and men. The poets' concept of the holiness of sex—and indeed, of all expressions of energy—is based on the quality and nature of their perception. That is, like Blake's Ezekiel, they viewed *all* things, not just some, *sub specie aeternitatis*. All things are one through the power of love. In the view of both poets, man has suffered a failure of vision which they, in their poetry, attempt to correct.

In his fall, Albion finds it impossible to maintain his Emanation in her noble and magnanimous role as Jerusalem. Love turns into the desire for possession—the desire to own a piece of property—and passion turns into lust, the latter in Shelley's poetry often descending into actual rape (Othman-Cythna; Jupiter-Thetis; Cenci-Beatrice). Albion experiences great difficulty in his attempt to overcome the Female Will (Vala, Rahab, and Tirzah) of his own creation and to restore her to her original position as Jerusalem. Throughout most of *The Four Zoas* and *Jerusalem* he is almost completely under the sway of Vala, Urizen, Rahab, and Tirzah and their cruel mystery religion and moral law, which restricts energy as "sin."

Thus, one of the most evil results of the fall is that Albion accepts Urizen and Vala's divisions between higher and lower, spirit and body, man and nature, outer and inner, good and evil, masculine and feminine. In other words, Albion has eaten of the fruit of the Tree of Knowledge of Good and Evil and falls into separation, the "wat'ry vision" that Urizen has prepared for him. The formerly androgynous Albion, following Urizen and Vala's lead regarding the necessity of caution, concealment, and prudence, hides—or attempts to hide—his Emanation, Jerusalem, in jealous secret fears (J.4:33). What had existed in Eden and Beulah as his joys, desires, creations, loves, graces—whatever beauty had emanated from him—he now looks on as sin. The Zoas—Tharmas, Los, Urizen, Luvah—who are his personified faculties, also separate from Albion, constantly warring among themselves and with their now separate feminine Emanations, whose names are as follows: Enion (Tharmas); Enitharmon (Los); Ahania (Urizen); and Vala (Luvah).[1] For in Eden the Zoas are also androgynous and in the fall they too look upon their feminine Emanations as sins. After the fall, Tharmas states: "I know / That I have sinn'd & that my Emanations are become harlots" (FZ.1.54).

This attitude of brooding secretly on sin (or what one conceives to be sin) makes it impossible for the Emanation to remain with her consort. Tharmas has come to look on his creative acts—mental or sexual—his love and graces, as harlots, and therefore Enion cannot remain one with him: "I have look'd into the secret soul of him I lov'd," she says, speaking of Tharmas, "And in the Dark recesses found Sin & cannot return" (FZ.1.44–45). Thus cast out—as Albion and his sons cast out Jerusalem in favor of Babylon—the Emanation (because of the male's sense of her sin) becomes cruel, possessive, jealous, proud, chaste, and vindictive. Enitharmon, for example, tells Los, "be thou assured I never will be thy slave. / Let Man's delight be Love, but Woman's delight be Pride. / In Eden our loves were the same; here they are opposite" (J.87:15–17). In Eden and Beulah, the female delights to give her handmaiden to her husband, but in the fall Los and Enitharmon evince all the pernicious qualities of the sexual selfhood, especially jealousy and possessiveness. They will not permit each other the freedom they formerly enjoyed: "She drave the Females all away from Los, / And Los drave the Males from her away" (FZ.1.243–244). Blake repeats this line almost verbatim when he discusses the separation of Ahania from Urizen (FZ.2.209–210).

This restrictive possessiveness, in their usual inversion of Christian morality, both Blake and Shelley define as lust, which they distinguish from passion. In *Visions of the Daughters of Albion,* Oothoon, Blake's prototypical woman, a true Emanation, does not define lust as "the moment of desire" (VDA.7:3), which is open, free, vigorous and honest. Instead, lust exists when "she who burns with youth, and knows no fixed lot, is bound / In spells of law to one she loathes." Such a one turns "the wheel of false desire" (VDA.5:21–22;27). Elsewhere, as one might suspect, Blake connects what he considers lust with Urizenic holiness, secrecy, and hypocrisy: "The open heart is shut up in integuments of frozen silence / That the spear that lights it forth may shatter the ribs and bosom" (J.43:33–34). The "modest" rose of "The Lilly" in the *Songs of Experience,* who puts forth a thorn (as the "humble" sheep does a "threat'ning horn") was in Blake's first draft (p. 171) "the lustful rose"— lustful being deleted in favor of the more equivocal term in order to rouse the faculties to act by not being too explicit (p. 793). Why would a *modest* rose put forth a thorn? Is there any connection between concealment and pain? Blake's answer: modesty, like holiness, purity, and righteousness, is a Urizenic virtue; and as Northrop Frye points out, "prudery and prurience are much the same thing."[2] This is the connection that Blake wished to establish in his deletion of "lustful" for "modest." Vala, for example, is a "virgin-harlot"—a seeming contradiction at first glance until one realizes that, to Blake, virginity (any kind of "mystery" or "veiling") is an aspect of the selfhood, the great Satan. Oothoon, however, is not "modest"; she has no defenses; it is the modest-lustful rose who puts forth a thorn (i.e., pain is the inevitable result when energy is suppressed). If Oothoon's lover Theotormon would consent, Oothoon, like any Emanation in Beulah, would catch for him "girls of mild silver, or of furious gold" (VDA.7:24). She has been released from the bondage of "sin" and possessiveness. But Theotormon remains bound by the hypocritical Urizenic code which demands secrecy, "subtil modesty" (VDA.6:7), and caution—none of which Oothoon has shown. Moreover, on her way to offer herself openly and unselfishly to Theotormon, an attitude he cannot understand or accept, she is seized and raped by Bromion (who may be considered the personified Urizenic aspect of Theotormon himself). Consequently, Oothoon has become a "harlot" (VDA.I.18); for as soon as an idea becomes inflexible, it falls over into its opposite.[3] Thus, Vala is a virgin-harlot. Oothoon blames Urizen for imposing restraints upon Theotormon's mind: "O Urizen! Creator of men! mistaken Demon of heaven!" (VDA.5:3). Urizen has taught Theotormon to expect modesty or concealment, what Oothoon calls "This knowing, artful, secret, fearful, cautious, trembling hypocrite" (VDA.6:17).

In her sermon to the mariners in *The Revolt of Islam,* Cythna tells them "to live, as if to love and live were one" (RI.VIII.xii.3304), but like Oothoon she counsels against lust, which to both poets is the restrictive, rapacious force that chains one to his selfhood as in the case of Othman, or is an aspect of Urizenic cruelty (as in the torture of Luvah) resulting from the suppression of energy. But passion is the opposite of lust. When Othman rapes Cythna, for example, he is lustful, but passionless, for in passion the "above" (spiritual) and the "below" (material) are combined, as Blake's Ezekiel stated they should be. This distinction between passion and lust is quite similar to another that Joseph Wood Krutch makes between joy and pleasure:

> Pleasure, which we seek as a compensation for the joy we so seldom feel, is both worth less and harder to come by. It requires some positive occasion and adequate occasions become harder and harder to create. Pleasure sickens from what it feeds on, joy comes easier the more often one is joyous.[4]

One may see the difference by comparing Othman's rape of Cythna, in which "selfishness mocks love's delight" (RI.VII.vi.2876), and the final section of *Epipsychidion*, previously quoted, which Carl Grabo describes not as Platonic but as "a dream of love fulfilment in which the sensuous and the ideal are blent to passion."[5] There may indeed be pleasure in lust, but no joy and no beauty. In *Prometheus Unbound*, for example, Jupiter's "mingling," as he calls it, with Thetis is very much like Othman's rape of Cythna—or, one may presume, Cenci's of Beatrice; for Cenci's "greater point" is to annihilate Beatrice's soul, if he can, and such annihilation is precisely what Thetis experiences with Jupiter, as if her entire being were dissolved with poison, since Jupiter here as elsewhere reveals nothing but his tyrannical selfhood. "Insufferable might!" Thetis cries out,

> God! Spare me! I sustain not the quick flames,
> The penetrating presence; all my being,
> Like him whom the Numidian septs did thaw
> Into a dew with poison, is dissolved,
> Sinking through its foundations. (PU.III.i.37–42)

Such a coupling is what Shelley elsewhere terms a "cold-blooded and malignant selfishness of sensuality,"[6] and what Blake would no doubt call "hermaphroditic" rather than androgynous, the latter being for him a perfectly free, perfectly proportioned blending of masculine and feminine or male and female, depending on the context. In the penultimate plate (99) of *Jerusalem*, Albion embraces Jerusalem while she makes the joyous gesture (such is Blake's interpretation) of the crucifixion—outflung arms—which everywhere in Blake signifies the giving up of the selfhood—the greatest freedom and the highest happiness.

Melville wrote to Hawthorne that he refused to believe in a temperance heaven, and that he would smuggle in a basket of champagne if necessary to strike glasses with his friend. So, too, Blake refused a passionless, and therefore a joyless heaven. He told Crabb Robinson that there was sorrow in heaven, for where there was the possibility of joy there was the possibility of pain. As I have previously noted, Blake's Eden is a place of intense creative activity. "The Treasures of Heaven are not Negations of Passion," he asserted, "but Realities of Intellect, from which all the Passions Emanate Uncurbed in their Eternal Glory" (VLJ, p. 615). Similarly, Shelley keeps passion in his utopia at the end of *Prometheus Unbound.* Though man is "just, gentle, wise" (PU.III.iv.197) he has not been made so through castration of his emotional nature but through an intensification of it, through what Blake calls its "uncurbed" outpouring. Man is freed, however, from the "guilt or pain" (PU.III.iv.198) which almost always accompany passion before the regeneration. As the third act of *Prometheus Unbound* closes, women become "gentle radiant forms" who no longer fear to express their emotions. Like Blake's Emanation, they have no pride, jealousy, envy or shame (PU.III.iv.153–163). Yeats points out that in Blake's view, "Passions, because most living, are most holy . . . and man shall enter eternity borne upon their wings."[7] That is why in Blake's designs to his poems he depicts Urizen so often as a chained, bent, cold, restricted figure: he has denied the passionate wings, what Jerusalem calls the "Wings of Cherubim" (J.22:35) with which he might rise again into Eden.

Passion is a form of Blakean energy expressed in love, and just as Blake's emphasis on energy ("evil") made the Christian God into "Nobodaddy" for him, the same emphasis in this context renders orthodox Christianity—in which hell is not opened to heaven and opposites cannot be "married"—even more unacceptable. For the "Wheel of Religion" that Urizen creates is a "terrible devouring sword" based on the memory of sin, on sorrow and punishment (J.77:13–19), an aspect of Albion's (or Urizen's) fall. In this view, hell is forever closed to heaven: there can be no "marriage" of the contraries Good and Evil such as Blake describes in *The Marriage of Heaven and Hell.* Blake's definition of Christianity, on the other hand, is simply and solely "Forgiveness of Sins." Since all sins (for evil is a negative error or mistake only) may be forgiven, "Hell is open'd to Heaven" and the prisoners pour up out of the torturous dungeons of "Nobodaddy" (J.77:34–45). As Northrop Frye has noted in defense of Blake's position:

Orthodox theology tells us that in the eternal world the fires of hell have heat without light, and that heaven is a blaze of golden light, the question of heat being slurred over. Remembering that passion and desire are spiritual heat, such doctrines tell us symbolically that desires are hellish and that we shall be tortured forever for having them, whereas those who have emasculated their passions will be admitted to a heaven in which the kind of divine love they enjoy, while its exact nature is unknown, is certain to be something very, very pure.[8]

This "something very pure" is what Albion becomes in his fall, in contrast and contradiction to the usual Christian notion (Milton's, for example) of a fall into lust. Not only does Albion's fallen viewpoint (his "caverned" perception) freeze his own loins, but even the hills congeal into steadfast, stony, unexpansive forms. Stated quite simply, wherever Urizen sits, it snows. Actually, of course, Albion does fall into lust, but as in Blake's other definitions (pure, holy, righteous, virgin, and so on) lust is not the free expression of sexual energy, but a repression of it, especially when the repression takes a sadomasochistic turn, as in the Druid Stone of Trial where the howling victims are bound down and Tirzah passes her knife of flint over them.

Failure to distinguish between Blake's notion of lust and passion has led to a number of mistakes in the interpretation of his theories of sex. One of these mistakes is indicated in Helen C. White's *The Mysticism of William Blake*, in which she states:

> This protest [against chastity] has been warmly applauded by some of Blake's critics who seem to forget that no amount of purely physical intensity of living can quite approximate high spiritual quality of living, that these two ideals belong to two distinct regions which, while not necessarily incompatible under ideal conditions, are certainly hostile to each other when the gates that bar the road to excess are broken down.

In White's view, Blake's idea of sex is "abstract"; it has no humanity: "As one reads of the relations of Oothoon, Bromion, and Theotormon he feels as if he were reading of the loves of the algebraic symbols A and B."[9] This second objection to Blake's "abstraction" comes from expecting a quality in Blake's poetry that it does not possess and that he did not attempt to achieve. To expect characterization in the ordinary sense in Blake's poetry is to be disappointed. White's first objection, however, requires a fuller answer, since it indicates an erroneous division— "purely physical intensity" versus "high spiritual quality" made by both White and the critics she mentions, though she disapproves while they approve of this physical intensity.

Blake would have been surprised to learn that he advocated "purely physical intensity," since "that call'd Body is a portion of Soul discern'd by the five Senses, the chief inlets of Soul in this age" (MHH.4, p. 149). These two—the physical and the spiritual realms—are, White states, "certainly hostile to each other when the gates that bar the road to excess are broken down." Yet Blake affirms, "The road of excess leads to the palace of wisdom" (MHH.7:3), and, "If the fool would persist in his folly he would become wise" (MHH.7:18), for "foolishness" or "excessiveness," gone full circle, touches its contrary, just as "excess of joy is like

Excess of grief" (FZ.9:730). The separation "spiritual" and "physical" into "two distinct regions" that White makes, like all separations, comes about (in Blake's view) because one eats of the Tree of Knowledge of Good and Evil. Blake made no such distinctions, any more than he separated God and Man, man and woman, art and religion, marriage and harlotry, religion and politics, or dung and the perception of the infinite. (I shall discuss all these "opposites" at some length later in this chapter.) To Blake, there is no "progression" except by "marrying" contraries (MHH.3, p. 149), "for everything that works is grounded on its opposite,"[10] in the words of Jung.

White's division is the same separation that Blake's Thel believes to exist. Thel refuses to learn from the Cloud, the Clod of Clay, the Lilly, and the Worm that all life is one and therefore that life in all its manifestations—even the very "lowest"—is holy. God exists in all things. The Lilly in the "humble grass" is "visited from heaven" (BT.1:15;19); the Cloud's steeds "drink of the golden springs / Where Luvah doth renew his horses" (BT.3:7–8); the Clod of Clay, who speaks for the infant Worm, calls herself the "meanest thing" (BT.4:11), yet she becomes the Bride of God who pours oil upon her head and says: "Thou mother of my children, I have loved thee / And I have given thee a crown that none can take away" (BT.5:1–4). Thel, however, refuses this knowledge (which appears as death to her, for it means dying to the selfhood, living not for ourselves alone as the Clod of Clay says); she fears the "little curtain of flesh on the bed of our desire" much as Urizen and Vala fear it; it seems to be something different from spirit or from "holiness." And so Thel "with a shriek / Fled back unhinder'd till she came into the Vales of Har" (BT.6:20–22).

In *Visions of the Daughters of Albion*, Theotormon, like Thel, fails to be convinced by the argument that "the soul of sweet delight can never be defil'd" (MHH.9:14). Oothoon attempts to show Theotormon that the so-called lower aspects of life are meant to blend with the higher ones, else man will always remain a fragmented being prying after Good and Evil, like Urizen, seeking a solid without fluctuation, a joy without pain. But Oothoon realizes that all things, higher and lower, are related:

> Sweetest the fruit that the worm feeds on, & the soul prey'd on
> by woe,
> The new wash'd lamb ting'd with the village smoke, & the bright
> swan
> By the red earth of our immortal river. (VDA.3:17–19)

In fact, all things are so intimately connected—ultimately one within Albion—that if any of the "lower" forms of life experience pain, every other being does also: "For not one sparrow can suffer & the whole Universe not suffer also / In all it Regions" (J.25:8–9). Thus, "A dog starv'd at his Master's Gate / Predicts the ruin of the State" (AI.9–10).

In Shelley's view, also, the below, the material, can become united with the above, the spiritual, through the power of love, and he too uses the worm as the symbol of such lowness:

> I know
> That Love makes all things equal: I have heard
> By mine own heart this joyous truth averred:
> The spirit of the worm beneath the sod
> In love and worship, blends itself with God. (EPI.125–129)

To Asia, love "makes the reptile equal to the God" (PU.II.v.43). Shelley's authority for this belief is "mine own heart," just as Asia replies to Demogorgon, when he says that only "eternal Love" will not decay, that her own heart had already supplied this answer (PU.II.iv.121–123). Cythna, too, states that one can find the "earnest" of the hope of regeneration only in the heart. This was Shelley's ultimate authority for the reconciliation of opposites. It was a lamp that he carried and never quite gave up even in his bitterest disillusionments, as Los carries a "globe of fire" when he sets out to explore the fallen interior of Albion's bosom in an effort to salvage whatever "Minute Particular" he can (J.31:2–7).

Part of the difficulty in seeing Woman and sex on their emanative or epipsychical level, in seeing *all* life as holy, lies in the attitude that society has taken toward Woman herself. Shelley points out that women have been considered pieces of property or "articles of luxury," since "they are the materials of usefulness or pleasure" to men. The institution of marriage was thus based on the "dread of insecurity." As men feared to lose their property, in like manner they feared to lose their women, and marriage arose as "a contrivance to prevent others from deriving advantage from that which any individual has succeeded in pre-occupying."[11]

Part of Cythna's mission in *The Revolt of Islam* is to raise the consciousness of women out of this "property" concept so that men can also become free, for in the Shelleyan formula, so long as women remain bound, the men who bind them are also slaves. Shelley's stress on the actual, practical equality of the sexes is different from Blake's idea of woman's function. Blake views woman as the "shadow" of man. In Blake's poetry, the female reveals her own freedom not so much in what she wants for herself but in the freedom she is willing to grant her consort, as in Oothoon's offer of gold and silver girls, whether or not we consider these actual "girls," or symbolically, "loves and graces." Blake demands the absolute annihilation of the female selfhood, else she descends into Rahab and Tirzah with the power to torture man with her separate will, though of course he did not view woman as a piece of property or an article of luxury. Indeed, without their Emanations, the sons of Eden themselves cannot experience the brotherhood of Eden, for if their Emanations do not first embrace emotionally, the males cannot blend in thunders of intellect, and therefore no creativity can take place. When this much has been said, however, it still remains true that the Emanations are definitely inferior (as Beulah is subordinate to Eden) to their male counterparts, and Blake states quite explicitly that the female life lives only from the light of the male. This difference of view between the two poets, I think, can be accounted for by a number of factors, some of them necessarily conjectural.

First of all, by temperament Shelley possessed a greater capacity to see things from a woman's perspective. With more of the feminine in his nature (unlike Mark Schorer, I say this without disparagement),[12] Shelley could put himself in the place of a woman and imaginatively understand the often debilitating effects of male supremacy. This attitude was strengthened by his marriage to Mary Godwin, who was more interested in literary pursuits than his first wife Harriet had been. Indeed, part of Mary's attraction for Shelley was her illustrious literary parentage—Mary Wollstonecraft and William Godwin—as he affirms in his dedication of *The Revolt of Islam*. Mary could "feel poetry and understand philosophy."[13] Secondly, Shelley was far more influenced by the women's rights literature of his time, for example, William Godwin's *Political Justice* (1793), Mary Wollstonecraft's *A Vindication of the Rights of Women* (1792), and Sir James Lawrence's *The Empire of the Nairs* (1811).

Blake also came under the influence of Mary Wollstonecraft (several years before she married William Godwin), whom he met at the bookseller Joseph Johnson's weekly dinners in 1791. He did a set of engravings for her *Original Stories From Real Life* (1791), which Johnson published. But, though Blake's *Visions of the Daughters of Albion* (1793) was probably written to echo her sentiments for the freedom of women in her *Rights of Women* (which Johnson had published in 1791), Oothoon ends the poem not on that note, but protesting that she will give her lover, Theotormon, all the freedom he wants and needs. This is characteristic of Blake. Unlike Shelley, he married a simple, illiterate woman, Catherine Boucher, whom he taught to read and write and whom he formed into what the writers of the Old Testament would have termed a perfect wife. Blake's attitude might have been different had he married Mary Wollstonecraft or someone like her. As it was, following out his interpretation of the Old Testament prophets, he told Crabb Robinson he had learned from the Bible that wives should be had in common.[14] There is a legend that Blake considered at one time bringing another woman into his house as a concubine but that he gave up the idea when Catherine wept.[15]

On the other hand, Shelley defines women's liberation in the twentieth-century sense. When he and his friend Thomas Jefferson Hogg

had a disagreement about the advisability of marriage, Shelley mar-
shalled all the reasons he could think of against it, concluding, "For
God's sake if you want more arguments read the marriage service [which
defined the woman as the property of the man] before you *think* of
allowing an amiable beloved female to submit to such degradation."[16]
Under such a property system, women are "victims of lust and hate, the
slaves of slaves"; all their "grace and power" are thrown "to the hyaena
lust" (RI.II.xxxvi.987–989). Peace is impossible when men and women
are not "free and equal" (RI.II.xxxvii.995), for as we have seen the
unhappy slave makes things miserable for his master: the oppression
flows back to bind the oppressor, and such is true no less for the man
who binds a woman than it is for the tyrant who binds other men. "Can
man be free if woman be a slave?" asks Cythna (RI.II.xliii.1045). If
woman remains "the bond-slave" of man, if love is forever equated with
property and possession, "life is poisoned in its wells" (RI.VIII.xiii.3314–
3315), and all of what Blake calls the emanative loves and graces are cut
down before they have a chance to flower.

Both Blake and Shelley stress the relationship of the "property-and-
possession" marriage to prostitution. In Blake's "London," for example,
life is quite literally poisoned in its well, its beginnings, for the harlot's
curse "Blasts the new born Infant's tear" and turns the marriage carriage
itself into a hearse (p. 216). The harlot can exist only where and when
Urizenic ideas of "purity," "holiness," and exclusive possession obtain,
that is, when the Sons of Albion take the two contraries Good and Evil,
separate them, and turn them into generalizations and abstractions, a
process of thought symbolized by the Tree of Knowledge of Good and
Evil.[17]

The social ramifications of this dichotomy, which takes place in the
fall, are at once apparent. In Los's words, "Love & Innocence" freeze
"into the gold & silver of the Merchant" (J.64:23). Blake asks:

> What is a Wife & what is a Harlot? What is a Church & What
> Is a Theatre? are they Two & not One? can they Exist Separate?
> Are not Religion & Politics the Same Thing? (J.57:8–10)

When energy is suppressed by Urizen and Vala's mystery religion (based
on the idea of a secret holiness), brothels and sadism emerge: brothels
are built with bricks of religion—an idea clearly expressed in "London."
On the social and religious levels, the chimney sweeper's cry falls in a
black cloud over the serpent temples of the world, making the church an
appalling institution where all worship their own selfhoods and pry after
"holiness":

> How the Chimney-sweeper's cry
> Every black'ning Church appalls.

Politically, the soldier who fights "corporeal" rather than "mental" war dies in the service of this selfhood, represented by the king in his palace:

> And the hapless Soldier's sigh
> Runs in Blood down Palace Walls. (p. 216)

But *most,* the Poet says in the final stanza of "London," he hears the harlot's curse, for prostitution is a more basic distortion and perversion of the essential creative energy within man from which all the other "mind forg'd manacles"—political, social and religious—are derived. Man's Edenic energy should flow out unchecked into acts of artistic creation and acts of love, but it is caught and damned up by Urizen and Vala to be used instead in religion and war. "War," Albion finally understands in his regeneration, "is energy Enslav'd" (FZ.9:152). The Covering Cherub (one of Rahab's forms) is a "Double Female," that is, "Religion hid in War" (J.89:52–53).

To overcome the double Tree of the Knowledge of Good and Evil and to replace it with the unified Tree of Life, the wife must become "evil" (energetic, passionate) and the harlot must be forgiven—continually if necessary—so that in Los's words she can become chaste. For the true chastity (as with "holy" the term functions with a double meaning) cannot be found in Vala's virginity or in harlotry. Both, while seeming opposites, actually generate each other; Blake equates the virgin Vala with the Whore of Babylon: all selfishness is whoredom. Urizen builds Vala within Man, and the mystery religion based on the containment of energy (virginity) which they devise inevitably creates harlotry because no flesh nor spirit can keep Urizen's iron laws, though guilt-ridden man attempts to do so. His failure, of course, creates more guilt—the same dull round over again.

In "A Little Girl Lost" the containment of energy creates guilt; life is poisoned in its wells; the little girl, Ona, does indeed become "lost." In this poem we can see what Blake considers a "sin": not act, but "hindering another." Ona returns from her innocent love making with a youth in the "holy light" of morning to be confronted by her "father white" (i.e., a representation of Nobodaddy, white being a color associated with the aged Urizen), who terrifies her and makes her feel guilty with his "holy book," Urizen's book of brass (p. 219). Thus, woman learns to conceal herself, to withhold herself in pride (which is selfishness), and to be jealous and possessive. To man, his Emanation becomes a "sin," and sex, therefore, a lustful, selfish indulgence rather than a passion, limited physically to a "dark, secret place" and metaphorically veiled like the ark of the covenant.

If a woman should attempt to remove this veil, as Oothoon does, she is branded a whore, for fallen man accepts the dichotomy of the double Tree, an acceptance that also does away with his own freedom. The jealous, possessive woman he creates by demanding chastity will not give him liberty but will give him pain instead (the inevitable concomitant of restriction), as the speaker in "My Pretty Rose Tree" discovers. In that poem, the speaker—like Theotormon bound by the Urizenic notion of chastity—refuses the flower of May in favor of the Rose Tree he already *possesses* (for he "tends" her by day and by night), but the Rose Tree is just as jealous as if he had accepted the May flower, and so the speaker is left to "delight" in the Rose Tree's thorns (p. 215). That is, she too is "modest" like the rose in "The Lilly" and puts up a defensive barrier that causes the male pain. He apparently enjoys this pain, however, for suppressed sexual energy may easily arise in its perverted form as sadomasochism (in this case, sadism on the Rose Tree's part, masochism on the speaker's part). For this reason, Luvah (Love) is tortured on the Druid Stone by Rahab and Tirzah.

The act of giving herself freely enjoyed by the Emanation in Beulah no longer exists in the fallen world, for in Beulah the females die for the males: "Males immortal live renew'd by female deaths; in soft / Delight they die" (FZ.1:66–67).[18] The females give up their selfhoods in those unquenchable burnings that Urizen attempts to escape when he separates himself from Eternity: "Why will you die, O Eternals?" he asks. Instead, in her fallen condition the Emanation plays coy with her consort, giving the appearance that she will yield, then fleeing as Enitharmon does from Los: "he siezed her in his arms; delusive hopes / Kindling, she led him into shadows & then fled outstretch'd / Upon the immense like a bright rainbow, weeping & smiling & fading" (FZ.2:380–382). Blake points out that the male himself is responsible for this reaction, since Albion creates the Female Will and then becomes bound by it, as Los notes. In some cases, when the female has overcome this Will herself, she finds her partner still bound by it. Thus, Theotormon, taught by Urizen to expect concealment, will accept neither Oothoon's gift of herself nor her offer of gold and silver girls.

Sexual energy could be expressed on its highest level, the Emanation or epipsyche, but when it is forced underground as "sin" it rises in the fallen form of prostitution, which to Blake and Shelley alike is the true license and lust. According to Shelley, the exclusive possession that obtains in marriage leads inevitably to prostitution: "Prostitution is the legitimate offspring of marriage and its accompanying errors," he asserts.[19] He wrote to Sir James Lawrence, author of *The Empire of the Nairs* (1811)—a people of Malabar whose customs gave women sexual freedom—that only after reading Sir James' book had he understood the "greatest argument" against marriage: "prostitution both *legal* and *illegal*."[20] Like Blake's Oothoon, Shelley contends that love cannot exist except in freedom:

> Love withers under constraint; its very essence is liberty; it is compatible
> neither with obedience, jealousy, nor fear; it is there most pure, perfect,

and unlimited, where its votaries live in confidence, equality, and unre-
serve.[21]

But such a relationship is a rare occurrence between men and women.
Plagued by all the evils of the selfhood, they are more intent on jealousy
and possession than they are liberty. In witnessing the usual "hermaphroditic" marriage, Oothoon asks:

> Can that be Love that drinks another as a sponge drinks water,
> That clouds with jealousy his nights, with weepings all the day,
> To spin a web of age around him, grey and hoary, dark,
> Till his eyes sicken at the fruit that hangs before his sight?
> Such is self-love that envies all; a creeping skeleton
> With lamplike eyes watching around the frozen marriage bed. (VDA.7:17–22)

Characteristically, Blake speaks in terms of male rather than female
freedom, for the female finds her freedom more in that liberty she is
willing to *give*—as Oothoon indicates.

The "frozen marriage bed"—the "marriage hearse"—on the one hand
and the observance of chastity for those who are unmarried on the other
lead inevitably to prostitution. "Society is never so self-righteous as when
accusing the harlot of sin and doing nothing to free her from it,"
Northrop Frye observes.

> Yet she is an inevitable result of its own blaspheming of love, and the
> plagues which blight the marriage hearse are no more an accidental result
> of that blasphemy than violent death is an accidental result of war.[22]

Shelley contends that women are made into prostitutes in the first place
through the unforgiving attitude assumed by society. For having followed "the impulse of unerring nature" society casts them forth and they
eventually become "vicious and miserable." All things are so closely
connected (as Blake indicates in "London"), however, that society itself
(and especially its male members) ultimately suffers for the degradation
of its women into the Urizenic categories "pure" and "impure":

> Young men, excluded by the fanatical idea of chastity from the soceity of
> modest and accomplished women, associate with these vicious and miser-
> able beings, destroying thereby all those exquisite and delicate sensibilities
> whose existence cold-hearted worldlings have denied; annihilating all
> genuine passion, and debasing that to a selfish feeling which is the excess
> of generosity and devotedness.[23]

Partly for this reason Shelley excoriates chastity as "a monkish and
evangelical superstition."[24] Similarly, when he describes Urizen's mystery religion, Blake sees "Every Emanative joy forbidden as a Crime /
And the Emanations buried alive in the earth with pomp of religion"
(J.9:14–15). The Eternals (the portion of Eternity or the Human Imagi-

nation that is not drawn down into the vortex of Albion's fall) look down
on the world of Generation and say, laughing,

> Have you known the Judgment that is arisen among the
> Zoas of Albion, where a Man dare hardly to embrace
> His own Wife for the terrors of Chastity that they call
> By the name of Morality? (J.36:44–49)

Shelley maintains that society "is a mixture of feudal savageness and
imperfect civilization," and that "the narrow and unenlightened morality of the Christian religion is an aggravation of these evils."[25] For this
reason, Blake completely abandons "moral precept" and law (Urizen's
books of brass and iron) in his idea of Christianity, subsuming it entirely
under the heading: forgiveness of sins. He makes his point abundantly
clear by asserting that Jesus was born not of a virgin but was the product
of an adulterous liaison on Mary's part for which Joseph forgave her:

> Was Jesus Chaste? or did he
> Give any Lessons of Chastity?
> The morning blush'd fiery red:
> Mary was found in Adulterous bed
> Earth groan'd beneath, & heaven
>   above
> Trembled at discovery of Love. (EG.e:1–6)

In this act, because she followed her energies, Mary was truly with child
by the Holy Ghost. At first, however, even though Mary says she loves
him, Joseph calls her "a Harlot & an Adulteress" (J.61:6). But he hears
the voice of God explaining the forgiveness of sins. No conditions are
made for this forgiveness. It is not necessary that a sinless being die to
atone for the sinful. And, as before, we might note Blake's different
attitude toward female sexuality; Mary must be forgiven for having had
a lover:[26]

> Doth Jehovah Forgive a Debt only on condition that it shall
> Be Payed? Doth he Forgive Pollution only on conditions of Purity?
> That Debt is not Forgiven! That Pollution is not Forgiven!
> Such is the Forgiveness of the Gods, the Moral Virtues of the
> Heathen whose tender Mercies are Cruelty. But Jehovah's Salvation
> Is without Money & without Price, in the Continual Forgiveness of
>   Sins,
> In the Perpetual Mutual Sacrifice in Great Eternity. (J.61:17–23)

God therefore tells Joseph to "Fear not then to take / To Thee Mary thy
Wife, for she is with Child by the Holy Ghost" (J.61:26–27).

That Blake thus equated the working of the Holy Ghost (energy,
passion, creativity, genius) with an act of adultery points up more

unequivocally than any other statement could his relentless fight for freedom, especially freedom from the Christian idea of "sin," which in Blake's view will bind man down to the oozy rock of generation, to his caverned skull with its limited five senses, until he comes to understand that *all* life and all its manifestations are holy. Even if a man commits what in Blake's opinion is a real sin—hindering another, murder, theft—he should be forgiven, for the gates to paradise open only to those who mutually forgive as the Eternals do, and this is the only way in which hell is opened to heaven, the harlot made a virgin. For discordant qualities are harmonized by love, much as the Witch of Atlas blends fire and snow to create Hermaphroditus, the navigator of her boat (WA.XXXV). Heaven and hell, a harlot and a wife, a church and a theater, politics and religion, soul and body are not "opposites," but they appear so to the partaker of the fruit of the double Tree. Hence, Blake stresses that Jesus forgave (loved) the woman taken in adultery, whereas the law of Moses commanded that she be stoned:

> He laid His hand on Moses' Law:
> The Ancient Heavens, in Silent Awe
> Writ with Curses from Pole to Pole,
> All away began to roll:
> The Earth trembling & Naked lay
> In secret bed of Mortal Clay,
> On Sinai felt the hand divine
> Putting back the bloody shrine,
> And she heard the breath of God
> As she heard by Eden's flood:
> Good & Evil are no more!
> Sinai's trumpets, cease to roar!
> Cease, finger of God, to write! (EG.e:11–23)

"Sir," said Dr. Johnson when Boswell attempted to defend a certain lady's morals, who had been divorced by act of parliament from her husband, "never accustom your mind to mingle virtue and vice. The woman's a whore, and there's an end on 't." But to Blake that was only the beginning: virtue and vice, chastity and harlotry, are the two forks of the Tree of Knowledge of Good and Evil, and had he heard the statement he would have thought Johnson an "angel." So long as man uses such abstract categories (in which he places living human beings for sacrifice, becoming the Wicker Man of Scandinavia), he remains bound down to the stems of vegetation, to the natural or unspiritual world—in short, to separation and suffering. At about the same time Boswell published his *Life* of Johnson (1791), Blake in *The Marriage of Heaven and Hell* (1790–1793) was attempting to "marry" the Johnsonian categories, to make man whole and thus free him from pain: "The head Sublime, the heart Pathos, the genitals Beauty, the hands & feet proportion" (MHH.10:1).

The distinction that Blake and Shelley make between passion and lust and their opinions regarding marriage and its relation to prostitution show their remarkable similarity of view. Both poets always worked toward greater freedom and joy in human relationships. On the basis of their imaginative perception, they derive their idea that the physical and spiritual realms are not separate but one. Their poetry attempts to establish this insight for their readers. If such a perception could be established, Shelley believed, most of the evils of the world could be eradicated. Since Blake (unlike Shelley) did not accept any absolute evils, he believed that fourfold vision would aid man to burst out of his cavern into the perception of Eternity.

Blake and Shelley's idea of the sanctity of the sexual impulse—indeed of all action, passion, or energy, of which sex is only a part—is an illuminating commentary on the world's usual attitude toward such matters, which has been neatly summed up by Mark Rampion in Aldous Huxley's *Point Counter Point,* and by a character, Mérodack, in Péladan's *Le Vice Suprême,* published in Paris in 1884. Mérodack snorts derisively, "Chercher l'infini entre le deux draps d'un lit, est-ce pas risée?" ("To look for the infinite between two bed sheets, isn't it ridiculous?"). Shelley would call Mérodack a "cold-hearted worldling" for denying the connection between the body and the spirit. In Shelley and Blake's view even the worm or the clod of clay becomes equal to God through love, for what is "higher" and "lower"? Is the act that creates life itself "lower"? It's a matter of one's perspective or one's perception. Sartrean Existentialism, for instance, tends to view the body with disgust. In Sartre's *La Nausée,* Roquentin's hand lies before him on the table like a dead crab, and he shouts, "quelle saleté, quelle saleté!" ("what filth, what filth!"). Blake's Ezekiel, however, soundly accounts for dung (which symbolizes all we think of as "lower") in the overall scheme of his metaphysics. Should we not do so, it has a way of confronting us in various, tortuous, underground forms, as Blake realized, of secrecy, war, hatred, pornography, sadism, and violence.[27] In several of Swift's late scatological poems—"Strephon and Chloe," "The Lady's Dressing Room," and "Cassinus and Peter," for example—the biological functions of woman (like those of the Brobdingnagian women) make her a nauseous, odious object of putrefaction. Cassinus' love for his lady simply will not sustain the knowledge that she defecates:

> Nor can Imagination guess,
> Nor Eloquence Divine express
> How that ungrateful, charming Maid,
> My purest Passion has betray'd.

Swift died insane, but I do not wish to argue *post hoc, ergo propter hoc;* I do not wish to say that his "excremental vision" (as Middleton Murry has termed it)[28] was responsible for his insanity. For Swift's idea is held, more or less, by most people, one would surmise, though they neither write poetry about it nor go insane. "Above all," states Freud, in explaining this attitude, "the coprophilic elements in the [sexual] instinct have proved incompatible with our aesthetic ideas," adding,

> excremental things are all too intimately and inseparably bound up with sexual things, the position of the genital organs—*inter urinas et faeces*—remains the decisive and unchangeable factor.[29]

D. H. Lawrence, on the other hand, expresses a view exactly like Blake's Ezekiel:

> If, in the midst of the Timaeus, Plato had only paused to say: "And now, my dear Cleon—(or whoever it was)—I have a bellyache, and must retreat to the privy: this too is part of the Eternal Idea of man," then we never need have fallen so low as Freud.[30]

Blake's vision brings the infinite "down" to transform these supposedly unchangeable factors, and in his ability to see such changes, Blake was free of hatred, obsessions, neuroses, and full of health and joy. Like his own Los, each day he stood before his fiery forge and created a thing of beauty. On his deathbed and lucid to the end in the disposition of his few worldly affairs, Blake sang impromptu hymns of his own composition to the glorious visions of his Eden opening out before him, saying to his wife, "my beloved, they are not mine—no—they are not mine."[31]

Freudians (and post-Freudians, though perhaps not so much as formerly) are both well-disposed and well-armed to discover dishonesty, self-deception, or rationalization in Blake and Shelley's idea of the holiness of sex. Since both poets stress the free expression of sexual desire, the Freudian might find it difficult to support his position that religious feelings are "nothing but" repressed sexual desires that are thus "sublimated." In this respect, Blake is already ahead of the Freudian by recognizing that Urizen's mystery religion based on human sacrifice and torture results from the suppression of libidinous energy. He departs from the Freudian in maintaining that that same energy, if allowed free expression, appears as well in true religion and art—indeed in all life. Suppression of sex creates a false religion, whereas the true one—brotherhood—exists in Eden where the Eternals can gratify their desires. On the other hand, logically following out the Freudian view, religion would cease to exist if the sex instinct could be fully gratified. Of the generally received Freudian definitions of love and sex, Theodor Reik states: "If love were only aim-inhibited sex its existence would not be imaginable with men and women who have no such inhibitions, who gratify their sexual wishes to the point of orgies."[32] Love, however, does not cease to exist under these conditions any more than religion does. At that point, the point of the orgy (assuming that there is a complete and utter gratification so that one could want nothing more!), religion and love should disappear. Instead, among primitive peoples, the orgy itself expresses *religious* feeling, an attempt to get in contact with cosmic forces by repeating the union of the divine, primordial couple (the young people copulate on the ploughed ground), to make the land, animals and women fruitful, and to celebrate the harvest, among many other things. "The orgy sets flowing the sacred energy of life," Mircea Eliade notes of many primitive societies.[33]

But to Mark Rampion, the character in Huxley's *Point Counter Point*, Shelley's depiction of this energy as sacred is dishonest. Rampion refers to Shelley's "awful incapacity to call a spade a spade" in his attitude toward sex (not a man and a woman in bed, but "just two angels holding hands"), and wishes that the skylark (not a *bird* but a *spirit*) would let fall some of its droppings on Shelley's head in order to convince him that a spade really is a spade. However, anyone who has studied Shelley more than superficially will realize that he did not deny the flesh; that denial was part of the ascetic Christianity he rejected, like Blake, along with its tyrannical God. What Shelley did deny was the flesh without what he (and Blake) called passion or the passions. In effect, they refused to separate the soul and the body, a separation that both poets could see exemplified not only in prostitution but in marriage as well when one was bound in chains to a jealous, possessive, cruel mate with whom he truly lived in lust.

Many others of the traditional Christian persuasion are little inclined to Mark Rampion's view yet cannot make that leap of the imagination whereby the droppings of the skylark or sexual intercourse—that is, all things—are seen *sub specie aeternitatis*. Though the Christian hungers and thirsts after God and may eat and drink Him in the attempt to become one with Him, he could never admit to having been embraced (in the Blakean sense) and remain religiously acceptable, however much his metaphors speak of the Bridegroom and His Bride. To Blake, this separation—the literal and the metaphorical—was simply another Urizenic-Tree-of-Knowledge-division. Thus, the union "below" of male and female must be the same as the union "above" of Albion and his Emanation—a union in which sexual differentiation ceases to exist on its highest Edenic level.

Blake's designs for Blair's *The Grave* (1808)—the only work of Blake's that enjoyed much of a vogue in his lifetime—especially reveal his attitude that all life is holy by showing men and women—and families—embracing in heaven. In these illustrations, some of the men are touching the women on the hip, thigh, or buttock. Apparently, many of Blake's contemporaries looked on those parts of the body as indecent, and a number of people expressed moral outrage when the book was first seen.[34] These expressions doubtless came from both those who called a spade a spade (the Mérodack, Rampion view) as well as from those who called a spade a not-spade (the ascetic Christian view), for sex is obscene to the libertine and the ascetic alike. These attitudes are not separate but generate each other, like all the seeming opposites discussed in this chapter. In S. Foster Damon's opinion, "Blake's . . . nudes are probably the first in English art which are completely devoid of any suggestion of sensuality."[35] Blake believed that "Art can never exist without Naked Beauty displayed" (p. 776), implying also that what is *concealed* (the whole complex of ideas surrounding Vala) must be *revealed* by the imagination. Early in his poetic career Blake said he intended to expunge "the notion that man has a body distinct from his soul" by "printing in the infernal method, by corrosives . . . melting apparent surfaces away, and displaying the infinite which was hid" (MHH.14, p. 154).

In Blake's vision, the appearance of the sexes indicates a split in the original androgynous unity of Albion. Therefore, the union of a male with his Emanation is a step towards regaining that unity. This idea follows inevitably from Blake's first assumption regarding Albion's nature and consequently the nature of the universe. In Shelley's poetry, the union of the psyche and the epipsyche is an approximation to this idea; both are closely tied to the deep well-springs of myth and ritual. The ideas of the Emanation and the epipsyche are Blake's and Shelley's transmutations of the mythic *hieros gamos*—the divine marriage of Heaven (higher) and Earth (lower). In their concepts of the Emanation and the Epipsyche, Blake and Shelley have reached a high state of development and refinement over earlier notions (a refinement that can also be seen in the Shekinah of the Kabbalah and the Sophia of the Gnostics). But like many of the earlier myths, both Blake's Jerusalem and Shelley's Asia represent a feminine, outward nature that must be rejoined to an inner, masculine cosmic being who will then become whole.

For those who do not perceive the universe in the form of a male and a female principle that must be blended before man can achieve wholeness—a concept that is very nearly universal, as the works of Jung, Sir James Frazer, and Mircea Eliade have demonstrated—Blake and Shelley's attitude toward the function of sex (that it blends opposites or heals divisiveness) will be difficult to understand and impossible to achieve. James Rieger, for example, in his comments on *Epipsychidion*, reveals that Whitman's "There Was a Child Went Forth" must be a complete conundrum to him, for the child who goes forth becomes one with the first object he sees simply by looking at it:

There was a child went forth every day,
And the first object he look'd upon, that object he became,
And that object became part of him for the day or a certain part
    of the day,
Or for many years or stretching cycles of years.

But to Mr. Rieger: "It is observably untrue that the copulation of bodies or of minds blends them or heals the sundering of nature for our sins." He adds: "Yeats's Bishop deludes himself in believing that the 'heavenly mansion' of which he prates is anything other than Crazy Jane's 'foul sty.' "[36] But the Bishop is deluded in Yeats' view precisely because he fails to recognize that within the foul sty he must find the heavenly mansion, or not find it at all. "Fair and foul are near of kin," Jane tells the uncomprehending Bishop, and goes on to explain how these opposites are also near of kin in our experience of love:

> A woman can be proud and stiff
> When on love intent;
> But Love has pitched his mansion in
> The place of excrement;
> For nothing can be sole or whole
> That has not been rent.

This paradox Blake's Ezekiel understood, but Byron's seasick Don Juan, by contrast, feeling "nausea, or a pain / About the lower region of the bowels," is hard pressed to sustain his tender feeling for the woman he loves because "Love, who heroically breathes a vein, / Shrinks from the application of hot towels, / And purgatives are dangerous to his reign, / Sea-sickness death." Ezekiel, like Crazy Jane, is able to combine the higher and the lower: spirit and body, fair and foul, excrement and love, dung and the infinite. The Narrator in *Don Juan*, however, ironically states that Juan's "love was perfect, how else, / Could [his] passion, while the billows roar, / Resist his stomach, ne'er at sea before?" (II.xxiii).

Some valuable insights into Blake's and Shelley's definitions of love can be gained by contrasting their views to those of Byron. In reply to Byron's *Cain* (1821), Blake dedicated his brief poem of 1822 *The Ghost of Abel* (pp. 779–781) to "Lord Byron in the Wilderness" in an attempt to show the latter how to overcome the dichotomies of the flesh and the spirit which so severely plagued him, for it was obvious to the sixty-five year old Blake in reading *Cain* that the young poet (Byron was then thirty-three) had very nearly strangled himself on the fruit of the double Tree.

It was obvious to Shelley, too. From Italy, he wrote Thomas Love Peacock that Byron's Venetian debaucheries were "sickening"; for, according to Shelley, Byron bargained with Italian families for their daughters and accepted whatever pieces of flesh his gondolieri picked up in the street for him.[37] Shelley contemns the "loveless intercourse of brutal appetite" that he found depicted in his friend Hogg's novel *Memoirs of Prince Alexy Haimatoff*.[38] To Shelley, such "loveless intercourse" (i.e., lust, esentially "cold-blooded" selfishness) was a perversion of what should be one of man's most selfless and passionate feelings.

One loves another, Shelley states, not because he or she is a source of pleasure or even happiness but because the other is "really worthy."[39] Stated in Blakean terms, Byron, however, could indulge in lust (not passion) because he accepted the Urizenic notion of chastity. Thus, there could be harlots. Although Byron's biographer Leslie Marchand says that "even his most casual encounters were lightened in his own mind at the time by a certain *romantic* aura," yet he speaks of Byron's "systematic pursuit of women who attracted him, by methods which had become almost *scientific* in their thoroughgoing design."[40] But Byron may speak for himself. In a long list sent to John Cam Hobhouse and Douglas Kinniard he designated his "pieces" for a year, stating, "Some of them are countesses, and some of them cobblers' wives; some noble, some middling, some low, & all whores."[41]

One of the greatest ironies of Byron and Shelley's friendship is that the often licentious Byron was afraid his illegitimate daughter Allegra would be corrupted by living in the Shelley household, where Shelley for some time took care of both Allegra and Allegra's mother, Claire Clairmont, Byron's former mistress. Though beset with his own tribulations at that moment, including the death of his daughter Clara, Shelley seems to have loved Allegra as if she had been his own child. But the author of *Cain* and *Don Juan* feared that Shelley would teach Allegra to be unchaste and to disbelieve in God. Shelley replied, moderately and judiciously as he could on occasion:

> I smiled at your protest about what you consider my creed. On the contrary, I think a regard to chastity is quite necessary, as things are, to a young female—that is, to her happiness—and at any time a good habit. As to Christianity—there I am vulnerable; though I should be as little inclined to teach a child disbelief, as belief, as a formal creed.[42]

Blake and Shelley believed that the immortal and the eternal are immanent in the mortal and the temporal. "Eternity is in love with the productions of time" (MHH.7:10), said Blake, noting the Shelleyan link, love, which connected these "opposites." The same link connects all other things, including Albion and his Emanation, the psyche and the epipsyche and man and woman. Blake addressed "A Little Girl Lost" to a more enlightened "future age" when "Love! sweet Love" would not be thought a crime (p. 219). It is an age that we still await. The child Blake was punished by his mother for saying he saw the Prophet Ezekiel under a tree in the fields.[43] But the mature Blake, who dined with Ezekiel, tells us that we do not even see the tree—only a green thing that stands in our way. Fortunately for us, however, "that child went forth every day, and . . . now goes, and will always go forth every day."

Conclusion

Blake's and Shelley's insights into the nature of man reveal a profound likeness based on their similar modes of perception. Though Shelley was less positive than Blake regarding the final eradication of all evils, both poets believed that through the cultivation of the imagination—the vision of the essential oneness and unity of all things—the viewer could recreate the universe and largely expel evil from it.

Blake and Shelley define evil as selfishness (the selfhood), tyranny, lust, war, the desire for power, hypocrisy, hate, deceit, and cruelty. These evils are manifested particularly in the concept of the tyrannical, orthodox Christian God, the heavenly paradigm of the earthly father, priest, and king. All these manifestations of evil, however, have their origin in the mind of man, who, in turning inward to the selfhood, thereby loses the divine vision of unity and falls into a state of multiplicity and separation.

In Blake's *The Four Zoas* and *Jerusalem,* the condition of oneness before the fall is characterized by the perfect androgynous blend of the universal male (Albion) and female (Jerusalem) principles. In Shelley's *Prometheus Unbound* and *The Revolt of Islam,* the male psyche and the female epipsyche are separated by a similar fall into the selfhood, seen in Prometheus by his hatred of Jupiter and in Laon by his killing of the tyrant's soldiers. These complementary principles must be reunited before man can achieve wholeness and overcome evil.

In Blake and Shelley's view, perception is not passive but active; it is the radical transformation of the usual "object" world given by the five senses. In this active participation of the viewer, subject and object may interact or become one. To these poets, all things must be seen *sub specie aeternitatis.* Though it appears not to be a part of the viewer, the outer world is in reality the projected forms, both good and evil, of his own being. When not transfigured through the perception of oneness that can be gained through poetry, both man and his world remain in a condition of evil, suffering, and constriction. Thus, Shelley and Blake wrote "prophetic" poetry in the attempt to raise their readers' understanding into the higher awareness of unity where dwell love, peace, and joy.

Essentially, Blake defines evil as a "negative accident," a sin, error, or mistake arising from suppressed energy. The single vision of reason, Urizen, acting in isolation from man's other three faculties of sensation, emotion, and imagination, is largely responsible for this suppression. It separates and solidifies things into abstractions. In *The Four Zoas,* once Urizen can be persuaded by Albion and the other Zoas to give up his domination and act in unison with them, the universe is regenerated. Of course, the other Zoas also seek to dominate Albion, but Urizen is the most difficult to convince of his error. Similarly, in *Jerusalem* Los battles this same domination in the form of the Spectre (rational demonstration, self-righteousness, moral law) and his most titanic artistic labors are continually required to keep the vision of Eternity, the world of Imagination, before Albion's eyes. Los says to the Spectre:

> Take thou this Hammer & in patience heave the thundering Bellows;
> Take thou these Tongs, strike thou alternate with me, labour
> obedient. (J.8:39–40)

The Spectre attempts to rebel, but Los compels him

> To labours mighty with vast strength, with his mighty chains,
> In pulsations of time, & extensions of space like Urns of Beulah,
> With great labour upon his anvils, & in his ladles the Ore
> He lifted, pouring it into the clay ground prepar'd with art,
> Striving with Systems to deliver Individuals from those Systems.
>
> (J.11:1–5)

Blake's "system" constitutes an apocalyptic deliverance into freedom: Jerusalem "overspread[s] all Nations as in Ancient Time" (J.97:2).

Shelley, however, accepted some evils as absolute, for example, the death, chance, and mutability found at the end of *Prometheus Unbound.* His skepticism (based on reason) always kept up a running battle with his belief (based on feeling) in the perfectibility of man. Consequently, his finest and most representative poem, *Prometheus Unbound,* contains a tentative and precarious utopia in contrast to Blake's total apocalypse at the end of his masterpiece, *Jerusalem. The Cenci,* moreover, presents in the character of Count Cenci an immedicable and radical evil. Thus Shelley, as he states in his Preface to *Hellas,* preferred not to "dogmatise upon a subject, concerning which all men are equally ignorant" (p. 478). Some readers, of course, have taken too much to heart Mary Shelley's pronouncements about Shelley's attitude toward evil in her comments on *Prometheus Unbound,* and therefore have failed to see what his general, overall attitude actually is, as balanced by both *Prometheus Unbound* and *The Cenci.* Moreover, Shelley's hesitancies and doubts stand out in greater contrast through comparison with Blake.

Though Blake and Shelley (the latter, by and large) do not have a tragic view of evil, the view they do have is nevertheless intellectually respectable and tenable. And this view is one the twentieth-century might profit by. Blake and Shelley speak of a perception based on love and energy that leads to the imaginative understanding of how the part relates to the whole (a kind of spiritual or poetic ecology). If we possessed or could develop such a vision, we might be able to see the tree before us, at least, even though we probably would not be able to see Ezekiel under it, as Blake did. No venerable giant redwood could fall victim to such a vision; pure rivers would run down to the sea again, as they did throughout countless ages. But we have lost contact (despite the flood of "how to" and pseudoscientific books on sex and the entire vulgarized paraphernalia surrounding the idea of personality development) with our libidinous and nonrational depths; and Western man, for the most part, exists like the protagonist in Ionesco's *Le Nouveau Locataire* enclosed by the suffocating furniture of his own devising. Though Byron died for Greek independence, Greece (i.e., the entire world) still stands in need of the deliverance of which Blake and Shelley speak. Blake's Luvah (love, energy) and Los (imagination, creativity) and Shelley's Asia (love, intuition) and Demogorgon (the will necessary to overcome evil) are as much needed today to counteract our Satanic mills and wheels as when Blake and Shelley first wrote. Tagore characterizes "the world of man's own manufacture" as one of "discordant shrieks and swagger," what he terms "huge productions of things, huge organizations, huge administrations of empire—all obstructing the path of life."[1] Blake and Shelley attempted to point out this path and to make men love it enough to follow it, for the true path lies not toward empire (what Blake calls "Caesar's laurel crown") but toward art (that is, spiritual transformation or vision). The twentieth century has suffered the devastating effects of the administrations of empire on an unparalleled scale. If "know thyself" remains a valid spiritual dictum, the poetry of Blake and Shelley speaks more forcefully to the human condition in the twentieth century than it did to their own time.

Notes

Introduction

1. S. Foster Damon, *William Blake: His Philosophy and Symbols* (Gloucester, Mass.: Peter Smith, 1958), p. xi.

2. *The Letters of Percy Bysshe Shelley*, 2 Vols., ed. Frederick L. Jones (Oxford: Clarendon Press, 1964), 2:127.

3. Carl Grabo, *The Magic Plant: The Growth of Shelley's Thought* (Chapel Hill: University of North Carolina Press, 1936).

4. David Lee Clark, ed., *Shelley's Prose* or *The Trumpet of A Prophecy* (Albuquerque: University of New Mexico Press, 1954).

5. James Rieger, *The Mutiny Within: The Heresies of Percy Bysshe Shelley* (New York: George Braziller, 1967), p. 218.

6. M. H. Abrams, *The Mirror and the Lamp: Romantic Theory and the Critical Tradition* (New York: W. W. Norton & Co., 1958), p. vi. Of course, Blake's *Tiriel* (1789), *Songs of Innocence* (1789), *Songs of Experience* (1794), *The Book of Thel* (1789), *The French Revolution* (1791), *The Marriage of Heaven and Hell* (1790–1793), *Visions of the Daughters of Albion* (1793), *America* (1793), *The Book of Urizen* (1794) and *Europe* (1794), appeared several years before the *Lyrical Ballads* (1798) ushered in the age of even the first generation of Romantics. This similar mode of perception is characteristic of the visionary or the seer in any age, as the investigations of Jung have demonstrated. As William J. McTaggart has pointed out regarding Shelley's Platonism, in "Some New Inquiries into Shelley's Platonism," *Keats-Shelley Memorial Bulletin* 21 (1970):43: "Saying that Shelley is a Platonist does not mean—as many seem to believe—that Shelley is a mere imitator, who simply recapitulates Plato. The ideas expressed in his poetry are Shelleyan ideas, but these ideas are born of a spirit he shares with Plato."

7. Philip Wheelwright, *The Burning Fountain: A Study in the Language of Symbolism* (Bloomington: Indiana University Press, 1954), p. 63.

8. Jacob Bronowski, *The Identity of Man* (Garden City: Natural History Press, 1965), p. 37.

9. Richard Feynman, *The Character of Physical Law* (Cambridge: Massachusetts Institute of Technology Press, 1967), p. 159.

10. Werner Heisenberg, *Physics and Philosophy: The Revolution in Modern Science* (New York: Harper & Brothers, 1958), p. 201.

11. Louis de Broglie, *The Revolution in Physics*, trans. R. W. Niemeyer, (New York: Noonday Press, 1953), pp. 218–219. Similarly, Michael Polanyi points out in *Personal Knowledge: Towards A Post-Critical Philosophy* (Chicago: University of Chicago Press, 1958), pp. 252–253, that "any philosophy that sets up strictness of meaning as its ideal is self-contradictory. For if the active participation of the philosopher in meaning what he says is regarded by it as a defect which

precludes the achievement of objective validity, it must reject itself by these standards."

12. J. Robert Oppenheimer, *The Flying Trapeze: Three Crises for Physicists* (London: Oxford University Press, 1964), p. 55. Former rigid attitudes involving the terms *rational* and *logical* have had to be abandoned in order to account for the new discoveries in physics. Studies on the breakdown of the classical world view in the sciences include: Jacob Bronowski, *The Common Sense of Science* (New York: Vintage Books, 1959); Jacob Bronowski, "The Logic of the Mind," *American Scholar* 35 (Spring 1966):233–242; Ernest H. Hutten, *The Language of Modern Physics: An Introduction to the Philosophy of Science* (London: George Allen & Unwin, 1956); Albert Szent-Gyorgyi, *The Crazy Ape* (New York: Philosophical Library, 1970).

13. Alexander Gilchrist, *Life of William Blake* (London: J. M. Dent & Sons, 1945), p. 257.

14. David Perkins, *The Quest For Permanence: The Symbolism of Wordsworth, Shelley and Keats* (Cambridge: Harvard University Press, 1959), p. 169.

15. Mark Schorer, *William Blake: The Politics of Vision* (New York: Henry Holt, 1946), p. 341.

16. George Santayana, "Shelley: or the Poetic Value of Revolutionary Principles," in *Essays in Literary Criticism,* ed. Irving Singer (New York: Charles Scribner's Sons, 1956), p. 205.

17. Northrop Frye, *Fearful Symmetry: A Study of William Blake* (Princeton: Princeton University Press, 1947), p. 143.

18. In these "abstract movements" Blake's Prophetic Books bear a close resemblance to his contemporary Beethoven's last five quartets—composed between 1824 and 1826—as Foster Damon has pointed out in *William Blake: His Philosophy and Symbols,* p. ix. Beethoven died the same year as Blake, 1827, and in his final years seems to have moved toward what Charles Lamb, in a letter to Bernard Barton, May 15, 1824, *The Letters of Charles Lamb* (London: Grey Walls Press, 1950), p. 154, defines in Blake's pictures as "great merit, but hard, dry, yet with grace." These same qualities are characteristic also of Blake's later poetry. And as Arthur Symons notes in discussing the terror and suffering in many of Blake's designs, in *William Blake* (London: Jonathan Cape, 1928), pp. 186–187: "Almost everyone can see the beauty of Raphael, only a certain number can see the beauty of Velásquez, not many can see the beauty of Blake."

19. I. A. Richards, *Coleridge On Imagination* (Bloomington: Indiana University Press, 1965), p. 196.

20. The childlike element of Zen—casualness, self-sufficiency, simplicity, spontaneity, teachability—is discussed by R. H. Blyth in *Zen in English Literature and Oriental Classics* (Tokyo: Hokuseido Press, 1942), p. 366.

21. Albert S. Gérard, *English Romantic Poetry: Ethos, Structure and Symbol in Coleridge, Wordsworth, Shelley, and Keats* (Berkeley and Los Angeles: University of California Press, 1968), p. 3.

22. Carl Jung, "A Psychological Approach to the Trinity," in *Psychology and Religion: West and East,* trans. R. F. C. Hull, *The Collected Works of C. G. Jung* (New York: Pantheon Books, 1958):11:183. By my references to the works of Jung throughout this study I do not intend to imply a point-by-point comparison between Jungian psychology and Blake's mythology, any more than I intend

such a comparison between Blake and twentieth-century scientific theories. What I do want to suggest is that the reader will find in Jung easily accessible analogues that may suggest to him further possibilities in Blake's ideas of which he was formerly unaware.

23. "Introduction: Shelley's Optimism," *Shelley: A Collection of Critical Essays,* ed. George M. Ridenour (Englewood Cliffs, N. J.: Prentice Hall, 1965), p. 2. Shelley's poetry has also been defended against the New Critics by Rodney Delasanta, "Shelley's 'Sometimes Embarrassing Declarations': A Defence," *Texas Studies in Literature and Language* 7 (Spring 1965): 173–179; Richard H. Fogle, "Romantic Bards and Metaphysical Reviewers," *ELH* 12 (March 1945): 221–250; Newell F. Ford, "Paradox and Irony in Shelley's Poetry," *Studies in Philology* 57 (July 1960):648–662. See also R. A. Foakes, *The Romantic Assertion: A Study in the Language of Nineteenth Century Poetry* (New Haven: Yale University Press, 1958).

Chapter One

1. Edith J. Morley, ed., *Henry Crabb Robinson on Books and Their Writers* (London: J. M. Dent & Sons, 1938), 1:330. Hereafter cited by the editor's name.
2. Mona Wilson, *The Life of William Blake* (New York: Jonathan Cape & Robert Ballou, 1932), p. 295.
3. Ernst H. Gombrich, *Art and Illusion: A Study of the Psychology of Pictorial Representation* (New York: Pantheon Books, 1960), pp. 248–249. More recent studies of perception are quoted from time to time later in this chapter; they have not altered Gombrich's basic conclusions.
4. Rudolf Arnheim, *Visual Thinking* (Berkeley and Los Angeles: University of California Press, 1969), p. 22.
5. Richard Haven, *Patterns of Consciousness: An Essay on Coleridge* (Amherst: University of Massachusetts Press, 1969), p. 20.
6. Gombrich, p. 104.
7. Jacob Bronowski, *The Common Sense of Science* (New York: Vintage Books, 1959), p. 78. Compare Sir Arthur Eddington's statement in *New Pathways in Science* (Ann Arbor: University of Michigan Press, 1959), p. 7: "It is the inexorable law of our acquaintance with the external world that that which is presented for knowing becomes transformed in the process of knowing." In his timely and suggestive work, *Personal Knowledge,* p. 142, which I have previously quoted, Michael Polanyi says that "scientific severity" in the Laplacean sense "threaten[s] the position of science itself," for it "presents us with a picture of the universe in which we ourselves are absent. In such a universe there is no one capable of creating and upholding scientific value; hence there is no science."
8. Erwin Schrödinger, *Mind and Matter* (New York: Cambridge University Press, 1959), p. 76.
9. Jacob Bronowski, "The Logic of the Mind," *American Scholar* 35 (Spring 1966):235. While some say that the science of psychology is too young to be exact, Bronowski contends (p. 239) that this is not the reason for its inexactness, since any system based on "self-reference" will contain paradox. Thus, the psychologist explains that in one person the inferiority complex causes rudeness; in another it may be revealed through politeness. As Polanyi states (*Personal*

Knowledge, p. 189), these "holes" are tacitly filled in, so that a scientific structure not only makes sense but possesses intellectual beauty.

10. Harold Bloom, "The Visionary Cinema of Romantic Poetry," in *William Blake: Essays For S. Foster Damon*, ed. Alvin H. Rosenfeld (Providence: Brown University Press, 1969), p. 19.

11. Northrop Frye, *Fearful Symmetry*, p. 7.

12. David Lee Clark, ed., *Shelley's Prose* or *The Trumpet of a Prophecy* (Albuquerque: University of New Mexico Press, 1954), p. 295. All references to Shelley's essays are cited from this edition.

13. Vitus B. Dröscher, *The Magic of the Senses: New Discoveries in Animal Perception*, trans. Ursula Lehrburger and Oliver Coburn (New York: E. P. Dutton, 1969), p. 3.

14. William Blake, "A Vision of the Last Judgment," *Blake: Complete Writings*, ed. Geoffrey Keynes (London: Oxford University Press, 1966), p. 617. All references to Blake are cited from this edition and hereafter appear within parentheses in the text.

15. G. E. Bentley, Jr., *Blake Records* (London: Oxford University Press, 1969), p. 302.

16. Northrop Frye, "Blake After Two Centuries," *University of Toronto Quarterly* 27 (October 1957):15.

17. Peter F. Fisher, "Blake and the Druids," *Journal of English and Germanic Philology* 58 (October 1959):600.

18. Milton O. Percival, *William Blake's Circle of Destiny* (New York: Octagon Books, 1964), p. 253.

19. Ross Greig Woodman, *The Apocalyptic Vision in the Poetry of Shelley* (Toronto: University of Toronto Press, 1964), p. 10.

20. *The Complete Poetical Works of Percy Bysshe Shelley*, ed. Thomas Hutchinson (London: Oxford University Press, 1964), III.ii.18–34. All references to Shelley's poems, prefaces, and notes to poems are cited from this edition and hereafter appear with parentheses in the text.

21. Morley, 1:328.

22. George Robert Stow Mead, *Fragments of A Faith Forgotten* (New York: University Books, 1960), pp. 446–447.

23. William Bonner, *The Mystery of the Expanding Universe* (New York: Macmillan, 1964), p. 137, italics mine. Another interesting analogue appears in what astronomers call the "red shift": the universe seems to be expanding, fleeing away from us. "The Starry Heavens all were fled from the mighty limbs of Albion" (J.70:32), Blake says in explaining the fall of his giant Man. See P. D. Ouspensky's *Tertium Organum* (New York: Vintage Books, 1970), first published in 1912, for a suggestive analogical study of the fourth dimension.

24. Charles Noël Martin, *The Role of Perception in Science*, trans. A. J. Pomerans (London: Hutchinson & Co., 1963), p. 73.

25. See "Universe" in S. Foster Damon, *A Blake Dictionary: The Ideas and Symbols of William Blake* (Providence: Brown University Press, 1965), p. 418.

26. M. O. Percival, *Blake's Circle of Destiny*, p. 15. See also Harold Bloom's Commentary in *The Poetry and Prose of William Blake*, ed. David V. Erdman (Garden City: Doubleday & Co., 1965), pp. 875–876.

27. I have discussed the fall as set forth in *The Four Zoas* only to the extent necessary to explain how inverted vision comes about, since perception and not

the fall itself is the subject of this chapter. For further analysis of the fall, see Northrop Frye, *Fearful Symmetry*, pp. 278–291 and Milton O. Percival, *Blake's Circle of Destiny*, chapter IX. Perhaps Blake himself was not sure how he finally wished the fall to come about; he left *The Four Zoas* in manuscript. In *Jerusalem* he turns to the battle of Los and the Spectre.

28. Mead, p. 319, italics mine.

29. "A Defence of Poetry," *Shelley's Prose*, p. 293.

30. The emphasis on suffering in Blake's designs led to much misunderstanding on the part of his nineteenth-century commentators. One noted, for example, that he "delights to draw evil things and evil beings in their naked and final state." See Doborah Dorfman, *Blake in the Nineteenth Century: His Reputation as Poet From Gilchrist to Yeats* (New Haven: Yale University Press, 1969), p. 49.

31. It is probably no accident that the Romantic age is called a "movement," for if Philip Wheelwright is correct in *Metaphor and Reality* (Bloomington: Indiana University Press, 1962), p. 49, "the verbal cannot be separated from the ontological and psychological factors in any real situation." The movement, song or sound of the spirit when all is well is a Romantic commonplace. On the other hand, when evil dominates, motion ceases and constriction sets in. For example, just after the Ancient Mariner kills the Albatross and his shipmates make themselves accomplices in the crime by approving the act, the ship is becalmed in a silent sea. For an archetypal interpretation of this aspect of Romantic poetry, see Maud Bodkin, *Archetypal Patterns in Poetry: Psychological Studies of Imagination* (London: Oxford University Press, 1963), pp. 30–37.

32. This is what happens in the fall of Adam Kadmon (who is similar to Blake's Albion) in the Kabbalah. See A. E. Waite, *The Holy Kabbalah* (New York: Macmillan Co., 1929), pp. 280–281.

33. Bennett Weaver, "*Prometheus Unbound*," University of Michigan Publications in Language and Literature, No. 27 (1957):9.

34. Glenn O'Malley, *Shelley and Synesthesia* (Evanston: Northwestern University Press, 1964), pp. 152–154.

35. Peter F. Fisher, *The Valley of Vision: Blake as Prophet and Revolutionary*, ed. Northrop Frye (Toronto: University of Toronto Press, 1961), p. 109. Chapters Four and Five of Fisher's work are particularly illuminating on the subject of perception.

36. Nicholas Berdyaev, *Truth and Revelation*, trans. R. M. French (New York: Harper & Brothers, 1953), p. 23.

37. See Chapter Three.

38. David Lee Clark, ed., *Shelley's Prose*, p. 173.

39. On this same subject, Jung states: "It is an almost ridiculous prejudice to assume that existence can only be physical. As a matter of fact the only form of existence we know of immediately is psychic. We might as well say, on the contrary, that physical existence is merely an inference, since we know of matter only in so far as we perceive psychic images transmitted by the senses." C. G. Jung, *Psychology and Religion* (New Haven: Yale University Press, 1938), p. 11. Compare Erwin Schrödinger's statement (previously quoted): the "objective world remains a hypothesis."

40. This "opening up and out" movement—so different from the containment and decorum sought by many of the preceding century's poets—is characteristic of much Romantic poetry as well as painting. The cloudscapes of Constable, for

example, open out into an expansive universe that is often Wordsworthian in its sublimity; the seascapes of Turner are sometimes Blakean in their violence. Desmond King-Hele, *Shelley: The Man and the Poet* (New York: Thomas Yoseloff, 1960), discusses (with special emphasis on Goethe) cloudscapes and their meaning for the Romantics. See especially pp. 219–220. M. H. Abrams, "The Correspondent Breeze: A Romantic Metaphor," *English Romantic Poets: Modern Essays in Criticism*, ed. M. H. Abrams (New York: Oxford University Press, 1960), pp. 37–38, points out that the Romantics correlated "the rising wind" (movement after torpor) with "an outburst of creative power." According to Abrams (p. 51), "the wind, as an invisible power known only by its effects, had an even greater part to play than water, light, and clouds in the Romantic revolt against the world-view of the Enlightenment."

41. Carl Grabo, *The Magic Plant,* p. 108.

42. Morley, 1:328–329.

43. José Ortega y Gasset, *History As A System* (New York: W. W. Norton & Co., 1961), p. 16; pp. 21–22.

44. Northrop Frye, *Fearful Symmetry,* p. 148. Blake refers to temperance, prudence, justice and fortitude as the "four iron pillars of Satan's throne" (M.29:48).

45. "A Treatise on Morals," David Lee Clark, ed., *Shelley's Prose,* p. 188.

46. Asloob Ansari, "Blake and the Kabbalah," *William Blake: Essays For S. Foster Damon,* p. 209.

47. O'Malley, p. 177.

48. Joseph Barrell, *Shelley and the Thought of His Time* (New Haven: Yale University Press, 1947), p. 178. Such a desire, however, is not "peculiar" to the Romantics but is an essential feature of the mythic consciousness in any age. See Chapters Five and Six of this study.

49. C. M. Bowra, *The Romantic Imagination* (Cambridge: Harvard University Press, 1949), p. 110. Chapter One of this book contains a brief but lucid exposition of the Lockian-Newtonian universe as contrasted to the typical Romantic view.

50. Northrop Frye, "New Directions From Old," *Fables of Identity,* p. 63.

51. "Dark," however, is more often used by Blake in its traditional sense of opaque, dull, evil. Such ambivalence (or interchangeability) indicates what Gombrich, *Art and Illusion,* p. 249, calls "the inherent ambiguity of all images."

52. Fëdor Dostoevski, *The Possessed,* trans. Constance Garnett (New York: Random House, 1963), pp. 336–341.

53. Morley, 1:329.

54. M. Esther Harding, *Journey Into Self* (New York: David McKay, 1956), p. 300.

55. *The Greater Holy Assembly of The Kabbalah,* trans. S. L. Mathers, *The Sacred Books and Early Literature of the East* (New York and London: Parke, Austin & Lipscomb, 1917), 4:276

56. A. E. Waite, *The Holy Kabbalah* (New York: Macmillan, 1929), p. 282.

57. Morley, 1:327.

58. Jacob Boehme, *Six Theosophic Points and Other Writings,* trans. John Rolleston Earle (Ann Arbor: University of Michigan Press, 1958), p. 38. This split between the "higher" and the "lower" has been a prominent theme in Western

literature under the form of the *Doppelgänger*. Dr. Jekyll and Mr. Hyde remains the most famous example of the type. It is noteworthy that the evil double (who has such a strong fascination for us) possesses almost all the power, force, and energy (often specifically sexual): Boehme's "dark world" in separation from the "light world"; Blake's "vices" in separation from "sublimities."

59. See Joseph A. Wittreich, Jr., "The 'Satanism' of Blake and Shelley Reconsidered," *Studies in Philology* 65 (October 1968):816–833.

60. Peter Coveney, *The Image of Childhood. The Individual and Society: A Study of the Theme in English Literature.* Rev. ed. (Baltimore: Penguin Books, 1967), p. 302.

61. H. W. Garrod, *Wordsworth: Lectures and Essays* (London: Oxford University Press, 1927), p. 144.

62. Philip Wheelwright, *The Burning Fountain,* p. 48; italics Wheelwright's.

63. Schrödinger, p. 51.

64. Northrop Frye, "The Imaginative and the Imaginary," *Fables of Identity,* p. 164.

65. Northrop Frye, "Blake's Treatment of the Archetype," *Discussions of William Blake,* ed. John E. Grant (Boston: D. C. Heath, 1961), p. 7.

66. Gilchrist, p. 301. This statement is reported by Samuel Palmer (one of the young artists who knew Blake in his last years) in a letter to Gilchrist dated August 23, 1855.

67. See Joseph H. Wicksteed, *Blake's Vision of the Book of Job* (London: J. M. Dent & Sons, 1910).

Chapter Two

1. *Biographia Literaria* (London: J. M. Dent & Sons, 1917), Chapter XIV, p. 166; Chapter IX, p. 76. All references to the *Biographia Literaria* are from this edition.

2. David Lee Clark, ed., *Shelley's Prose,* p. 295; p. 277.

3. E. D. Hirsch, *Wordsworth and Schelling: A Typological Study of Romanticism* (New Haven: Yale University Press, 1960), p. 113; pp. 145–146.

4. Morley, 1:342.

5. Keats to John Hamilton Reynolds, May 3, 1818. *John Keats: Selected Poems and Letters,* ed. Douglas Bush (Boston: Houghton-Mifflin, 1959), p. 273.

6. Basil Willey, *The Seventeenth Century Background: Studies in the Thought of the Age in Relation to Poetry and Religion* (Garden City: Doubleday, 1953), p. 287, italics mine.

7. *Biographia Literaria,* Chapter XII, p. 148.

8. Morley, 1:337.

9. T. S. Eliot, *The Sacred Wood: Essays on Poetry and Criticism* (London: Methuen & Co., 1950), p. 154. Eliot, however, makes this same lack of "impersonal ideas" the basis of his condemnation of Blake. Several paragraphs later in the same essay (p. 157) he states that Blake should have been controlled by "impersonal reason," "common sense" and the "objectivity of science."

10. Morley, 1:326.

11. The Tree also represents man's "double" nature, a curious blend (or dichotomy) of opposites he feels within himself: good and evil, soul and body, hate and love, virtue and vice, joy and pain. The drama and the novel are

especially concerned with the inherent paradoxes and ironies arising from this situation. Dmitri Karamazov, for example, says that he falls headlong into the pit, pleased and full of pride, but in the very depths begins a hymn of praise. Since Blake for the most part attempts to transcend this double aspect of man's nature, to "marry" contraries, it may seem that he does not speak as immediately to the human condition as, say, Conrad or Shakespeare, in whom the opposites appear in all their human, colorful and dramatic panoply. Consider, for example, the effect upon us of *Hamlet* or *Heart of Darkness* in which doubleness is not transcended. By contrast, to some Blake may seem not profound but merely obscure, lacking in a "tragic sense." The darkness is more interesting, more complex than the light.

12. For a discussion of the Tree as an archetype, see chapter 2 of Hazard Adams' *William Blake: A Reading of the Shorter Poems* (Seattle: University of Washington Press, 1963).

13. Harold Bloom in *Blake's Apocalypse: A Study in Poetic Argument* (Garden City: Doubleday & Co., Anchor Books, 1965), p. 276, compares the First Spirit to the Spectre of Urthona (that is, Los's reasoning Spectre) in *Jerusalem*.

14. See Chapter Four.

15. "Blake and the Druids," p. 598.

16. Philip Wheelwright, *Metaphor and Reality*, p. 41.

17. Shelley's attitude on this point was quite similar to Blake's. "I think, if I may judge by its merits, the 'Prometheus' cannot sell beyond twenty copies," Shelley wrote to Charles Ollier, March 6, 1820 (*Letters*, 2:174); and to Leigh Hunt, May 26, 1820: "Have you read my Prometheus yet? but that will not sell—it is written only for the elect" (*Letters*, 2:200). Despite these statements, however, both Blake and Shelley desired to have readers, for regeneration or reformation of vision was part of their purpose in writing.

18. Gilchrist, p. 351.

19. Morley, 1:328.

20. Ibid.

21. "This episode is evidently a tribute to Shelley," he states, adding that it would be unlikely that Blake did not know of the son-in-law of his friends William Godwin and Mary Wollstonecraft. See "Oxford, Bard of" in S. Foster Damon, *A Blake Dictionary*, p. 314. Daniel Hughes, however, follows Gilchrist in believing that the Bard is the poetaster Edward Garead Marsh; see his paper, "Blake and Shelley: Beyond the Uroboros," in *William Blake: Essays For S. Foster Damon*, p. 69.

22. Morley, 1:329.

23. Blake's idea of "contraries" has been analyzed by, among others: Hazard Adams, *William Blake: A Reading of the Shorter Poems*, especially pp. 47–48; Northrop Frye, *Fearful Symmetry*, pp. 188–190; and Peter F. Fisher, *The Valley of Vision*, pp. 5–14.

24. See Chapter Four for a discussion of the selfhood in Blake and Shelley.

25. "A Defence of Poetry," David Lee Clark, ed., *Shelley's Prose*, p. 295.

26. *Biographia Literaria*, Chapter XIV, p. 166.

27. Northrop Frye, *Fearful Symmetry*, p. 293.

28. All stories of the Double are recognitions of what Antonin Artaud—in his *The Theatre and Its Double*, trans. Mary Caroline Richards (New York: Grove

Press, 1958), p. 51—terms "the second phase of Creation," when the idea makes its physical appearance, for nothing "appears" except by contraries, by doubleness, and hence by "evil." See also Stella Kramrisch, "The Triple Structure of Creation in the *Rig Veda*," *History of Religions* 2 (Summer 1962):140–175. The second part of the study is contained in the same volume (Winter 1963):256–285.

29. Northrop Frye, *Fearful Symmetry*, p. 66.

30. See Chapter Four for further discussion of the Father (God)-Son relationship.

31. F. R. Leavis, "Introduction" to Peter Coveney, *The Image of Childhood*, p. 16.

32. Edward J. Rose, "The Structure of Blake's *Jerusalem*," *Bucknell Review* 11 (May 1963):39.

33. Nathaniel Hawthorne, *Selected Tales and Sketches* (New York: Holt, Rinehart & Winston, 1965), p. 221.

34. T. S. Eliot, *Collected Poems: 1909–1935* (New York: Harcourt, Brace & World, 1936), pp. 214–215.

35. W. B. Yeats, *Essays and Introductions* (New York: Macmillan Co., 1961), pp. 134–135.

36. Hazard Adams, *Blake and Yeats: The Contrary Vision* (Ithaca: Cornell University Press, 1955), p. 105. Southey told Crabb Robinson that *Jerusalem* was "a perfectly mad poem," that "Oxford Street is in Jerusalem." See Morley, 1:41.

37. Besides its relationship to evil, the idea of the indefinite has far-reaching implications for Blake's theories of art. For commentary on this point, see George Mills Harper, *The Neoplatonism of William Blake* (Chapel Hill: University of North Carolina Press, 1961), pp. 101–109, and Milton O. Percival, *Blake's Circle of Destiny*, Chapter IV.

38. Edward J. Rose, "The Structure of Blake's *Jerusalem*," p. 50.

Chapter Three

1. October 16, 1811. Percy Bysshe Shelley, *The Letters of Percy Bysshe Shelley*, 2 vols., ed. Frederick L. Jones (Oxford: Clarendon Press, 1964), 1:150. Hereafter cited as *Letters*.

2. David Lee Clark, in his edition of *Shelley's Prose*, stresses Shelley's relation to the British empiricists. Both Carl Grabo, *The Magic Plant*, and James A. Notopoulos, *The Platonism of Shelley* (Durham: Duke University Press, 1949), emphasize Shelley's Platonism. It is from Plato, for the most part, that Shelley derived his idea of evil as transitory, appearance (not reality), and accident. C. E. Pulos, *The Deep Truth: A Study of Shelley's Scepticism* (Lincoln: University of Nebraska Press, 1954), discusses Shelley's skepticism as the factor that enabled him to reconcile the other elements of his thought.

3. Newman Ivey White, *Shelley*, 2 vols. (New York: Alfred A. Knopf, 1940), 2:125–126.

4. Spinoza, whom Shelley translated, in a similar fashion affirms that God exists necessarily, though freely. See the first section of his *Ethics*, "Concerning God," in *Ethics and De Intellectus Emendatione*, trans. A. Boyle (London and Toronto: J. M. Dent & Sons, 1925), p. 16. Shelley read Spinoza's works as early

as 1812, before the publication of *Queen Mab* in 1813. His translations are from the years 1817, 1819, 1820, and 1821. During these same years, he wrote and revised *The Revolt of Islam* (1817–1818) and *Prometheus Unbound* (1818–1820).

5. Bennett Weaver, "*Prometheus Unbound*," p. 14, italics mine.

6. "Essay on Life," David Lee Clark, ed., *Shelley's Prose*, p. 173.

7. The continuity of Shelley's optimism/pessimism (that is, he did not become progressively more pessimistic to any great extent), has been stressed by Donald H. Reiman, "Shelley's 'The Triumph of Life': A Critical Study," Illinois Studies in Language and Literature No. 55 (1965):3–272; G. M. Matthews, "On Shelley's 'The Triumph of Life,' " *Studia Neophilologica* 34 (1962):104–134; and Newman Ivey White, *Shelley*, 2:371. Mr. White, for example, states: "when Shelley wrote 'The Triumph of Life' he had a profound and almost morbid conviction of the pains and penalties of living. But it is a misconception of Shelley's character and writings to assume either that this was something new or that it negates his fundamental optimism. He held these same beliefs, and expressed them with equal poignance, in *Prometheus Unbound*, which asserts the perfectibility of the human spirit." However, some readers do interpret *The Triumph of Life* as an expression of Shelley's deepening pessimism. See, for example, Stuart Curran, *Shelley's Cenci: Scorpions Ringed With Fire* (Princeton: Princeton University Press, 1970), p. 151. Gerald McNiece in *Shelley and the Revolutionary Idea* (Cambridge: Harvard University Press, 1969), p. 155, asserts that "early and late [Shelley] presented his love as a desolation masked, his hope as a veil concealing despair."

8. Carl Grabo, *Prometheus Unbound: An Interpretation* (Chapel Hill: University of North Carolina Press, 1935), p. 111.

9. Earl Wasserman, *Shelley's Prometheus Unbound: A Critical Reading* (Baltimore: Johns Hopkins University Press, 1965), p. 198.

10. Milton Wilson, *Shelley's Later Poetry: A Study of His Prophetic Imagination* (New York: Columbia University Press, 1959), p. 209.

11. *Letters*, 1:237–238.

12. *Letters*, 2:211.

13. *Letters*, 2:319. For an account of what is known as the "Hoppner Scandal" in Shelley's life, see Newman Ivey White, *Shelley*, 2:306–315. See also *Letters*, 2:317–320.

14. January 15, 1822. *Letters*, 2:382.

15. *Letters*, 2:405. Byron, however, did Shelley the final justice of recognizing the latter's goodness and unselfishness. And Byron thoroughly understood his own character (probably far better than Shelley did his own on many occasions) when he wrote Mary Shelley (after Shelley's death) in December 1822: "As to friendship, it is a propensity in which my genius is very limited. I do not know the *male* human being, except Lord Clare, the friend of my infancy, for whom I feel any thing that deserves the name. All my others are men-of-the-world friendships. I did not feel it for Shelley, however much I admired and esteemed him; so that you see not even vanity could bribe me into it, for, of all men, Shelley thought highest of my talents—and perhaps of my disposition." Lord Byron, *Selected Poetry and Letters*, ed. Edward E. Bostetter (New York: Rinehart & Co., 1951), p. 422; italics Byron's.

16. "An Address to the Irish People," David Lee Clark, ed., *Shelley's Prose*, p. 45.

17. Melvin M. Rader, in an article first published in 1930, "Shelley's Theory of Evil," *Shelley: A Collection of Critical Essays*, ed. George M. Ridenour (Englewood Cliffs: Prentice-Hall, 1965), pp. 103–110, recounts many critics' views to this effect, but states (p. 110) that Shelley distinguished between objective evil, which cannot be overcome, and subjective, which can be overcome. The latter can be overcome by lack of hatred and seeing "existence under the form of eternity." The objective evil comprises the death, chance, and mutability spoken of in *Prometheus Unbound*. More recently, George Bornstein in *Yeats and Shelley* (Chicago: University of Chicago Press, 1970), pp. 201–213, has defended Shelley against the charge of superficiality on this score.

18. David Lee Clark, ed., *Shelley's Prose*, pp. 50–51.

19. Edmund W. Sinnot, in *The Biology of the Spirit* (New York: Viking Press, 1955), p. 95, states that education "promotes virtue through precept rather than through preference"—that is, it does not promote virtue at all. Blake, as pointed out, had no use at all for education, since it perpetuated and intensified man's "double" nature.

20. "Essay on the Devil, and Devils," David Lee Clark, ed., *Shelley's Prose*, p. 273.

21. David Lee Clark, ed., *Shelley's Prose*, p. 204.

22. *Letters*, 1:77–78.

23. "Essay on the Devil, and Devils," David Lee Clark, ed., *Shelley's Prose*, p. 265.

24. David Lee Clark, ed., *Shelley's Prose*, p. 156.

25. David Lee Clark, ed., *Shelley's Prose*, p. 198.

26. To Maria Gisborne, November 16, 1819. *Letters*, 2:154.

27. Hogg formed relationships—or attempted to—with Shelley's sister Elizabeth and with both of Shelley's wives, Harriet Westbrook and Mary Godwin. He finally married (after Shelley's death) Jane Williams, with whom Shelley was closely associated in his last years and may or may not have loved. For an account of these relationships, see Newman Ivey White, *Shelley*, 1:170–174, 391–393, 400–402.

28. November 10, 1811. *Letters*, 1:171; italics Shelley's.

29. "A Defence of Poetry," David Lee Clark, ed., *Shelley's Prose*, pp. 282–283.

30. The "cold hypocrite" (FZ.7a.142) weeps as he makes others suffer while he secretly enjoys their pain. This is characteristic of Rahab and Tirzah. Although this precise reaction is not seen in Mercury, he does profess to pity Prometheus while at the same time he follows the orders of his cruel God and looses Jove's Furies upon him. The Furies, in their turn, do not conceal their intense and utter joy in the pain they inflict. Taken together, Mercury and the Furies exemplify an idea very close to that of Blake's.

31. See Chapter Four.

32. If one thinks Shelley's portrait of a tyrant could not be fairly close to the facts and that the Poet does not reveal a very high degree of psychological insight, he forgets the reports, for example, of Hitler's ascetic way of life; he ate no meat, drank no alcoholic beverages, and—as recommended by the Surgeon General of the United States—eschewed tobacco. On the other hand, one has little to fear from Dmitri Karamazov and the local gypsies. Although Dmitri desires his father's death, and is culpable to that extent, it is Ivan's evil,

intellectual *idea* "all is permissible" as carried out by Smerdyakov that actually kills him.

33. I am indebted to those forged writings of about A.D. 500 which go under the name of "Dionysius the Areopagite" (called "Pseudo-Dionysius") for this idea of the relationship of good and evil. Quoted in Victor Gollancz, *Man and God* (Boston: Houghton Mifflin Co., 1951), p. 94. Plato makes a similar assertion in *The Republic*.

34. David Lee Clark, ed., *Shelley's Prose*, p. 52.

35. *The Short Novels of Dostoevsky*, trans. Constance Garnett (New York: Dial Press, 1958), p. 149. The Underground Man's idea of "sheer spite" is that it ensures freedom—man cannot become a piano key. As we can see, Shelley's view of Cenci's "sheer spite" is quite different: slavery to evil.

36. Robert F. Whitman, "Beatrice's 'Pernicious Mistake' in *The Cenci*," *PMLA* 71 (June 1959):251.

37. For a different opinion regarding Cenci and Jupiter, see Charles L. Adams, "The Structure of *The Cenci*," *Drama Survey* 4 (Summer 1965):145. Adams also defends the play as "structurally effective" (p. 147). On the other hand, Joan Rees, "Shelley's Orsino: Evil in *The Cenci*," *Keats-Shelley Memorial Bulletin*, No. 12 (1961):3–6, maintains that the play fails as drama because Shelley's own opinions are in it. Joseph W. Donohue, Jr., in "Shelley's Beatrice and the Romantic Concept of Tragic Character," *Keats-Shelley Journal* 17 (1968):72, also concludes that Shelley "failed to create a unified tragic structure."

38. It is interesting to note, however, that even in Beatrice and in *The Cenci* as a whole Shelley is less successful than in *Prometheus Unbound* or *Adonais*. I doubt if this can be accounted for simply and solely on the basis of the difference in form, whatever Shelley's failings as a dramatist. It appears that he succeeded most, in his longer poems, when he was under the sway of feeling and belief rather than reason and skepticism. Walter Peck, in his biography *Shelley: His Life and Work*, 2 vols. (Boston and New York: Houghton Mifflin Co., 1927), 2:137, maintains that this is "the key to Shelley's view of the universe. He *felt*, rather than reasoned his way toward the millennium."

39. *Heart of Darkness* in *Youth and Two Other Stories* (Garden City, N. Y.: Doubleday, Page & Co., 1920), p. 135.

40. Similarly, Shelley might have looked a bit closer at his characterization of the Pope, who in Act IV sends an order for Cenci's execution. Ernest S. Bates, in *A Study of Shelley's Drama The Cenci* (New York: Columbia University Press, 1908), p. 49, states that his "desire for dramatic irony led Shelley to make use of an unmotivated act at variance with the whole conduct of the Pope throughout the rest of the play."

41. See Bruno Bettelheim's Foreword to Dr. Miklos Nyiszli, *Auschwitz: A Doctor's Eyewitness Account*, trans. Tibere Kremer and Richard Seaver (New York: Fawcett World Library, 1960), p. ix.

42. Nyiszli, p. 100.

43. See Bruno Bettelheim, *The Informed Heart: Autonomy in A Mass Age* (New York: Free Press of Glencoe, 1964), p. 186; and George Steiner, "Humane Literacy," in *Language and Silence: Essays on Language, Literature and the Inhuman* (New York: Atheneum, 1967), p. 5. As recounted by Dr. Bettelheim, one privileged prisoner who took part in experiments on human beings despised the

other prisoners for their lack of culture (he read Plato and Galsworthy). In several of the essays in his book Steiner attempts to come to grips (as he states in the Preface) with the question: how can a man read Goethe and Rilke, and presumably read them with understanding, and then go to his morning's work at Auschwitz? I suspect Shelley could have been read in the same way and conclude that he did not become better by reading Plato, but that he read Plato (other reasons to one side) because he was a good man. But that, of course, could not be the reason why an administrator of Auschwitz would read him. Frankly, one remains baffled by this question, and what it does to Shelley's (and for that matter Blake's) theory of "beautiful idealisms of moral excellence" to raise one's "perception into the infinite" is dreadfully apparent. "The only gain of civilization for mankind," asserts the Underground Man in a sinister pronouncement that each decade of the twentieth century has borne out, "is the greater capacity for variety of sensations—and absolutely nothing more. And through the development of this many-sidedness man may come to finding enjoyment in bloodshed. In fact, this has already happened to him. Have you ever noticed that it is the most civilized gentlemen who have been the subtlest slaughterers?" *The Short Novels of Dostoevsky,* p. 144.

44. Peter Butter, *Shelley's Idols of the Cave* (Edinburgh: Edinburgh University Press, 1954), p. 78.

45. Ibid. p. 83.

46. Carlos Baker, *Shelley's Major Poetry: The Fabric of A Vision* (Princeton, N. J.: Princeton University Press, 1948), p. 109.

47. Carl Grabo, *The Magic Plant,* p. 211.

48. Shelley's description of these horrors, which I have just quoted, is strikingly similar to Comenius' in his *The Labyrinth of the World,* trans. Matthew Spinka (Chicago: National Union of Czechoslovak Protestants in America, 1942), p. 16: "For some gathered refuse, distributing it among themselves; others rolled timber and stones to and fro, or hoisted them up by pulleys, and then let them down again; others dug in the ground. . . . The rest worked with bells, mirrors, bellows, rattles, and other trinkets. Some played even with their own shadow, measuring, chasing, or catching it. All of this was done so earnestly that many sighed and perspired, while others even harmed themselves with over-exertion. Moreover, there were everywhere officers who directed and allotted the tasks with great zeal, while the rest obeyed with equal alacrity." Like Comenius, Shelley in the very act of writing the poem (there is no reason to believe he had abandoned his former purpose) wishes to make the reader perceive his condition, for improvement may follow upon such understanding. In a letter to Horace Smith, June 29, 1822, a few days before his death, Shelley wrote, "The destiny of man can scarcely be so degraded that he was born only to die." *Letters,* 2:442.

49. Thus Harold Bloom in *Shelley's Mythmaking* (New Haven: Yale University Press, 1959), p. 274, states that the Poet's words which end the poem, "Then what is Life?" is a "despairing cry."

50. Donald H. Reiman, "Shelley's 'The Triumph of Life': A Critical Study," Illinois Studies in Language and Literature No. 55 (1965):28.

51. In using "mutiny" rather than "mystery" I follow Donald H. Reiman's reading in his variorum edition contained in his "Shelley's 'The Triumph of

Life' " (see preceding note), p. 164. Although there are some other differences between Hutchinson's text (the one I have used throughout this study) and Reiman's, in the quotations I have used from *The Triumph of Life* they are too minor to change the meaning and I have followed Hutchinson otherwise.

52. As Newman Ivey White states, *Shelley*, 2:370.

53. Reiman, p. 67.

54. To Thomas Love Peacock, July 12, 1816. *Letters*, 1:480.

55. "Essay on Christianity," David Lee Clark, ed., *Shelley's Prose*, p. 209.

56. *Shelley*, 2:631.

57. "A Defence of Poetry," David Lee Clark, ed., *Shelley's Prose*, p. 292. The strong influence, however, was upon Shelley. Demonstrably, these writers have exerted, unfortunately, no *moral* influence on the world, however great their esthetic impact has been. One is reminded of the great, white, faceless hump of Moby Dick rising out of the primordial waters. See note 43.

58. James Rieger, *The Mutiny Within: The Heresies of Percy Bysshe Shelley* (New York: George Braziller, 1967), p. 211; Harold Bloom, *Shelley's Mythmaking*, p. 267, respectively. Ross Grieg Woodman maintains, *The Apocalyptic Vision*, p. 188, that the Shape's function "is to come between the poet and the object of his quest, which is reunion with the One."

59. Reiman, p. 64. Carlos Baker, in *Shelley's Major Poetry*, supports the view that the Shape does represent the highest ideal. If Rousseau had actually drunk from her cup, not just touched his lips to it, "he could have quenched his youthful thirst for knowledge of the mysteries [of his origins]" (p. 267). That he does not do so is a "failure of nerve" (p. 268). As I interpret Shelley's line (404) "Touched with faint lips the cup she raised," Rousseau does drink from the cup.

60. David Lee Clark, ed., *Shelley's Prose*, p. 67.

61. Although it appears as if he might attempt to. See Reiman, p. 210, who restores three lines of Shelley's manuscript missing in Hutchinson.

62. Both White (*Shelley*, 2:370) and Reiman (p. 63) make this comparison. One should remember, however, that the speaker is Rousseau, a "distorted" member of the Dance of Death behind the Chariot. In making the connection between the Shape and the Witch of Atlas, Mr. Reiman states: "In Shelley's symbolic mythology, the union of the sun (or a star) and a terrestrial creature of water or earth symbolized the infusion of celestial energy into the terrestrial world . . . , but such a union of the Absolute and the limited, the Eternal and the temporal, inevitably resulted in the distortion of the Ideal." The distortion, however, is not the result of the blend of the higher and the lower (which Shelley so well accomplishes elsewhere in his poetry through synesthetic imagery) but of Rousseau's own being and hence vision. Perhaps Shelley, if he had lived to finish the poem, would have "corrected" Rousseau much as Blake does Milton.

63. *Shelley's Later Poetry*, p. 54.

64. Newman Ivey White, *Shelley*, 2:125. Global events since World War I have not, of course, been conducive to any kind of Promethean belief in man's regeneration, quick or gradual, as stressed in my discussion of *The Cenci*. Still, one cannot help but believe that there is some truth in Newton Arvin's statement in his article " 'The House of Pain': Emerson and the Tragic Sense," *Hudson Review* 12 (Spring 1959):48: "It may . . . be that there can exist a kind of complacency of pessimism, as there is certainly a complacency of optimism; and

that many of us in this age are guilty of it. We hug our negations, our doubts, our disbeliefs, to our chests, as if our moral and intellectual dignity depended on them."

Chapter Four

1. For a discussion of Blake's relationship to the political situation of his day, see David V. Erdman, *Blake, Prophet Against Empire: A Poet's Interpretation of the History of His Own Time* (Princeton, N.J.: Princeton University Press, 1954), especially Chapter 7.

2. Northrop Frye, *Fearful Symmetry*, p. 66.

3. Peter F. Fisher, *The Valley of Vision*, p. 188.

4. Carl Grabo, *Prometheus Unbound*, p. 35.

5. Northrop Frye, *Fearful Symmetry*, p. 57.

6. To Elizabeth Hitchener, July 25, 1811. *Letters*, 1:126.

7. When Bacon asserts in his essay "Of A King": "A King is a mortal god on earth, unto whom the living God hath lent his own name as a great honour," Blake snorts in the margin of his copy, "O Contemptible & Abject Slave!" (p. 401). Lest anyone should be left in doubt as to his exact meaning, Blake drew, in Keynes' description, "A representation of hinder parts, labelled: 'The devil's arse,' and depending from it a chain of excrement ending in: 'A King' " (p. 400).

8. Blake used these terms in a double sense. The meaning depends on the context. As noted in Chapter One, *dark*, when applied to Urizen, generally represents his opaque, constricted attitudes; the same term applied to Urthona indicates that he is at work on his anvils in the depths of Albion's being in an attempt to awaken Albion's suppressed imaginative energy. Similarly, *virgin, chaste,* or *holy* when applied to Rahab or Tirzah (and *holy* when referring to Urizen) are always pejorative; yet Jerusalem herself was a virgin in Eternity (J.20:5–10)—that is, she was Albion's innocent lover, truly at one with him as wife, sister, and daughter; and Oothoon asserts that she is "pure" after Bromion rapes her (VDA.2:28). In the same manner, Blake writes that "All Life Is Holy" (p. 74). Blake also uses the term *God* on two levels: God the evil tyrant, and God the Divine Humanity. In all instances, however, the context makes the meaning clear.

9. Morley, 1:326. For further discussion of Blake's idea of Jesus, see Northrop Frye, *Fearful Symmetry*, pp. 78–84.

10. Blake also scathingly denounces Nobodaddy in another short notebook piece, "When Klopstock England Defied" (pp. 186–187), which S. Foster Damon in *A Blake Dictionary* (p. 229) terms "a brief ritual of scatologic magic."

11. See Chapter Five for a discussion of the Blakean Emanation and the Shelleyan "epipsyche"—Shelley's name for the feminine half of the male psyche.

12. Hazard Adams, *Blake and Yeats*, p. 72.

13. Reiman, p. 31.

14. Morley, 1:343.

15. David Lee Clark, ed., *Shelley's Prose*, p. 124.

16. S. Foster Damon, "Wicker Man," *A Blake Dictionary*, p. 447.

17. S. Foster Damon, *William Blake: His Philosophy and Symbols*, p. 120.

18. The cave is one of Shelley's major symbols for the mind of man (as in Cythna's sea-cave in *The Revolt of Islam*); and like Blake, Shelley uses it pejoratively or not, depending on the context. At the end of *Prometheus Unbound*, Prometheus and his company of immortals withdraw to a most beautiful cave of marble to engage in the arts; Demogorgon rises out of a cave to overthrow the evil Jupiter; Blake's Urthona, in the apocalypse, sounds his hammer in the deep caves beneath the rejuvenated earth. For further discussion of the symbol, see Chapter 9, Neville Rogers, *Shelley at Work: A Critical Inquiry* (Oxford: Clarendon Press, 1956), and Peter Butter, *Shelley's Idols*, pp. 55–58.

19. March 10, 1812. *Letters*, 1:271; italics Shelley's. In the same letter Shelley also wrote (pp. 270–271): "I cannot recount all the horrible instances of unrestricted & licensed tyranny that have met my ears." He gives several instances, however, among them this one: "A poor boy whom I found starving with his mother, in a hiding place of unutterable filth and misery, whom I rescued, and was about to teach to read, has been snatched on a charge of false and villainous effrontery to a magistrate of *Hell*, who gave him the alternative of the *tender* or of military servitude. He preferred neither yet was compelled to be a soldier. This has come to my knowledge this morning. I am resolved to prosecute this business to the very jaws of government snatching (if possible) the poison from its fangs." (Italics Shelley's.) This type of official was apparently what Blake referred to as "fly-blows of Bacon," that is, "A Flogging Magistrate" (p. 400).

20. David Lee Clark, ed., *Shelley's Prose*, p. 169.

21. *On Christian Doctrine*, trans. D. W. Robertson, Jr. (Indianapolis and New York: Bobbs-Merrill Co., 1958), pp. 31–32.

22. Reiman, p. 33.

23. Both Robert F. Whitman in "Beatrice's 'Pernicious Mistake,' " (p. 243), and James Rieger, *The Mutiny Within* (p. 126) believe that Beatrice is motivated by revenge in murdering Cenci.

24. Melvin R. Watson, "Shelley and Tragedy: The Case of Beatrice Cenci," *Keats-Shelley Journal* 7 (Winter 1958): 14;21.

25. David Lee Clark, ed., "A Refutation of Deism," *Shelley's Prose*, p. 122.

26. Newman Ivey White, *Shelley*, 2:143.

27. Reiman, pp. 30–31.

28. David Lee Clark, ed., "Essay on Marriage," *Shelley's Prose*, pp. 215–216.

29. Northrop Frye, *Fearful Symmetry*, p. 393.

30. Joseph Wicksteed, *Blake's Vision of the Book of Job*, p. 19; italics Wicksteed's.

31. Northrop Frye, "Blake's Treatment of the Archetype," *Discussions of William Blake*, p. 11. For further discussion of Blake's concept of God see Chapter VII of Milton O. Percival, *Blake's Circle of Destiny*.

32. Joan Rees, "Shelley's Orsino: Evil in *The Cenci*," *Keats-Shelley Memorial Bulletin*, No. 12, (1961):3.

33. Shelley's concept of the unseen Power or one Spirit has often been identified with the Platonic and Neoplatonic "One." See, for example, Carl Grabo, *Prometheus Unbound*, and James A. Notopoulos, *The Platonism of Shelley*.

34. July 25, 1811. *Letters*, 1:126.

35. "An Address to the Irish People," David Lee Clark, ed., *Shelley's Prose*, p. 43.

36. David Lee Clark, ed., *Shelley's Prose*, p. 77, italics Shelley's.

37. "Essay on Christianity," David Lee Clark, ed., *Shelley's Prose*, pp. 201–202.

38. Jean L. De Palacio, "Music and Musical Themes in Shelley's Poetry," *Modern Language Review* 59 (July 1964):359.

39. In Northrop Frye's view (*Fearful Symmetry*, p. 186), the rhythm of Blake's Prophecies also approaches the condition of music, in which "any number of notes, within limits impossible to define by strict rules, may be contained within a single rhythmic unit." See Glenn O'Malley, *Shelley and Synesthesia*, Chapter 6, for an analysis of the stream-of-sound imagery in *Prometheus Unbound*. In Chapter One, from a different perspective (vision and regeneration), I have already discussed this aspect (sound or song) of Blake and Shelley's "prophetic" imagination.

40. Based on Erasmus Darwin's description, Carl Grabo in *A Newton Among Poets: Shelley's Use of Science in Prometheus Unbound* (Chapel Hill: University of North Carolina Press, 1930), p. 173, identifies the bubbles as "hydrogen gas which the action of the sun liberates from the vegetation at the bottom of lakes and pools. This liberated gas, as in Darwin's description, is electrically ignited and flows in the form of a meteor back to the waters of the earth."

41. One cannot discuss Blake's and Shelley's ideas of the nature of good and evil without giving some attention to the similarity of the imagery in which these ideas are contained and made viable, as I have briefly indicated in this chapter and elsewhere. Much, however, remains to be done, and the poetry of both poets would be greatly illuminated by such a comparative study. Even in the very smallest metaphorical reference, they are often so alike that the younger poet appears to have dipped into Blake's Prophecies and carried off whatever he could use for his own purposes. Thus, Blake always uses the caterpillar to define Urizen's cruel "State Religion" and government: the caterpillar and the fly feed on his tree of mystery ("The Human Abstract," p. 217), and Rational Demonstration "creeps into State Government like a caterpiller to destroy" (M.41:11). Shelley in his essay "A Proposal For An Association of Philanthropists," refers to the songs "Rule, Britannia" and "God Save the King" as "abstracts of the caterpillar creed of courtiers." David Lee Clark, ed., *Shelley's Prose*, p. 65.

42. Reiman, p. 44.

Chapter Five

1. Though Harold Bloom in *Shelley's Mythmaking*, p. 106, has distinguished Blake's Beulah-land from what he calls Shelley's "Namby-Pamby land" (the "childish" speeches of Ione and Panthea), this Blakean love making is at least as amusing as any similar incident in Shelley. Of course, Blake's idea of Time (masculine) and Space (feminine) has much larger, cosmic ramifications. See "Time" (p. 404) and "Space" (p. 379), for example, in S. Foster Damon, *A Blake Dictionary*.

2. For further discussion of Blake's "religion of art" see Yeats, "William Blake and the Imagination," *Essays and Introductions*, pp. 111–115.

3. These cities are similarly personified as women in the Book of Revelation. The City of God, the new Jerusalem, "prepared as a bride adorned for her husband" (21:2) descends out of heaven from God. Blake's Jerusalem is also the

bride of the Lamb (J.46:27–28). The union of the Bride and the Bridegroom, in Blake's view, is the reintegration of Albion and his Emanation, Man and nature, masculine and feminine: another aspect of the contraries ("higher" and "lower") discussed in Chapter One.

4. The "wheel without wheel" (FZ.7b.179) is always an image of evil: rational demonstration, the Ratio, Urizenic religion, the selfhood, and so on in Blake's Prophecies. On the other hand, the "wheel within wheel" (J.15:20) is an image of Edenic harmony.

5. Piloo Navavutty in "*Materia Prima* in a Page of Blake's Vala," *William Blake: Essays For S. Foster Damon,* p. 295, identifies Vala with the *Materia Prima* of the alchemists.

6. Edward J. Rose, "Circumcision Symbolism in Blake's *Jerusalem,*" *Studies in Romanticism* 8 (Autumn 1968):18.

7. Erich Fromm, *Escape From Freedom* (New York: Holt, Rinehart & Winston, 1961), 183–184, italics Fromm's. Blake, of course, does not touch the Underground Man's idea that man would play you some nasty trick out of sheer spite no matter what bubbles of bliss were given him. Blake's method, however, at least might *reduce* the number of his nasty tricks.

8. Wilhelm Reich, *Ether, God and Devil* and *Cosmic Superimposition* (New York: Farrar, Straus & Giroux, 1973), pp. 64–65, italics Reich's. See also his *The Mass Psychology of Fascism,* trans. Vincent R. Carfagno (New York: Farrar, Straus & Giroux, 1970).

9. S. Foster Damon, "Zelophehad," *A Blake Dictionary,* p. 457.

10. Notopoulous, pp. 278–279.

11. David Lee Clark, ed., *Shelley's Prose,* p. 170.

12. "On the Manners of the Ancient Greeks," David Lee Clark, ed., *Shelley's Prose,* p. 220.

13. "Essay on Love," David Lee Clark, ed., *Shelley's Prose,* p. 170.

14. Shelley conveys this totality primarily through his Venus symbolism, Venus being the Morning Star (Lucifer), which is masculine, and also the Evening Star (Vesper or Hesperus), which is feminine. Thus, the Woman (Love) in Canto One who cherishes the defeated snake (Good) in her bosom Shelley associates with Vesper, her lover with Lucifer. These two blend into Venus, the "mighty planet" (I.lvi.627) within the Temple of the Spirit. For an account of what Glenn O'Malley terms the "Venus complex"—that is, "an intricate system of themes, imagery and symbolism," see his *Shelley and Synesthesia,* pp. 58–69. Asia is also a Venus figure.

15. For an account of Shelley's relationship to Emilia, what his wife Mary termed his "Italian Platonics," see Newman Ivey White, *Shelley,* 2:247–269; 323–326.

16. Perkins, p. 172.

17. Baker, p. 218.

18. Newman Ivey White, *Shelley,* 2:259–263.

19. O'Malley, p. 89.

20. Barrell, p. 163.

21. Butter, p. 40. "Platonism" in *Epipsychidion* (in regard to Shelley's relationship to Emily) may be defined as the distinction between "spiritual" (Platonic) love and "physical" love. This is the contrast noted by Pausanias in Plato's

Symposium between "common love" (the earthly Aphrodite) and "heavenly love" (the heavenly Aphrodite). Pausanias, however, applies the term heavenly love to a homosexual relationship between males. (Thus, the popular definition of "Platonic" has never been correct.) The idea of the epipsyche itself (as distinguished from Shelley's actual situation) owes more to Aristophanes' description (in the *Symposium*) of the original androgynous nature of man, which was split into two halves by Zeus (love becoming thus "the desire for the whole"), and to Diotima's assertion (here I oversimplify) that love is the pursuit of the Good and the Beautiful. To find the epipsyche is to find psychological and spiritual wholeness, and philosophically, the ideal Good, True, and Beautiful.

22. Shelley extolled several women in his life, early and late, who turned out to be much like Elizabeth Hitchener, whom he called a "brown demon" and "a hermaphroditical beast of a woman," writing to Thomas Jefferson Hogg, December 3, 1812 (*Letters,* 1:336) that he was astonished at his "fatuity." Miss Hitchener lived for a time (1812) with Shelley and his first wife Harriet Westbrook. The precise cause of Shelley's disillusionment is unknown, but he was at first most devoted to her, calling her, in a letter dated October 16, 1811, (*Letters,* 1:152), the "sister of my soul." Near the end of his life, however, he still possessed the tendency to idealize. After terming Emily Viviani a "Seraph of Heaven" among a rather long list of fulsome epithets in *Epipsychidion,* Shelley later wrote John Gisborne (June 18, 1822) that he could not look at *Epipsychidion,* for "the person whom it celebrates was a cloud instead of a Juno; and poor Ixion starts from the centaur that was the offspring of his own embrace." Shelley saw his "mistake" as "seeking in a mortal image the likeness of what is perhaps eternal" (*Letters,* 2:434). In Blake's terms, Shelley simply failed to distinguish between the individual and his State.

23. Carl Grabo, *The Magic Plant,* p. 202.

24. To Maria Gisborne, November, 16, 1819. *Letters,* 2:154.

25. Ibid.

26. Mircea Eliade, *Patterns in Comparative Religion: A Study of the Element of the Sacred in the History of Religious Phenomena,* trans. Rosemary Sheed (Cleveland and New York: World Publishing Co., 1963), pp. 51–52.

27. Mircea Eliade, *Patterns in Comparative Religion,* p. 57, fn. 2; italics Eliade's.

28. See Mircea Eliade, *Mephistopheles and the Androgyne: Studies in Religious Myth and Symbol,* trans. J. M. Cohen (New York: Sheed & Ward, 1965), p. 118.

29. A. E. Waite, *The Holy Kabbalah,* p. 204. Indeed, all the hypostases of the Sephirotic tree, as they descend to the phenomenal world, are male-female.

30. Mircea Eliade, *Mephistopheles and the Androgyne,* p. 100.

31. Carl Grabo, *Prometheus Unbound,* p. 49.

32. Earl R. Wasserman, *Shelley's Prometheus Unbound,* p. 70. This is the distinction I refer to in Note 21.

33. Earl R. Wasserman, *Shelley's Prometheus Unbound,* p. 90.

34. Carl Grabo, *A Newton Among Poets,* p. 129.

Chapter Six

1. As I have noted in the discussion of Albion's fall (Chapter Four), Vala is the Emanation or consort of Luvah (Love, emotion, passion) who aids Urizen in

Albion's fall by presenting a vision of the outer world of nature. "As everything we see is an exteriorization of our emotions," S. Foster Damon observes in *A Blake Dictionary* (p. 428), "she is quite properly the Emanation of Luvah." Or, as explained by Northrop Frye: "What we see in nature is our own body turned inside out." *Fearful Symmetry*, p. 349. Vala also represents that world of nature itself, a lower form of Jerusalem, and is thus the wife of Albion as well as the consort of Luvah. Very seldom in Blake's Prophecies is there a one-to-one relationship, since all things exist ultimately *within* Albion himself.

2. Northrop Frye, *Fearful Symmetry*, p. 74.

3. "Falling over into the opposite," Jung terms "enantiodromia." See C. G. Jung, *Civilization in Transition*, trans. R. F. C. Hull, vol. 10, *The Collected Works of C. G. Jung* (New York: Pantheon Books, 1964). Jung deals with the concept throughout the book, but the essays "The Spiritual Problem of Modern Man," "After the Catastrophe" and "Good and Evil in Analytical Psychology" are especially relevant. Jung's *Mysterium Coniunctionis,* trans. R. F. C. Hull, vol. 14, *The Collected Works of C. G. Jung* (New York: Pantheon Books, 1963), deals with psychic opposites as revealed in alchemy.

4. Joseph Wood Krutch, *The Great Chain of Life* (Boston: Houghton Mifflin Co., 1956), p. 227.

5. Carl Grabo, *The Magic Plant*, p. 342.

6. "Review of Thomas Jefferson Hogg's *Memoirs* of *Prince Alexy Haimatoff*," David Lee Clark, ed., *Shelley's Prose*, p. 305.

7. W. B. Yeats, "William Blake and the Imagination," *Essays and Introductions,* p. 113.

8. Northrop Frye, *Fearful Symmetry*, pp. 196–197.

9. Helen C. White, *The Mysticism of William Blake* (New York: Russell & Russell, 1964), p. 220; p. 236.

10. C. G. Jung, *The Archetypes and the Collective Unconscious,* trans. R. F. C. Hull, *The Collected Works of C. G. Jung* (New York: Pantheon Books, 1959):9, Pt. 1:32. We can clearly see this "grounding" in Blake's description of the respective realms of Urthona (North-Nadir) and Urizen (South-Zenith). Before the fall, the Eternal Man, Albion, is in a condition of unity because these opposite poles "work" together.

11. "Essay on Marriage," David Lee Clark, ed. *Shelley's Prose*, p. 215.

12. Mark Schorer speaks in *The Politics of Vision* (p. 391) of Shelley's "invertebrate effeminate temper that wrapped itself in the veils of a sickly reverie." This is a prejudice that has looked at criticism ("the beautiful and ineffectual angel"), not at Shelley's life itself.

13. Thomas Love Peacock, "Memoirs of Percy Bysshe Shelley," *The Works of Thomas Love Peacock* (London: Constable & Co., 1934):8:92.

14. Morley, 1:337. This statement is in German ("Eine Gemeinschaft der Frauen Statt finden sollte") in Crabb Robinson's diary.

15. Wilson, *Life of William Blake*, p. 70.

16. May 9, 1811. *Letters*, 1:81, italics Shelley's.

17. It is well known that in some primitive societies, for example, prostitution as well as "sin" was unknown until the arrival of Christian missionaries who taught the natives to wear trousers and skirts and planted the Tree of Knowl-

edge of Good and Evil—another taboo that the primitive could add to his already long list, for he himself was by no means free in the Blakean sense.

18. Since Blake sees energy as perhaps resulting in a person's literal children if it is manifested in sex, and in his mental, intellectual "children" or creations—loves and graces—if it is manifested in art, here he is probably punning on the verb *die* in the Elizabethan sense as "orgasm." Thus, it is hardly surprising that Urizen wants to escape this "death" on its sexual as well as artistic level, for he is seeking a solid that will not fluctuate.

19. "Even Love is Sold," David Lee Clark, ed., *Shelley's Prose,* p. 116.

20. August 17, 1812. *Letters,* 1:323, italics Shelley's. Shelley was aware, however, of the practical aspects of the problem, for in this same letter, though he says he is convinced of the "unholiness of the act" of placing love in a prison (he was then married to Harriet Westbrook) he realized "that in the present state of society, if love is not thus villainously treated, she, who is most loved, will be treated worse by a misjudging world." Similarly, he wrote to Elizabeth Hitchener: "I think marriage an evil, an evil of immense and extensive magnitude, but I think a previous reformation in morals, and that a general & a great one is requisite before it may be remedied." November 26, 1811. *Letters,* 1:196.

21. "Even Love is Sold," David Lee Clark, ed., *Shelley's Prose,* p. 115.

22. Northrop Frye, *Fearful Symmetry,* p. 74.

23. "Even Love is Sold," David Lee Clark, ed., *Shelley's Prose,* p. 117.

24. Ibid.

25. "Even Love is Sold," David Lee Clark, ed., *Shelley's Prose,* p. 115.

26. Perhaps Joseph could have given a gold or silver *boy* to Mary to show *his* unselfishness. This indicates what one might not suspect on the prima facie evidence, considering that he was such a great breaker of tablets: That Blake tended to have a more conventional notion of female sexuality (her need of only one mate) than Shelley did. Similarly, Shelley stresses women's equality to men, while Blake states that woman's life is a reflection of man's.

27. It is well known, for example, that the publicly repressed Victorians (who delicately spoke of *limbs* rather than *legs*) were privately most pornographically minded. When such suppression exists, Jung states, "a gruesome fantasy of fornication is spawned in the unconscious by way of compensation." See Jung's "Answer to Job," *Psychology and Religion: West and East,* p. 446. Pornography in its sadomasochistic forms can be explained in much the same way. That is, suppression creates a violence in the expression of sex that compensates for that same suppression.

28. Chapter 28 of John Middleton Murry's *Jonathan Swift: A Critical Biography* (New York: Noonday Press, 1955), is titled "The Excremental Vision."

29. Sigmund Freud, "Contributions to the Psychology of Love," trans. Joan Riviere, *Collected Papers* (London: Hogarth Press and the Institute of Psychoanalysis, 1949):4:215.

30. D. H. Lawrence, "The Novel," *Reflections On the Death of A Porcupine and Other Essays* (Bloomington: Indiana University Press, 1969), p. 107.

31. Mona Wilson, *Life of William Blake,* p. 295. See also John Thomas Smith, "Blake," in *Nineteenth-Century Accounts of William Blake,* ed. Joseph Anthony Wittreich, Jr. (Gainesville, Florida: Scholars' Facsimiles & Reprints, 1970), p.

486. The twentieth-century pioneer in Blake scholarship—S. Foster Damon—states that as he first took up his studies (his seminal work, *Blake: His Philosophy and Symbols,* appeared in 1924) he thought Blake a madman, but that as he worked, "plane after plane of sanity was opened." *Blake: His Philosophy and Symbols,* p. ix.

32. Theodor Reik, "A Psychologist Looks at Love," *Of Love and Lust: On the Psychoanalysis of Romantic and Sexual Emotions* (New York: Farrar, Straus & Co., 1949), p. 23. Dr. Reik adds: "I know that sex meant something other to Freud than it means to most of his students, to whom it signifies sex and nothing more; but the word has proved stronger than his will to change its meaning. The result of the confusion has been disastrous." See also Rollo May, *Love and Will* (New York: W. W. Norton & Co., 1969), especially Chapter Two.

33. Mircea Eliade, *Patterns in Comparative Religion,* p. 357. "For nonreligious man," states Eliade in *The Sacred and the Profane: The Nature of Religion,* trans. Willard R. Trask (New York: Harper & Row, 1961), p. 168, "all vital experiences—whether sex or eating, work or play—have been desacralized. This means that all these physiological acts are deprived of spiritual significance, hence deprived of their truly human dimension."

34. The Frontpiece (Plate 9)—"a naked Angel descending headlong and rousing the dead with the sound of the last Trumpet" was said to have "alarmed the devout people of the North, and made maids and matrons retire behind their fans." To Crabb Robinson, Blake's depiction in this series of the soul uniting with the body was "about the most offensive of his inventions" (Plate 10). Another sold his copy as "unfit to lie on the parlour table." A contemporary reviewer found two of the plates particularly offensive: "The Day of Judgment" (Plate 12) and "The Meeting of a Family in Heaven" (Plate 11). "At the awful day of Judgment," he states, "before the throne of God himself, a male and female figure are described in most indecent attitudes. It is the same with the salutation of a man and his wife meeting in the pure mansions of Heaven." Mona Wilson, *Life of William Blake,* p. 187. See *Blake's Grave: A Prophetic Book* (Providence: Brown University Press, 1963). Sure "pure" mansions were indubitably Urizenic to Blake.

35. S. Foster Damon, "Nudity," *A Blake Dictionary,* p. 303.

36. Rieger, p. 188.

37. December 17 or 18, 1818. *Letters,* 2:58.

38. "Review of Thomas Jefferson Hogg's *Memoirs of Prince Alexy Haimatoff,*" David Lee Clark, ed., *Shelley's Prose,* p. 304.

39. To Elizabeth Hitchener, November 11, 1811. *Letters,* 1:173.

40. Leslie Marchand, *Byron: A Biography* (New York: Alfred A. Knopf, 1957):2:767; italics mine. Of course in Byron's defense it must be stated that wherever he went women threw themselves at him and sometimes got no more than they asked for in his often harsh treatment of them.

41. January 19, 1819. *Byron: A Self-Portrait: Letters and Diaries, 1798–1824,* ed. Peter Quennell (New York: Charles Scribner's Sons, 1950):2:440.

42. May 26, 1820. *Letters,* 2:199.

43. Frederick Tatham, "Life of William Blake," *Nineteenth-Century Accounts of William Blake,* p. 216.

Conclusion

1. Rabindranath Tagore, "The Religion of An Artist," and "Talks in China," *A Tagore Reader,* ed. Amiya Chakravarty (New York: Macmillan Co., 1961), pp. 211, 240.

Select Bibliography

Abrams, M. H. "The Correspondent Breeze: A Romantic Metaphor." In *English Romantic Poets: Modern Essays in Criticism,* edited by M. H. Abrams. New York: Oxford University Press, 1960.

_____. *The Mirror and the Lamp: Romantic Theory and the Critical Tradition.* New York: W. W. Norton & Co., 1958.

Adams, Charles L. "The Structure of *The Cenci.*" *Drama Survey* 4 (Summer 1965):139–148.

Adams, Hazard. *Blake and Yeats: The Contrary Vision.* Ithaca: Cornell University Press, 1955.

_____. *William Blake: A Reading of the Shorter Poems.* Seattle: University of Washington Press, 1963.

Altizer, Thomas J. J. *The New Apocalypse: The Radical Christian Vision of William Blake.* East Lansing: Michigan State University Press, 1967.

Ansari, Asloob Ahmad. "Blake and the Kabbalah." In *William Blake: Essays For S. Foster Damon,* edited by Alvin H. Rosenfeld. Providence: Brown University Press, 1969.

Arnheim, Rudolf. *Visual Thinking.* Berkeley and Los Angeles: University of California Press, 1969.

Artaud, Antonin. *The Theater and Its Double.* Translated by Mary Caroline Richards. New York: Grove Press, 1958.

Arvin, Newton. " 'The House of Pain': Emerson and the Tragic Sense." *Hudson Review* 12 (Spring 1959):37–53.

Augustine, St. *On Christian Doctrine.* Translated by D. W. Robertson, Jr. Indianapolis and New York: Bobbs-Merrill Co., 1958.

Baker, Carlos. *Shelley's Major Poetry: The Fabric of A Vision.* Princeton: Princeton University Press, 1948.

Barrell, Joseph. *Shelley and the Thought of His Time.* New Haven: Yale University Press, 1947.

Bates, Ernest Sutherland. *A Study of Shelley's Drama The Cenci.* New York: Columbia University Press, 1908.

Bayley, John. *The Romantic Survival: A Study in Poetic Evolution.* London: Constable & Co., 1957.

Bentley, G. E., Jr. *Blake Records.* London: Oxford University Press, 1969.

Berdyaev, Nicholas. *Truth and Revelation.* Translated by R. M. French. New York: Harper & Brothers, 1953.

Bettelheim, Bruno. *The Informed Heart: Autonomy in A Mass Age.* New York: Free Press of Glencoe, 1964.

Blake, William. *Blake: Complete Writings.* Edited by Geoffrey Keynes. London: Oxford University Press, 1966.

Bloom, Harold. *Blake's Apocalypse: A Study in Poetic Argument.* Garden City: Doubleday & Co., Anchor Books, 1965.

———. "Commentary." In *The Poetry and Prose of William Blake,* edited by David V. Erdman. Garden City: Doubleday & Co., 1965.

———. *Shelley's Mythmaking.* New Haven: Yale University Press, 1959.

———. "The Visionary Cinema of Romantic Poetry." In *William Blake: Essays For S. Foster Damon,* edited by Alvin H. Rosenfeld. Providence: Brown University Press, 1969.

———. *The Visionary Company: A Reading of English Romantic Poetry.* Garden City: Doubleday & Co., 1961.

Blyth, R. H. *Zen in English Literature and Oriental Classics.* Tokyo: Hokuseido Press, 1942.

Bodkin, Maud. *Archetypal Patterns in Poetry: Psychological Studies of Imagination.* London: Oxford University Press, 1963.

Boehme, Jacob. *Six Theosophic Points and Other Writings.* Translated by John Rolleston Earle. Ann Arbor: University of Michigan Press, 1958.

Bonner, William. *The Mystery of the Expanding Universe.* New York: Macmillan Co., 1964.

Bornstein, George. *Yeats and Shelley.* Chicago: University of Chicago Press, 1970.

Bowra, C. M. *The Romantic Imagination.* Cambridge: Harvard University Press, 1949.

Broglie, Louis de. *The Revolution in Physics.* Translated by Ralph W. Niemeyer. New York: Noonday Press, 1953.

Bronowski, Jacob. *The Common Sense of Science.* New York: Vintage Books, 1959.

———. *The Identity of Man.* Garden City: Natural History Press, 1965.

———. "The Imaginative Mind in Art" and "The Imaginative Mind in Science." In *Imagination and the University.* Toronto: University of Toronto Press, 1964.

———. "The Logic of the Mind." *American Scholar* 35 (Spring 1966):233–242.

———. *Science and Human Values.* Rev. ed. New York: Harper & Row, 1965.

———. *William Blake: A Man Without A Mask.* London: Secker & Warburg, 1943.

Butter, Peter. *Shelley's Idols of the Cave.* Edinburgh: Edinburgh University Press, 1954.

Byron, George Gordon, Lord. *Byron: A Self-Portrait: Letters and Diaries, 1798–1824.* Edited by Peter Quennell. 2 Vols. New York: Charles Scribner's Sons, 1950.

———. *Selected Poetry and Letters.* Edited by Edward E. Bostetter. New York: Rinehart & Co., 1951.

Chernaik, Judith. *The Lyrics of Shelley.* Cleveland: The Press of Case Western Reserve University, 1972.

Clark, David Lee. "Introduction: The Growth of Shelley's Mind." In *Shelley's Prose or The Trumpet of A Prophecy,* edited by David Lee Clark. Albuquerque: University of New Mexico Press, 1954.

Coleridge, Samuel Taylor. *Biographia Literaria.* London: J. M. Dent & Sons, 1917.

Comenius, John Amos. *The Labyrinth of the World.* Chicago: National Union of Czechoslovak Protestants in America, 1942.

Conrad, Joseph. *Heart of Darkness.* In *Youth and Two Other Stories.* Garden City: Doubleday, Page & Co., 1920.

Coveney, Peter. *The Image of Childhood. The Individual and Society: A Study of the Theme in English Literature.* Rev. ed. Baltimore: Penguin Books, 1967. Originally published in 1957 by Rockcliff Publishing Corporation as *Poor Monkey: The Child in Literature.*

Curran, Stuart, and Wittreich, Joseph Anthony, Jr., eds. *Blake's Sublime Allegory: Essays on The Four Zoas, Milton, Jerusalem.* Madison: University of Wisconsin Press, 1973.

Curran, Stuart. *Shelley's Cenci: Scorpions Ringed With Fire.* Princeton: Princeton University Press, 1970.

Damon, S. Foster. *A Blake Dictionary: The Ideas and Symbols of William Blake.* Providence: Brown University Press, 1965.

_____. *William Blake: His Philosophy and Symbols.* Gloucester, Mass.: Peter Smith, 1958.

Delasanta, Rodney. "Shelley's 'Sometimes Embarrassing Declarations': A Defence." *Texas Studies in Literature and Language* 7 (Spring 1965):173–179.

Donohue, Joseph W., Jr. "Shelley's Beatrice and the Romantic Concept of Tragic Character." *Keats-Shelley Journal* 17 (1968):53–73.

Dorfman, Deborah. *Blake in the Nineteenth Century: His Reputation as Poet From Gilchrist to Yeats.* New Haven: Yale University Press, 1969.

Dostoevsky, Fyodor. *Notes From Underground* in *The Short Novels of Dostoevsky.* New York: Dial Press, 1958, pp. 129–222.

_____. *The Possessed.* Translated by Constance Garnett. New York: Random House, 1963.

Dröscher, Vitus B. *The Magic of the Senses: New Discoveries in Animal Perception.* New York: E. P. Dutton, 1969.

Eddington, Sir Arthur. *New Pathways in Science.* Ann Arbor: University of Michigan Press, 1959.

Eliade, Mircea. *Mephistopheles and the Androgyne: Studies in Religious Myth and Symbol.* Translated by J. M. Cohen. New York: Sheed & Ward, 1965.

_____. *Patterns in Comparative Religion: A Study of the Element of the Sacred in the History of Religious Phenomena.* Translated by Rosemary Sheed. Cleveland and New York: World Publishing Co., 1963.

_____. *The Sacred and the Profane: The Nature of Religion.* Translated by Willard R. Trask. New York: Harper & Row, 1961.

Eliot, T. S. *Collected Poems: 1909–1935.* New York: Harcourt, Brace & World, 1936.

_____. *The Sacred Wood: Essays On Poetry and Criticism.* London: Methuen & Co., 1950.

Erdman, David V. *Blake, Prophet Against Empire: A Poet's Interpretation of the History of His Own Times.* Princeton: Princeton University Press, 1954.

Feynman, Richard. *The Character of Physical Law.* Cambridge: Massachusetts Institute of Technology Press, 1967.

Fisher, Peter F. "Blake and the Druids." *Journal of English and Germanic Philology* 58 (October 1959):589–612.

_____. *The Valley of Vision: Blake as Prophet and Revolutionary.* Edited by Northrop Frye. Toronto: University of Toronto Press, 1961.

Foakes, R. A. *The Romantic Assertion: A Study in the Language of Nineteenth Century Poetry.* New Haven: Yale University Press, 1958.

Fogle, Richard H. "Romantic Bards and Metaphysical Reviewers." *ELH* 12 (March 1945):221–250.

Ford, Newell F. "Paradox and Irony in Shelley's Poetry." *Studies in Philology* 57 (July 1960):648–662.

Forster, E. M. *Aspects of the Novel.* New York: Harcourt, Brace, 1927.

Freud, Sigmund. "Contributions to the Psychology of Love." Translated by Joan Riviere. In *Collected Papers.* 5 Vols. London: Hogarth Press and the Institute of Psycho-analysis, 1949.

Fromm, Erich. *Escape From Freedom.* New York: Holt, Rinehart & Winston, 1961.

Frosch, Thomas R. *The Awakening of Albion: The Renovation of the Body in the Poetry of William Blake.* Ithaca: Cornell University Press, 1974.

Frye, Northop. "Blake's Treatment of the Archetype." In *Discussions of William Blake,* edited by John E. Grant. Boston: D. C. Heath, 1961.

————. *Fables of Identity: Studies in Poetic Mythology.* New York: Harcourt, Brace & World, 1963.

————. *Fearful Symmetry: A Study of William Blake.* Princeton: Princeton University Press, 1947.

Garrod, H. W. *Wordsworth: Lectures and Essays.* London: Oxford University Press, 1927.

Gérard, Albert S. *English Romantic Poetry: Ethos, Structure, and Symbol in Coleridge, Wordsworth, Shelley, and Keats.* Berkeley and Los Angeles: University of California Press, 1968.

Gilchrist, Alexander. *Life of William Blake.* London: J. M. Dent & Sons, 1945.

Gombrich, Ernst H. *Art and Illusion: A Study in the Psychology of Pictorial Representation.* New York: Pantheon Books, 1960.

Guinn, John Pollard. *Shelley's Political Thought.* The Hague: Mouton, 1969.

Grabo, Carl. *The Magic Plant: The Growth of Shelly's Thought.* Chapel Hill: University of North Carolina Press, 1936.

————. *The Meaning of The Witch of Atlas.* Chapel Hill: University of North Carolina Press, 1935.

————. *A Newton Among Poets: Shelley's Use of Science in Prometheus Unbound.* Chapel Hill: University of North Carolina Press, 1930.

————. *Prometheus Unbound: An Interpretation.* Chapel Hill: University of North Carolina Press, 1935.

Harding, M. Esther. *Journey Into Self.* New York: David McKay, 1963.

Harper, George Mills. *The Neoplatonism of William Blake.* Chapel Hill: University of North Carolina Press, 1961.

————. "The Divine Tetrad in Blake's Jerusalem." In *William Blake: Essays For S. Foster Damon,* edited by Alvin H. Rosenfeld. Providence: Brown University Press, 1969.

Haven, Richard. *Patterns of Consciousness: An Essay on Coleridge.* Amherst: University of Massachusetts Press, 1969.

Heisenberg, Werner. *Across the Frontiers.* Translated by Peter Heath. New York: Harper & Row, 1974.

————. *Physics and Philosophy: The Revolution in Modern Science.* New York: Harper & Brothers, 1958.

Hirsch, E. D., Jr. *Wordsworth and Schelling: A Typological Study of Romanticism.* New Haven: Yale University Press, 1960.

Hughes, Daniel. "Blake and Shelley: Beyond the Uroboros." In *William Blake: Essays For S. Foster Damon,* edited by Alvin H. Rosenfeld. Providence: Brown University Press, 1969.

Hutten, Ernest H. *The Language of Modern Physics: An Introduction to the Philosophy of Science.* London: George Allen & Unwin, 1956.

Jung, C. G. *Psychology and Religion: West and East.* Translated by R. F. C. Hull. *The Collected Works of C. G. Jung.* New York: Pantheon Books, 1958.

_____. *The Archetypes and the Collective Unconscious.* Translated by R. F. C. Hull. *The Collected Works of C. G. Jung.* New York: Pantheon Books, 1963.

_____. *Civilization in Transition.* Translated by R. F. C. Hull. *The Collected Works of C. G. Jung.* New York: Pantheon Books, 1964.

_____. *Mysterium Coniunctionis.* Translated by R. F. C. Hull. *The Collected Works of C. G. Jung.* New York: Pantheon Books, 1963.

Kabbalah, The. Translated by S. L. Mathers. In *The Sacred Books and Early Literature of the East.* 14 vols. New York and London: Parke, Austin & Lipscomb, 1917.

Keats, John. *Selected Poems and Letters,* edited by Douglas Bush. Boston: Houghton Mifflin Co., 1959.

King-Hele, Desmond. *Shelley: The Man and the Poet.* New York: Thomas Yoseloff, 1960.

Kramrisch, Stella. "The Triple Structure of Creation in the *Rig Veda.*" *History of Religions* 2 (Summer 1962):140–175.

_____. "The Triple Structure of Creation in the *Rig Veda.*" *History of Religions* 2 (Winter 1963):256–285.

Krutch, Joseph Wood. *The Great Chain of Life.* Boston: Houghton Mifflin Co., 1956.

Lamb, Charles. *The Letters of Charles Lamb.* London: Grey Walls Press, 1950.

Lawrence, D. H. "The Novel," *Reflections On the Death of A Porcupine and Other Essays.* Bloomington: Indiana University Press, 1969.

Marchand, Leslie A. *Byron: A Biography.* 3 vols. New York: Alfred A. Knopf, 1957.

Martin, Charles Noël. *The Role of Perception in Science.* Translated by A. J. Pomerans. London: Hutchinson & Co., 1963.

Matthews, G. M. "On Shelley's 'The Triumph of Life.' " *Studia Neophilologica* 34 (1962):104–134.

May, Rollo. *Love and Will.* New York: W. W. Norton & Co., 1969.

McNiece, Gerald. *Shelley and the Revolutionary Idea.* Cambridge: Harvard University Press, 1969.

McTaggart, William J. "Some New Inquiries into Shelley's Platonism." *Keats-Shelley Memorial Bulletin* 21 (1970):41–59.

Mead, George Robert Stow. *Fragments of A Faith Forgotten.* New York: University Books, 1960.

Mellor, Anne Kostelanetz. *Blake's Human Form Divine.* Berkeley: University of California Press, 1974.

Morley, Edith J., ed. *Henry Crabb Robinson on Books and Their Writers.* 3 Vols. London: J. M. Dent & Sons, 1938.

Nanavutty, Piloo. "*Materia Prima* in a Page of Blake's Vala," In *William Blake:*

Essays For S. Foster Damon, edited by Alvin H. Rosenfeld. Providence: Brown University Press, 1969.

Notopoulos, James A. *The Platonism of Shelley.* Durham: Duke University Press, 1949.

Nyiszli, Miklos. *Auschwitz: A Doctor's Eyewitness Account.* Translated by Tibere Kremer and Richard Seaver. Greenwich, Conn.: Fawcett Publications, 1960.

O'Malley, Glenn. *Shelley and Synesthesia.* Evanston, Ill.: Northwestern University Press, 1964.

Oppenheimer, J. Robert. *The Flying Trapeze: Three Crises for Physicists.* London: Oxford University Press, 1964.

Ortega y Gasset, José. "The Sportive Origin of the State." In *History As A System.* New York: W. W. Norton & Co., 1961.

Ouspensky, P. D. *Tertium Organum.* Translated by Nicholas Bessaraboff and Claude Bragdon. New York: Vintage Books, 1970.

Palacio, Jean L. de. "Music and Musical Intervals in Shelley's Poetry." *Modern Language Review* 59 (July 1964):345–359.

Paley, Morton D., and Phillips, Michael, eds. *William Blake: Essays in Honour of Sir Geoffrey Keynes.* London: Oxford University Press, 1973.

Pauli, Wolfgang. "The Influence of Archetypal Ideas on the Scientific Theories of Kepler." Translated by Priscilla Silz. In Carl Jung, *The Interpretation of Nature and the Psyche.* New York: Pantheon Books, 1955.

Peacock, Thomas Love. *The Works of Thomas Love Peacock.* 10 Vols. London: Constable & Co., 1934.

Peck, Walter Edwin. *Shelley: His Life and Work.* 2 vols. Boston and New York: Houghton Mifflin Co., 1927.

Percival, Milton O. *William Blake's Circle of Destiny.* New York: Octagon Books, 1964.

Perkins, David. *The Quest For Permanence: The Symbolism of Wordsworth, Shelley and Keats.* Cambridge: Harvard University Press, 1959.

Polanyi, Michael. *Personal Knowledge: Towards A Post-Critical Philosophy.* Chicago: University of Chicago Press, 1958.

Praz, Mario. *The Romantic Agony.* Translated by Angus Davidson. Cleveland and New York: World Publishing Co., 1965.

Pulos, C. E. *The Deep Truth: A Study of Shelley's Scepticism.* Lincoln: University of Nebraska Press, 1954.

Rader, Melvin M. "Shelley's Theory of Evil." In *Shelley: A Collection of Critical Essays,* edited by George M. Ridenour. Englewood Cliffs: Prentice-Hall, 1965.

Rees, Joan. "Shelly's Orsino: Evil in *The Cenci.*" *Keats-Shelley Memorial Bulletin,* No. 12 (1961), pp. 3–6.

Reich, Wilhelm. *Ether, God and Devil and Cosmic Superimposition.* Translated by Therese Pol. New York: Farrar, Straus & Giroux, 1973.

————. *The Mass Psychology of Fascism.* Translated by Vincent R. Carfagno. New York: Farrar, Straus & Giroux, 1970.

Reik, Theodor. "A Psychologist Looks At Love." In *Of Love and Lust: On the Psychoanalysis of Romantic and Sexual Emotions.* New York: Farrar, Straus & Co., 1949.

Reiman, Donald H. "Shelley's 'The Triumph of Life': A Critical Study." Illinois

Studies in Language and Literature No. 55 (1965): 3–272.

Richards, I. A. *Coleridge on Imagination*. Bloomington: Indiana University Press, 1965.

Ridenour, George M. "Introduction: Shelley's Optimism." In *Shelley: A Collection of Critical Essays*, edited by George M. Ridenour. Englewood Cliffs: Prentice-Hall, 1965.

Rieger, James. *The Mutiny Within: The Heresies of Percy Bysshe Shelley*. New York: George Braziller, 1967.

Rogers, Neville. *Shelley at Work: A Critical Inquiry*. Oxford: Clarendon Press, 1956.

Rose, Edward J. "Circumcision Symbolism in Blake's *Jerusalem*." *Studies in Romanticism* 8 (Autumn 1968):16–25.

———. "The Structure of Blake's *Jerusalem*." *Bucknell Review* 11 (May 1963):35–54.

———. "Wheels Within Wheels in Blake's *Jerusalem*." *Studies in Romanticism* 11 (Winter 1972):36–47.

Santayana, George. "Shelley: or the Poetic Value of Revolutionary Principles." In *Essays in Literary Criticism*, edited by Irving Singer. New York: Charles Scribner's Sons, 1956.

Schneer, Cecil J. *The Search for Order: The Development of the Major Ideas in the Physical Sciences From the Earliest Times to the Present*. New York: Harper & Brothers, 1960.

Schorer, Mark. *William Blake: The Politics of Vision*. New York: Henry Holt & Co., 1946.

Schrödinger, Edwin. *Mind and Matter*. New York: Cambridge University Press, 1959.

Shelley, Percy Bysshe. *The Complete Poetical Works of Percy Bysshe Shelley*. Edited by Thomas Hutchinson. London: Oxford University Press, 1965.

———. *The Letters of Percy Bysshe Shelley*. Edited by Frederick L. Jones. 2 Vols. Oxford: Clarendon Press, 1964.

———. *Shelley's Prose* or *The Trumpet of A Prophecy*. Edited by David Lee Clark. Albuquerque: University of New Mexico Press, 1954.

Sinnott, Edmund W. *The Biology of the Spirit*. New York: Viking Press, 1955.

Spinoza, Benedict De. *Ethics* and *De Intellectus Emendatione*. Translated by A. Boyle. London and Toronto: J. M. Dent & Sons, 1925.

Steiner, George. *Language and Silence: Essays on Language, Literature and the Inhuman*. New York: Atheneum, 1967.

Sutherland, John. "Blake: A Crisis of Love and Jealousy." *PMLA* (January 1972):424–431.

Suzuki, D. T. *An Introduction to Zen Buddhism*. New York: Philosophical Library, 1949.

Symons, Arthur. *William Blake*. London: Jonathan Cape, 1928.

Szent-Gyorgyi, Albert. *The Crazy Ape*. New York: Philosophical Library, 1970.

Tagore, Rabindranath. "The Religion of An Artist," and "Talks in China." In *A Tagore Reader*, edited by Amiya Chakravarty. New York: Macmillan Co., 1961.

Vogler, Thomas A. *Preludes to Vision: The Epic Venture in Blake, Wordsworth, Keats, and Hart Crane*. Berkeley: University of California Press, 1971.

von Neumann, John. *The Computer and the Brain.* New Haven and London: Yale University Press, 1963.

Wagenknecht, David. *Blake's Night: William Blake and the Idea of Pastoral.* Cambridge: Harvard University Press, 1973.

Waite, A. E. *The Holy Kabbalah.* New York: Macmillan Co., 1929.

Wasserman, Earl R. *Shelley: A Critical Reading.* Baltimore: Johns Hopkins University Press, 1971.

_____. *Shelley's Prometheus Unbound: A Critical Reading.* Baltimore: Johns Hopkins University Press, 1965.

Watson, E. Grant. *The Mystery of Physical Life.* London: Abelard-Schuman, 1964.

Watson, Melvin R. "Shelley and Tragedy: The Case of Beatrice Cenci." *Keats-Shelley Journal* 7 (Winter 1958):13–21.

Weaver, Bennett. *"Prometheus Unbound."* University of Michigan Publications in Language and Literature No. 27 (1957).

Wheelwright, Philip. *The Burning Fountain: A Study in the Language of Symbolism.* Bloomington: Indiana University Press, 1954.

_____. *Metaphor and Reality.* Bloomington: Indiana University Press, 1962.

White, Helen C. *The Mysticism of William Blake.* New York: Russell & Russell, 1964.

White, Newman Ivey. *The Unextinguished Hearth: Shelley and His Contemporary Critics.* New York: Octagon Books, 1966.

_____. *Shelley.* 2 Vols. New York: Alfred A. Knopf, 1940.

Whitman, Robert F. "Beatrice's 'Pernicious Mistake' in *The Cenci.*" *PMLA* 74 (June 1959):249–253.

Wicksteed, Joseph H. *Blake's Vision of the Book of Job.* London: J. M. Dent & Sons, 1910.

Willey, Basil. *The Seventeenth Century Background: Studies in the Thought of the Age in Relation to Poetry and Religion.* Garden City: Doubleday & Co., 1953.

Wilson, Milton. *Shelley's Later Poetry: A Study of His Prophetic Imagination.* New York: Columbia University Press, 1959.

Wilson, Mona. *The Life of William Blake.* New York: Jonathan Cape & Robert Ballou, 1932.

Wittreich, Joseph Anthony, Jr., ed. *Nineteenth-Century Accounts of William Blake.* Gainesville, Fla.: Scholars' Facsimiles & Reprints, 1970.

_____. "The 'Satanism' of Blake and Shelley Reconsidered." *Studies in Philology* 65 (October 1968):816–833.

Woodman, Ross Greig. *The Apocalyptic Vision in the Poetry of Shelley.* Toronto: University of Toronto Press, 1964.

Wright, Andrew. *Blake's Job: A Commentary.* London: Oxford University Press, 1972.

Yeats, William Butler. "William Blake and His Illustrations to *The Divine Comedy,*" and "William Blake and the Imagination." In *Essays and Introductions.* New York: Macmillan Co., 1961.

Index

Blake's and Shelley's writings are indexed under
their titles or first lines